T0306069

Labor, Global Supply Chains, and the Garment Industry in South Asia

This book argues that larger flaws in the global supply chain must first be addressed to change the way business is conducted to prevent factory owners from taking deadly risks to meet clients' demands in the garment industry in Bangladesh.

Using the 2013 Rana Plaza disaster as a departure point, and to prevent such tragedies from occurring in the future, this book presents an interdisciplinary analysis to address the disaster which resulted in a radical change in the functioning of the garment industry. The chapters present innovative ways of thinking about solutions that go beyond third-party monitoring. They open up possibilities for a renewed engagement of international brands and buyers within the garment sector, a focus on direct worker empowerment using technology, the role of community-based movements, developing a model of change through enforceable contracts combined with workers movements, and a more productive and influential role for both factory owners and the government. This book makes key interventions and rethinks the approaches that have been taken until now and proposes suggestions for the way forward. It engages with international brands, the private sector, and civil society to strategize about the future of the industry and for those who depend on it for their livelihood.

A much-needed review and evaluation of the many initiatives that have been set up in Bangladesh in the wake of Rana Plaza, this book is a valuable addition to academics in the fields of development studies, gender and women's studies, human rights, poverty and practice, political science, economics, sociology, anthropology, and South Asian studies.

Sanchita Banerjee Saxena is the Executive Director of the Institute for South Asia Studies and the Director of the Subir and Malini Chowdhury Center for Bangladesh Studies at the University of California, Berkeley, USA.

Routledge Contemporary South Asia Series

For the full list of titles in the series please visit: www.routledge.com/
Routledge-Contemporary-South-Asia-Series/book-series/RCSA.

Labor, Global Supply Chains, and the Garment Industry in South Asia

Bangladesh After Rana Plaza

Edited by
Sanchita Banerjee Saxena

 Routledge
Taylor & Francis Group

LONDON AND NEW YORK

First published 2020
by Routledge
2 Park Square, Milton Park, Abingdon, Oxon OX14 4RN

and by Routledge
52 Vanderbilt Avenue, New York, NY 10017

Routledge is an imprint of the Taylor & Francis Group, an informa business

First issued in paperback 2021

British Library Cataloguing-in-Publication Data
A catalogue record for this book is available from the British Library

Library of Congress Cataloging-in-Publication Data
A catalog record has been requested for this book

ISBN: 978-1-138-36680-0 (hbk)
ISBN: 978-1-03-209164-8 (pbk)
ISBN: 978-0-429-43003-9 (ebk)

Typeset in Times New Roman
by codeMantra

For my father, who showed me what truly matters

Contents

List of figures

List of tables

List of contributors

Dr Dorothee Baumann-Pauly is the Director of Research at the NYU Stern Center for Business and Human Rights, managing its strategic, industry-specific research agenda. She is the co-editor of *Business and Human Rights: From Principles to Practice* (Routledge 2016), the first textbook on business and human rights.

Shikha Silliman Bhattacharjee is a Research Fellow at Global Labor Justice and Content Director at HELM Social Design Studio. She holds a JD from University of Pennsylvania Law School and is pursuing a PhD from UC Berkeley in Jurisprudence and Social Policy. Her recent publications include reports on gender-based violence in Gap, H&M, and Walmart garment supply chains (2018) and gender justice on garment supply chains (2019).

Dr Shelley Feldman was an International Professor (1984–2016) and is currently a visiting scholar in Feminist, Gender, & Sexuality Studies at Cornell University, and Research Fellow at the Max Weber Centre for Advanced Cultural and Social Studies, Erfurt, Germany. Her relevant publications include *Historicizing Garment Manufacturing in Bangladesh: Gender, Generation, and New Regulatory Regimes*; *Bengali state and nation making: Partition and displacement revisited*; and with C. Geisler, *Land Expropriation and Displacement in Bangladesh*.

Dr Kohl Gill, a quantum physicist turned entrepreneur, founded LaborVoices after observing patterns of opaque supply chains and high mobile phone penetration while working with the US Department of State. He has a BS in physics from Caltech and a PhD in physics from UC Santa Barbara.

Dr Jakir Hossain is a professor at the Institute of Bangladesh Studies, University of Rajshahi, Bangladesh. He holds a PhD in international studies from the University of Trento, Italy. His research interests are international labor standards, decent work, occupational safety and health, participation and representation, and labor governance.

Chaumtoli Huq is an Associate Professor of Law at CUNY School of Law with an expertise in labor and employment law and human rights. She is the founder/editor of an innovative law and media non-profit called Law@theMargins (www.lawatthemargins.com).

Dr. Rubana Huq is the President of Bangladesh Garment Manufacturers and Exporters Association. She is also the Managing Director of Mohammadi Group, which is engaged in energy, media, manufacturing and real estate. Apart from her corporate entity, Dr. Huq obtained her PhD degree from Jadavpur University in Kolkata.

Dr Naila Kabeer is Joint Professor in Departments of International Development and Gender Studies at the London School of Economics and Political Science. Her single-authored books include *Reversed Realities: Gender Hierarchies in Development Thought, The Power to Choose: Bangladeshi Women and Labour Market Decision in London and Dhaka,* and *Gender and Social Protection in the Informal Economy.*

Ayush Khanna cofounded LaborVoices, a platform to guide workers to jobs that pay and treat them fairly. He has an MS in information systems from UC Berkeley and a BS in computer science from Mumbai University, India.

Dr Khondaker Golam Moazzem is Research Director at the Centre for Policy Dialogue in Bangladesh. His recent research includes *Least Developed Countries in the Global Value Chain: Trends, Determinants and Challenges* and *Strengthening the Social Dialogue Mechanism within a Weak Enabling Environment: The Case of Bangladesh's RMG Sector.*

Dr Shahidur Rahman is a Professor of Sociology in the Department of Economics and Social Sciences at BRAC University, Bangladesh. He completed a PhD in sociology at Monash University. His current research is involved in a three-year research on "Changes in Governance in garment production network." He is the author of *Broken Promises of Globalization: The Case of the Bangladesh Garment Industry* (Lexington Books, 2014).

Dr Sanchita Banerjee Saxena is the Executive Director of the Institute for South Asia Studies at UC Berkeley and the Director of the Subir and Malini Chowdhury Center for Bangladesh Studies. She holds a PhD in political science from UCLA. She is the author of *Made in Bangladesh, Cambodia, and Sri Lanka: The Labor Behind the Global Garments and Textiles Industries.*

Dr Dina M. Siddiqi is a Clinical Associate Professor in the Faculty of Liberal Studies at New York University. She has published extensively on gendered labor in Bangladesh's garment industry, Islam and transnational feminism, and the cultural politics of minorities and secularism.

Dr Meenu Tewari is an Associate Professor of Economic Development and International Planning at the University of North Carolina at Chapel Hill. She studies economic development, skill formation, and upgrading within regional and global production networks. Her latest book *Development with Global Value Chains: Upgrading and Innovation in Asia* (eds. D. Nathan, M. Tewari, and S. Sarkar) was published in November, 2018, by Cambridge University Press.

Dr Kristy Ward is a postdoctoral research associate at the Sydney Southeast Asia Centre at the University of Sydney. Her research interests include labor activism, gender and migration, and urbanization in Southeast Asia. She has published on gender and work Cambodia, forced migration, and the politics of urban aid and development programmes.

Preface

For those of us working on labor issues in global supply chains, April 24, 2013 will always be known as the deadliest garment factory accident in history. At this time, I was just finishing my first book, *Made In Bangladesh, Cambodia, and Sri Lanka: The Labor Behind the Global Garments and Textiles Industries* (2014, Cambria Press), and I requested an extension from the publisher to be able to (somewhat briefly) address this horrific disaster and what, some would argue, was a turning point in the industry. Now, more than five years later, this edited volume brings together 15 different authors from a variety of disciplines and approaches to try and understand whether the deep concerns following the Rana Plaza disaster have been addressed and if not, what new approaches might look like.

This volume brings together contributors from a wide variety of disciplines (law, anthropology, urban and regional studies, gender studies, business and human rights, international relations, area studies, labor studies, economic development, sociology, and political science), as well as the private sector and international organizations. This project is a wonderful example of collaborative research across borders, and includes the participation of scholars and practitioners from top institutions in the United States, the United Kingdom, Australia, and Bangladesh. Some of the authors I have known for many years and others I have never met, but I have admired each of their perspective and desire to develop a fresh approach to addressing the inherent flaws in this sector.

The Rana Plaza tragedy was significant in many ways because the horrific and preventable nature of the disaster made policymakers, factory owners, international buyers, and the global community realize that it could no longer be "business as usual" for the garment industry. This tragedy created an opportunity for all those involved in the sector to make improvements and enact positive change. It was also significant because this was the first time that "solutions to the labor problem" were proposed. However, as this volume argues, there are serious issues with these main strategies that have been employed and they are not really a true departure from what had been tried in the past. Instead of recognizing the inherent strength of marginalized populations and working towards harnessing that strength, these "solutions," instead, have created new structures designed to "help," but which, in fact, kept individuals more vulnerable.

There is a real opportunity for this volume to make key interventions and to rethink the approaches that have been taken until now and to forge a path forward. We would like to use this volume as a way to engage with international brands, the private sector, and civil society to strategize about how to move forward. Bringing together this group of authors to think about these issues is the first attempt to try and do this and to make a significant impact on the industry and on those who depend on it for their livelihood.

Acknowledgements

This book would not have come to fruition without the vision of Dorothea Schaefter, Senior Editor, Asian Studies at Routledge. I was fortunate to have met her at various conferences over the years. Dorothea's enthusiasm for this project convinced me that an edited volume on this subject was necessary and would indeed be possible. I would also like to thank an anonymous reviewer at Routledge for his/her comments and feedback.

It is a privilege to know many of the authors who have been a part of this collaboration. I admire their work and their desire to truly understand this sector from nuanced perspectives. Early conversations with many colleagues, but in particular with Dina Siddiqi, Dorothee Baumann-Pauly, and Sarah Labowitz, helped shaped the ideas for this volume.

I spent the best month of my life at the Rockefeller Foundation Bellagio Residency Program in Italy as a Resident Fellow during May–June, 2016. The opportunity to think, write, and interact with amazing scholars in a spectacular setting allowed me to put together the key arguments for this volume, develop the ideas for each section, and research possible authors who could contribute. I am grateful for this fellowship and to my cohort who gave me valuable feedback on early versions of the manuscript.

Earlier versions of the main arguments presented in the introductory chapter of this volume were articulated in an opinion piece in *The Globe and Mail* with Sarah Labowitz ("Monitoring working conditions at factories won't stop future tragedies," August 10, 2015), and in *Economic & Political Weekly* (Vol. LIII, No 16, "Beyond Third Party Monitoring: Post Rana Plaza Interventions," April 21, 2018).

Over the last few years, I benefited from feedback at various presentations on early drafts of this manuscript that were made at the Bangladesh Studies Network Meeting at the University of Edinburgh; the Transnational Law Institute Workshop at Kings College, London; The Centre for Urban and Policy Governance at The School of Habitat Studies Seminar at the Tata Institute of Social Sciences, Mumbai; and at the United Nations Forum on Business and Human Rights, Geneva.

When I was working on the book after my Bellagio fellowship in the Fall of 2016, I received the devastating news that my father was stricken with a very rare and aggressive form of cancer with a very poor prognosis. I immediately stopped work on the volume and focused my energies on his treatment. During one of our many drives to see his doctor, he asked me about my plans for my next book. I told him that I had taken a break and would possibly return to the book at a later time. He was dismayed to learn that I had to temporarily stop my work due to his health, but I promised him that one day I would return to it. My father embraced everyday beauty and questioned injustice in an effort to try and better understand the world around him. He was an eternal optimist and always had hope for a better future. My father followed his passions until the very end and taught me to do the same. This book is for him.

List of abbreviations

Accord	The Accord for Fire and Building Safety
Alliance	The Alliance for Bangladesh Worker Safety
AFL-CIO	American Federation of Labour-Congress of Industrial Organizations
AFWA	Asia Floor Wage Alliance
AUW	Asian University for Women
BEPZA	Bangladesh Export Processing Zones Authority
BGMEA	Bangladesh Garment Manufacturers and Exporters Association
BKMEA	Bangladesh Knitwear Manufacturers and Exporters Association
BLAST	Bangladesh Legal Aid and Services Trust
BDT	Bangladesh Taka
BFC	Better Factories Cambodia
BWB	Better Work Bangladesh
BMI	Body Mass Index
BWF	Bonded Warehouse Facilities
CPD	Centre for Policy Dialogue
COO	Chief Operating Officer
CTO	Chief Technical Officer
CCC	Clean Clothes Campaign
CoC	Code of Conduct
CEACR	Committee of Experts on the Application of Conventions and Recommendations
CHRB	Corporate Human Rights Benchmark
CSR	Corporate Social Responsibility
CAPs	Corrective Action Plans
CM	Cut and Make
DIFE	Department of Inspection for Factories and Establishments
ESAF	Enhanced Structural Adjustment Facility
ETI	Ethical Trading Initiative
EU	European Union
EBA	Everything But Arms
EPZ	Export Processing Zone

FIR	First Information Report
GATT	General Agreement on Tariffs and Trade
GSP	Generalized System of Preferences
GLJ	Global Labor Justice
GDP	Gross Domestic Product
HRW	Human Rights Watch
IFCTU	International Confederation of Free Trade Unions
ILC	International Labour Conference
ILRF	International Labor Rights Forum
ILO	International Labour Organization
IMF	International Monetary Fund
LLRC	Labour Law Reform Committee
L/C	Letters of Credit
LPS	Lightning Protection System
MOU	Memorandum of Understanding
MOLVT	Ministry of Labour and Vocational Training
MoRD	Ministry of Rural Development
MoWCD	Ministry of Women and Child Development
MFA	Multi-Fibre Arrangement
NAP	National Action Plan
NCR	National Capital Region
NFPA	National Fire Protection Association
NI	National Initiative
NTPA	National Tripartite Plan of Action
NIP	New Industrial Policy
NYU	New York University
NGO	Non-Governmental Organizations
OSH	Occupational Safety and Health
OECD	Organization for Economic Cooperation and Development
PC	Participatory Committee
RMG	Readymade Garment
RCC	Remediation Coordination Cell
SEWA	Self-Employed Women's Association
SLD	Single-Line Diagram
SPYM	Society for the Promotion of Youth and Masses
SMO	Special Monitoring Organization
SOP	Standard Operating Procedures
SC	Steering Committee
SAF	Structural Adjustment Facility
TCLF	Textile, Clothing, Leather and Footwear
TNCs	Transnational Corporations
UN	United Nations
WLC	Women's Leadership Committee
WPCs	Workers' Participation Committees
WRC	Worker Rights Consortium
WDM	World Development Movement

1 Introduction

How do we understand the Rana Plaza disaster and what needs to be done to prevent future tragedies

Sanchita Banerjee Saxena

Sector background

The export garment manufacturing sector in Bangladesh began in the late 1970s following the establishment of the Multi-Fibre Arrangement (MFA) in 1974. The MFA, though it was only supposed to be a temporary measure, was in effect for 20 years, until 1994. This arrangement restricted garment and textile imports to the United States, Canada, and the European Union by allocating quotas to countries throughout the developing world (Saxena 2014). Bangladesh's industry began with fewer than 12 garment firms; by 1985, there were 450 independent companies; and by 2015, close to 7,000 firms and subcontractors (Labowitz and Baumann-Pauly 2015). By the 1990s, women accounted for more than 90% of the almost four million workers, and by 2016, garment exports accounted for 82% of the country's total exports. Today, the industry employs 5.1 million people (Ali 2006, Khan 2009, Saxena 2007, Winterbottom et al. 2017).

Foreign buyers looked to Bangladesh as a source of cheap labor, and thus, readymade garments became the country's main export in a short time. The focus on "CM" (cut and make) orders and a strategy of producing basic garments (e.g. T-shirts) quickly made Bangladesh South Asia's "success" story (Saxena 2014). This success came in many forms: increased gross domestic product, improved development opportunities, and women's empowerment (Chapter 2, this volume).

The economic achievement in Bangladesh, however, also came with a very real price, one that resulted in an industry where low-cost garments are made in hazardous conditions with low wages in unregulated factories by workers whose physical and mental health is tested on a daily basis. Thus, in order to maximize profits, in effect, Western brands not only outsourced production, but also outsourced labor exploitation and environmental degradation in order to ensure that prices would remain so low.[1] And Bangladesh was not new to disasters due to unsafe factories. More than 500 workers died between 2005 and 2012 in fires and building collapses in factories throughout the country (Bair et al. 2017).

Rana Plaza disaster

April 24, 2013 will be known as the day of the deadliest garment factory accident in history. More than 1,125 people died and 2,000 were injured when an eight-story building in the outskirts of the capital of Bangladesh, Rana Plaza, collapsed. The building, which was originally built as a shopping complex, was not meant to serve as a garment factory filled to capacity with more than 3,000 workers and their machines. Four stories had been added to the building without proper permits or documentation. According to Shakya (2013), the Dhaka building safety agency, the entity that is authorized to issue construction permits, simply could not keep up with the explosive growth of the industry over the last few decades. Large cracks in the building had appeared the day before the disaster, and other than the garment factory, all other parts of the building were closed that day. When garment workers pointed out the cracks to their supervisors, they were reprimanded and told to go back to work; otherwise, they would lose their jobs. This speaks to a much deeper and broader issue about the necessity of enabling workers' rights that goes far beyond discussions about building inspections; this will be discussed later in the chapter.

It is hard to describe the effects of the tragedy on the families and communities in Bangladesh. In addition to the horrific loss of life, many families lost their primary wage earner. For those who survived, the disaster led to both short-term and long-term physical and psychological disabilities. More than five years later, the recovery process for many of these survivors has been very difficult and lengthy.

The necessity of third-party monitoring

In the aftermath of the tragedy, according to Stein (2016), a variety of public and private actors made funding commitments to improve Bangladesh's garment sector in the form of loans to factories for safety improvements, grants to nongovernmental organizations and the International Labour Organization (ILO) for worker and management training programs, a trust fund for victims of the Rana Plaza collapse and their families, and more.[2]

In addition, Western companies invested in two organizations designed to strictly monitor and inspect a portion of Bangladesh's registered factories.[3] The Accord for Fire and Building Safety (Accord) is an agreement between global unions and over 180 retailers and brands from 20 countries in Europe, North America, Asia, and Australia. The Accord is a legally binding agreement where all those signed agree to arbitration or enforcement of fees can be pursued in their national legal system. Companies commit to sourcing and maintaining purchasing volumes in Bangladesh for five years. The Alliance for Bangladesh Worker Safety (Alliance) is an agreement of 28 mainly US-based retailers. It is similar to the Accord in its mandate, but the agreement is not legally binding nor are labor groups or unions a part of the Alliance.[4]

This move by Western brands has been touted as unprecedented and innovative, and while these organizations have made some important progress,[5] for example in the areas of factory safety (Anner 2018, Schüßler et al. 2018), this volume challenges this predominant narrative by arguing that these plans are not really a departure from what has been tried in the past. Historically, there have been many attempts to ensure labor rights in the global supply chain. Locke (2013) highlights several of these including social clauses within trade agreements, ILO and United Nations (UN) decent work conventions, transnational nongovernmental organizations (NGOs), global corporations and industry associations, and multi-stakeholder initiatives (p. 11).[6] He describes the trajectory of compliance initiatives; earlier, the focus was completely on enforcement and policing through upholding codes of conduct. These later developed into capability and capacity building programs designed to provide technical assistance to factories to make the much-needed improvements. The role of the third-party monitor has also changed from that of inspector to one of a consultant who works in collaboration with the factories in question (Locke 2013, p. 174–175).

Chaumtoli Huq argues, in her chapter, that while the Accord and Alliance agreements were historic in the sense that there had not been a unified effort by global brands to address safety issues in the global garment industry until after Rana Plaza,[7] they were not a radical departure from the existing framework of corporate social responsibility programs by global brands of the past. While perhaps the Accord stands out as a new development in that it is a binding agreement between global brands, unions, and NGOs, it is still limited by its sole focus on factory inspections. The Accord and Alliance also do not cover all of the factories that produce garments in Bangladesh.

Many of the studies analyzing labor rights argue that there is a need for third-party accountability in order to push factories toward compliance with standards because countries in the Global South lack strong institutions and have high levels of corruption and instability which makes it difficult for internal actors to enforce regulation (Ruggie 2003, Nadvi and Waltring 2004, Vogel 2008, Belal et al. 2015, Rubenstein 2007). Workers and civil society are often seen as lacking in significant power to be able to pressurize owners or the state to enforce the right policies. The reality is that lead firms typically prefer to move production to countries with weak government regulation, which allows them to impose their own standards, codes of conduct, and auditing practices; thus, they play a paradoxical role – on the one hand trying to substitute for limited government capacity, while on the other, seeking out locations where precisely capacity is limited and prices are kept extremely low.

Against this context, surrogate account holders are seen as better equipped to pressurize power wielders to do what is "right" in terms of labor improvements (Rubenstein 2007). Surrogates can take the form of supranational bodies, civil society organizations, or partnerships among corporations. Both the Accord and, to a lesser extent, the Alliance were designed to serve this role (Sinkovics 2016, Reinecke and Donaghey 2015). Both these initiatives focus on the corporation as the "solution" to improving labor conditions; Chaumtoli Huq will discuss this in more detail in Chapter 4.

Critiques to this third-party monitoring model[8]

As the above snapshot demonstrates, the Accord and Alliance, while perhaps well intentioned, have not met their intended goals, even by their own standards. While 85%–88% of factories have fixed the individual safety problems, a very small percentage has completed the entire remediation process successfully. Both these plans address a narrowly defined universe of factories with a very small subset of safety issues (Table 1.1).

There are several notable flaws with the third-party monitoring model. First, this book argues that the singular emphasis by Western retailers on monitoring and compliance has neglected the larger issues around the entire global supply chain. There has been very little discussion around the indirect sourcing model prevalent in Bangladesh which results in the most compliant factories depending heavily on subcontractors as a part of their regular business practice to increase margins and boost production while keeping costs low. Because subcontractors fall out of the purview of monitoring and inspection, as Saxena and Baumann-Pauly demonstrate in their chapter, this complex system makes it relatively easy for Western brands to turn a blind eye to the potentially dangerous activities that their "compliant" direct suppliers may be engaging in.

According to empirical research conducted by the New York University (NYU) Stern School of Business, Center for Business and Human Rights, the garment production involves more than twice as many facilities than

Table 1.1 Snapshot of the garment industry (March 2017)[a]

28.1 billion	Value of the garment sector, 2015–2016
82%	Garments as a percentage of total exports in Bangladesh, 2016
5.1 million	Number of workers in the industry
7,179	Estimated number of RMG factories in Bangladesh
2,256	RMG factories actively engaged in remediation under the Accord and the Alliance ("active factories")
31%	Accord and Alliance active factories as a percentage of the total number of factories in Bangladesh
744	Alliance inspections
1,600	Accord inspections
2,334	Total inspections
79	Factories covered by the Accord and Alliance that have completed the entire remediation process successfully

a Winterbottom et al. (2017). Research Brief: "Bangladesh Factory Safety - Four Years after Rana Plaza." NYU Stern. Center for Business and Human Rights.

brands and retailers currently monitor directly.[9] While many brands are adamant about their "zero tolerance policy" for unauthorized subcontracting, the policy is largely ineffective in practice. Bangladeshi manufacturers openly discuss the extensive network of small, less compliant factories and how they play an important role in meeting the demands of the larger factories that maintain the primary relationships with Western buyers.[10] Their chapter explains how current business models of brands and retailers set incentives for the development of elaborate production networks in Bangladesh and how, thanks to these networks, the garment business has remained profitable post-Rana Plaza, despite fierce international competition, labor law reforms, and political blockages. The authors argue that unless business models change and all factories in Bangladesh are brought under a monitoring system that upgrades the entire sector, a large portion of the garment workers in Bangladesh will remain unsafe and other tragedies that cost workers' lives cannot be excluded. The presences of this large informal sector also means new ways of thinking about improvements in the industry that go beyond traditional approaches. Tewari (this volume), for example, writes about the necessity of local initiatives that improve labor rights from the bottom-up:

> The state can be the actor that can bring continuity by holding open the space for new organizational partnerships to emerge even as private supply chains and markets shift. This is especially important in countries and contexts where 90% of the total employment is in the informal sector, outside the reach of both labor laws as well as the monitoring protocols and codes of conduct of buyers and private companies.

Tied in with this, focusing only on monitoring factories as a solution to prevent future disasters does not address the extreme pressures suppliers face from brands to produce large quantities, at the lowest price and in the shortest time possible. Anner (2018) finds that since Rana Plaza, the price paid to Bangladeshi supplier factories has declined by 13%. On average, lead times declined by 8.14% between 2011 and 2015, as workers are constantly pushed by lead factories to produce their products quicker and faster; this is fueled by the desire for "fast fashion" in the United States and Europe leading to increased profit margins for global brands. Real wages have also dropped by 6.47% since the wage increase of December 2013. Schüßler et al. (2018) also write, "…some labour rights abuses, such as forced overtime, low wages, and verbal abuse remain entrenched in garment factories, reflecting an unchanged business model in the industry." The constant threat by brands to source elsewhere leads factory owners to accept these impossible conditions in order to maintain their business. Thus, the extreme competition and insecurity around future work creates a perverse incentive structure and an environment of taking risks, even for factories that may have passed all the inspections (Piore 1997, Saxena 2014, Gearheart 2016).

Locke (2013) argues that compliance programs do little to change the root causes of poor working conditions. Many of the problems faced in global supply chains cannot simply be attributed to unethical factory managers in need of capacity building, auditing, or policing. Much of it is due to the pressures and policies that have been put in place by global brands to maximize profit and minimize risks of not meeting consumer demands in a timely manner. Compliance issues related to hours of work, wages, precarious contracts, child labor, undeclared subcontracting, and even fire and building safety are all related to the downward pressure on prices and lead times that drive manufacturers to cut costs and seek flexibility by almost any means possible (Labowitz and Baumann-Pauly 2014). Women bear the disproportionate brunt of the negative impacts of these business practices, leading to gender-based violence in the industry that is systemic in nature (Chapter 12, this volume). The Rana Plaza disaster was not an isolated incident, but part of a much larger crisis of decent working conditions that is endemic to the entire global supply chain that has been in place for decades (Siddiqi 2017, Chapter 2, this volume). Unfortunately, there has been little attention paid to this, which has allowed global brands to continue to maintain their business practices even in the light of horrific disasters that have taken place.[11] As Kabeer (this volume) writes:

> We need to move from a narrow 'spotlight' perspective on working conditions in global value chains, a perspective that draws our gaze to the locus of production alone, to a 'flood light' approach which illuminates the broader political economy of supply chain capitalism within which these production processes are located.

Third, because a dialogue around business practices by global brands is left out of the discussion, it is easy to point the finger at the most visible offender when one of these disasters occurs – the Bangladeshi factory owner. While factory owners certainly bear responsibility for improving working conditions, as Shakya (2013) writes:

> ...to make a lone producer and a select few of his buyers culprits of this devastating accident of unprecedented scale, and to let the bigger powers off the hook, is to spank a racist while turning a blind eye to the regime of apartheid.

By making the factory owner the main focus of both international blame and condemnation, as well as holding him as the sole person responsible to prevent future disasters, global brands can be absolved of any accountability and feel absolutely no pressure to change their lucrative business practices. This also, as Siddiqi (2017) writes, conditions us to see labor violations and strategies for change only as a consequence of "local" factors and frames the problem in terms of the individual as opposed to the larger system (Chapter 6, this volume, Schüßler and Lohmeyer 2017). Ultimately, the power relationships between brands and suppliers are not challenged when the focus is only on factory-level compliance, as Ward (this volume) concludes:

> ...supply chain continuity drives the fundamental premise of compliance monitoring and corporate codes. If the root causes of labour rights violations are supply chain practices driven by brands and a lack of worker agency and ability for collective action – which manifest as poor factory conditions – then focusing on factory level remediation is a band-aid solution. Employment conditions are improved, but not to the extent that asymmetrical power relations between employers and workers, and brands and factories are disrupted.

Initiatives focused primarily on monitoring and policing also allow brands to appear as if they are serious about labor rights and factory conditions. Because as Locke (2013) writes: "Should the factories fail to remedy various workplace problems, brands are expected to switch their orders to supposedly more 'ethical' producers" (p. 24). When global brands terminate business relationships, they lose any leverage they might have had in improving conditions for workers, while leaving these workers in highly risky environments where improvements may never occur. Some even go as far as to argue that compliance initiatives are not designed to protect labor rights or improve conditions at all, but are really designed only to limit the legal liability of the global brands and prevent damage to their reputations (Bartley 2005).

In addition to holding Bangladeshi factory owners solely responsible for factory improvements, research by Winterbottom and Baumann-Pauly (2017) suggests that they are financially liable. The cost of addressing existing factory safety issues greatly exceeds the funds committed thus far, which leaves many factories without the finances to implement more costly improvements (Chapter 13, this volume). Factory owners must be in compliance to maintain relationships with both the Accord and Alliance and they must also fund the improvements themselves; if they cannot afford them, no one is obligated to assist them. Anner (2018) cites a figure of USD 11 million per year as the budget for the Accord to pay its approximately 94 specialized engineers and other support staff. However, no portion of this budget is earmarked for factories going through the remediation process. The result is a deep chasm in the industry; elite firms that are able to finance the improvements will continue their relationships with suppliers and workers will benefit from the upgrades. Many of the firms, however, cannot fund the recommended corrections, leaving their workers vulnerable and at risk. The international donor community has also not pledged funding to address issues like poor infrastructure, but have focused primarily on inspection and empowerment programs.

Fourth, with this singular focus on monitoring, most suppliers tend to be reluctant to enable rights that challenge deeply embedded labor relations or social norms, hoping to avoid disruption to the production process.

Consequently, issues such as gender discrimination, freedom of speech, and workers' skills development are still mainly neglected. A focus on the "failed building" as the main cause and culprit of the disaster puts the focus narrowly on factory safety, rather than broader issues of ill health and unsafe conditions (Ashraf 2017). Sinkovics et al. (2016) find that while the Accord achieved their mandate in some of the factories under their purview (safer and better equipped working environments), due to the high cost of compliance, companies were forced to terminate initiatives that focused on some of the social grounded needs of workers. Surrogate accountability often lacks insights into context-dependent socially grounded needs of workers and can even impair social, economic, or cultural rights (Belal and Roberts 2010, Lund-Thomsen 2008, Sinkovics et al. 2014).

As a result, the focus tends to be on the implementation of measurable and more visible standards (Barrientos and Smith 2007, Barrientos et al. 2011). For example, Winterbottom et al. (2017) find that after reviewing 100 remediation reports, there were an average of 59 noncompliance issues per factory. Electrical safety issues accounted for the majority (51%) of safety issues identified, followed by fire safety (30%) and structural safety (19%) issues. Prentice and De Neve (2017) also discuss a tendency to narrowly focus on safety and infrastructure issues that can be seen and audited. We argue that this tendency to focus on quantifiable, "checking the box" type of solutions (like the number of factories inspected or the number of unions registered) often ignores how effective these solutions truly are and ignores many other important areas that threaten workers' health and well-being on a day-to-day basis. Bhattacharjee (this volume), for example, discusses how the critical issue of gender-based violence in factories can be addressed.

In Ward's chapter, comparing the experiences of Bangladesh with Cambodia, she finds that in Cambodia, the first country to implement the ILO's Better Factories program, compliance with some labor standards has increased. Yet program synthesis reports from 2015 also show compliance regression in the area of freedom of association and union representation. Moreover, contextual drivers of labor compliance differ, making implementation of standardized models highly variable. Her chapter compares the cases of Cambodia and Bangladesh to consider whether programs such as Better Factories strengthen state and brand legitimacy without corresponding rights and safety gains for workers. She argues that as a complementary and parallel mechanism to state legislative enforcement, third-party monitoring alone runs the risk of eroding, rather than ensuring, worker rights in the long term. Locke (2013) also finds that

> ...these improvements seem to have reached a plateau: basic improvements have been achieved in some areas (e.g. health and safety) but not in others (e.g. freedom of association, limits on excess overtime). Moreover, these improvements appear to be unstable in that many factories cycle in and out of 'compliance' over time.
>
> (p. 31)

Saxena (2014) finds in her comparative study of the industry in Bangladesh, Cambodia, and Sri Lanka that not only do top-down programs not address issues related to enabling workers' rights and empowerment, but, as some conditions improve, these programs are used as a justification to exclude workers from discussions around larger sector issues:

> In the cases of Sri Lanka and Cambodia, such positive development in the factories have been seen as justifications for excluding labor from meaningful dialogue about further changes at both the factory and the national level. In Bangladesh, though change has been much slower and improvements have been incremental, the workers themselves...have been very involved in efforts to affect changes.
>
> (p. 163)

Ultimately, the strategy to develop top-down interventions by third parties is often misguided as it ignores local movements that are already in place. According to Ashraf (2017), "Both the Accord and the Alliance have been developed by external actors (retailers based in Europe and North America, global trade unions, and transnational NGOs, and the ILO) with little or selective participation from Bangladesh-based institutions..." (p. 251). Bangladesh has had a long history of a vibrant and visible labor movement that has worked to make changes in the industry, long before third-party monitoring and corporate codes of conduct. However, instead of supporting these local struggles, parallel programs with the involvement of international labor organizations, rather than local labor groups, are instituted in order to address issues that emerged after the disaster. In addition, the importance of collaborating with official trade unions (another solution that is quantifiable, i.e. the number of unions established per factory) is often highlighted as a solution to workers' rights, but as a result, other vibrant civil society movements, often outside the structure of formal unions, are rejected. In Bangladesh, factory-level unions in the garment industry often tend to be hierarchical, politically connected, and male dominated; these have not always been the most effective channels of representation for labor. On the other hand, garment federations, which are made up of NGOs, women's groups, and some unions, have often been far more instrumental in pushing for change than individual factory unions (Saxena 2014).

Siddiqi's chapter in this volume builds on earlier work on dominant narratives around the garment industry as they inform transnational policies and practices of solidarity. She argues, hegemonic Euro-American framings of "the problem" privilege some issues while occluding or dismissing others. The emergence of the Accord-Alliance "solution" and corresponding ILO initiatives to form factory-level unions illustrates the limited nature of such interventions. Both leave untouched long-term structural issues that fundamentally shape workers' experiences on the shop floor and with respect to organizing. Siddiqi draws on the experiences of primarily non-NGO trade union leaders as they negotiated with the state during mass protests in 2006, 2010, and 2013. At moments of crisis like this, she argues, the state uses a set of colonial laws, especially those on sedition and dissent, to discredit and repress worker organizing. This chapter shows how evoking the rhetoric of the garment industry's survival being a question of national interest allows the state to create a space of exception where routine labor laws do not apply.

When can this model be effective?

As Locke (2013) argues, private sector initiatives can only be effective if there are mutual benefits for the buyer and supplier, and then eventually for the worker (p. 17). Factory management needs to be convinced that improvements are necessary and important, and each member of the larger coalition of relevant actors must have a stake in the outcomes. Evidence gathered since the establishment of the Alliance and Accord shows limited impact on improvements for workers and on engaging the relevant stakeholders.[12]

This volume presents innovative ways of thinking about broader solutions to improve labor conditions that go beyond third-party monitoring initiatives, with a narrow focus on fire safety, by examining the role of community-based movements, focusing on direct worker empowerment using technology, developing a model of change through enforceable contracts combined with workers movements, and ensuring a more productive and influential function for factory owners, the government, and buyers. Many of the chapters provide examples of innovation, whether outside of Bangladesh, within the country, or in the area of international law that addresses many of the criticisms of monitoring and compliance initiatives articulated earlier.

Beyond third-party monitoring: renewed role for the domestic private sector, the government, and buyers

Rubana Huq (this volume) reviews the measures that have been put in place to improve standards of safety and labor after the Rana Plaza collapse, compliance and auditing pressures, implementation of measurable standards of work and safety, and the extent to which retailers and manufacturers in Bangladesh are now taking responsibility for improving working conditions and the quality of life of factory workers. In her chapter, she also focuses on the structure to form a local Bangladeshi platform for monitoring safety standards that is a departure from third-party monitoring.

Baumann-Pauly et al. (2015) and Locke (2013) find that while the government of Bangladesh should be the principal regulator of the garment sector, it lacks the political will, technical capacity, and resources necessary to protect the basic rights of its own workers. In some cases, they chose not to enforce certain laws due to the fear of driving up costs and driving up sources of economic development and employment. This is similar to problems faced by other garment producing countries and in global supply chains generally.

Rahman (this volume) finds that the government in Bangladesh has historically failed to protect the rights of workers; more than 2,200 garment workers have died and hundreds have been injured between 2000 and 2013 in Bangladesh. Although these incidents have been widely reported in national and international press, no major steps have been taken by the government to prevent the recurrence of such events. Soon after the Rana Plaza disaster, however, the government initiated various methods of ensuring compliance with labor standards. The main aim of his chapter is to understand why there has been this shift – what labor policies have been adopted by the government since the Rana Plaza disaster and how has the government negotiated the challenges raised after 2013. The changing role of the Bangladeshi government's policies post-Rana Plaza brings the government "back" into the picture, and is critical for examining institutional solutions to address the issues of labor rights in global supply chains.

There is evidence that when buyers enter into more collaborative, mutually beneficial, and long-term relationship with suppliers, working conditions do improve. Increased communication and interaction can lead to more collaborative and transparent relations between buyers and suppliers (Locke 2013). Large global garment buyers in Europe are experimenting with new approaches to manage labor standards that go beyond third-party monitoring, with a focus on transparency, supply chain consolidation, and collective governance initiatives (Schüßler et al. 2018). Saxena and Baumann-Pauly (this volume) also discuss the direct strategic sourcing model where buyers work with specific factories on a long-term basis as an alternative to the current system of insecure relationships that is in place.[13] Moazzem (this volume) argues that the post-Rana Plaza initiatives are a step forward in implementing the decent work agenda in the apparel sector value chain; however, the activities pursued have primarily focused on workplace safety issues and, only partly, on workers' rights issues. Survey data find that participation of buyers and suppliers is largely confined to brands, retailers, international buyers, and large- and medium-scale suppliers; participation of the local and international buying houses and small-scale enterprises and sub-contractee enterprises is either low or absent. He argues that a high level of commitment from *all* stakeholders including buyers at all levels, suppliers, the government, international organizations, workers' organizations, consumer groups and rights-based organizations is needed in order to ensure significant changes in the sector.

Local and direct oversight: involving the community and individual workers

Tewari (this volume) addresses many of the criticisms of the limitations of third-party monitoring in her chapter, which draws on lessons learned from an innovative place-based experiment in relational sourcing in India's Mewat region (2009–2012, and ongoing). She makes a case for place-based approaches to facilitating improved working conditions and fostering greater social accountability in complex global value chains. Tewari argues that new solutions and new thinking are needed that go beyond the current focus on the single firm. Her fundamental argument is that we need to move beyond the workplace and into the community where the most vulnerable, informal garment workers live and work to really make a difference to preventing horrific tragedies such as Rana Plaza from occurring again. To ensure that benefits reach them, we need to target the places, localized labor markets, and communities that they are a part. In addition to "place" the state needs to get involved by forging new sourcing models that involve networked ties between public sector agencies, branded buyers, and locally rooted community associations (or NGOs) that can provide continuous oversight, accountability, and learning as global (and local) work reaches those who are the most unprotected at the base of the garment industry's value chains. These changed ways of conducting business will not only change incentives that firms face, and limit the room to maneuver in taking risks, but by building up local relationships, workers can become a central part of a local movement to create safer working conditions and decent work.

Gill and Khanna (this volume) also address direct engagement by the workers by examining the role that technology can play in enabling possible solutions. Their chapter also addresses the barriers these solutions need to address in order to be successful at scale. They advocate for a worker-centric approach to improving labor rights, which they describe as:

> Workers are a key stakeholder in the supply chain, and need to be treated as such to enable a successful outcome...when workers feel empowered by the same information that is being shared with brands, they have a compelling reason to share the full, true story. The only way to collect reliable data is to deliver value to the source—workers, themselves...Making them a part of the process means that they will actually participate and provide reliable data on a continuous basis, which is a lot more valuable than a one-off conversation every other year.

Interventions to address gender-based violence in the garment industry

Silliman Bhattacharjee's chapter (this volume) analyzes the personal experiences of violence reported by women garment workers in Bangladesh, Cambodia, India, Indonesia, and Sri Lanka. Women described sexual harm and suffering; and industrial discipline practices, including physical violence, verbal abuse, coercion, threats, retaliation, and forced overtime. She argues that gender-based violence in the garment industry is not simply a factory-level problem that can be corrected by improved compliance monitoring. Rather, it is a predictable outcome in an industry dominated by lead firms that seek to release fast fashion trends at reduced costs by using a business model predicated on outsourcing apparel production to a flexible workforce employed on short-term contracts and required to meet unrealistic production targets for below living wages. The daily race to meet production targets is sustained through gendered industrial discipline practices that leave women particularly vulnerable to abuse. What approaches might prove effective in addressing gender-based violence in garment supply chains? Learning from the successes and limitations of the Bangladesh Accord model, her chapter makes a case for substantive obligations on lead firms through binding, contractually enforceable agreements, combined with the leadership of workers' collectives and women garment workers themselves to eliminate gender-based violence.

Organization of the volume

This volume is organized into four main sections: *Leading to the Disaster, Dealing with the Aftermath, Rethinking Solutions, and A Way Forward.* The two chapters in *Leading to the Disaster* provide a larger context to the circumstances that led to the Rana Plaza disaster. Feldman and Hossain's chapter offers us an overview of the industry, the policies guiding production and exports, and the building of an industrial labor force to situate post-Rana Plaza interventions. They take a long view of the sector to situate Bangladesh manufacturing in the global economy and highlight its changing structure, organization, and conditions of production and compliance. Saxena and Baumann-Pauly describe the highly prevalent, but largely ignored subcontracting sector in the Bangladesh's garment industry and argue that ignoring this hidden reality will result in future tragedies that will take workers' lives.

Dealing with the Aftermath includes three distinct chapters that examine varying aspects of the post-Rana Plaza disaster. C. Huq's chapter focuses on the opportunities and limitations of the Accord and Alliance programs. She argues that without a labor rights focus to these programs and greater accountability measures, their impact will be limited. There are, however, opportunities to redirect the focus of these programs toward building the capacity of workers to demand better working conditions. Ward's chapter provides a critique of Accord- and Alliance-type interventions by examining the limitations of the Better Factories Cambodia program, a top-down, third-party monitoring program executed by the International Labour Organization in Cambodia. Finally, Siddiqi discusses the challenges of labor organizing, especially after national tragedies, that fall outside of the formal factory-level union structure.

The six chapters under *Rethinking Solutions* examine new and innovative ways of thinking about the post-Rana Plaza environment that goes beyond third-party monitoring. The first set of chapters focus on the transformations to the garment industry specifically in Bangladesh. These chapters focus on a changing role for the domestic private sector (R. Huq), a changing role for the Bangladeshi government (Rahman), and a new relationship with buyers (Moazzem). The next set of chapters focus on solutions from an international perspective and include community-based solutions (Tewari), the use of technology to empower workers (Gill and Khanna), and interventions to address gender-based violence (Bhattacharjee). Finally, Kabeer concludes this volume by presenting a way forward.

Conclusion

This volume presents an interdisciplinary approach to addressing the crisis of labor rights from the perspective of workers, brands, international protections, community organizations, and governments. It is a unique contribution to the field, with chapters that are unified around the central theme of global supply chains that stretch around the world, as well as the sourcing decisions and business models that animate those chains, and how these pertain to poor labor conditions. As Kabeer (this volume) concludes in her final chapter:

> The rapid development of the sector, and its contribution to the country's growth rates and foreign exchange earnings, appeared to hold out the promise of helping the country to transition from aid dependency to greater self-reliance through trade. But while it has gone from the handful of factories that existed in its early years to becoming the second largest exporter of garments after China, it is evident that the market conditions under which it has to compete have steadily worsened as the fast fashion business model has come to dominate global value chains. It is by no means clear that employers in the industry would have voluntarily improved labour standards in their factories if the terms on which they supply their garments had improved over time but what is clear is that their ability to do so has been severely constrained by the increasingly exploitative business practices of global buyers.

The volume does three things through its collection of chapters that are both theoretically analytical and "solution" oriented. First, it puts Rana Plaza into a larger context to help readers understand the structural, managerial, and political conditions within which poor labor standards flourish. Second, the book productively critiques the existing plans that are in place and highlights their limitations with the hopes of new and improved methods to address these critical concerns. And finally, many of the authors provide a way forward by examining innovations, new ideas, and novel approaches that can all be part of a larger set of "solutions" to address workers' rights post-Rana Plaza and beyond.

It is clear that third-party monitoring initiatives are limited in their scope and focus and will not likely prevent future tragedies from occurring. To effectively address the gaps going forward, there must be a concerted effort by all actors in the global supply chain, public and private, from consumers to donors, international organizations, local industry, civil society, to governments to engage in a dialogue. This book argues that in order to prevent horrific tragedies like Rana Plaza from occurring in the future, larger flaws in the global chain must be addressed, direct and long-term buying relations with factories must be established, the government of Bangladesh must assume responsibility for properly regulating garment production, and linkages with existing movements must be created with the hope that this will change the way business is conducted and reduce the incentives of factory owners to take deadly risks in order to meet the demands of their clients.

Notes

1 See Saxena (2014), chapter 1 about the contradictions prevalent in this industry.
2 See Stein (2016), p. 2 for timeline of financial commitments.
3 See http://ssrn.com/abstract=2577535 for details on the Accord and Alliance governance structure, p. 6.
4 See Ashraf (2017), pp. 254–257 for more details distinguishing these two agreements.
5 See Anner (2018) where he finds that there have been limited gains in overtime, work intensity, wages, and the right to organize. There have, however, been improvements in building safety.
6 For a list of private, voluntary initiatives aimed at regulating global labor standards, see Locke (2013), p. 9.
7 There are examples of private sector initiatives to improve labor conditions in other industries such as electronics, taken on by companies such as Apple and Hewlett-Packard (Locke 2013).
8 Many authors have written about the mixed results of the various compliance models in a variety of sectors (Barrientos and Smith 2007, Egels-Zanden 2007, Korovkin and Sanmiguel-Valderrama 2007, Yu 2008, Nadvi et al. 2011, Saxena 2014, Chapter 5 in this volume).
9 The Bangladesh Garment Manufacturers and Exporters Association estimates that there are 4,296 RMG factories in Bangladesh. The NYU Stern Center for Business and Human Rights, however, has estimated that there are more than 7,100 facilities producing for the RMG industry. Further research by the BRAC University's Centre for Entrepreneurship Development in Dhaka has estimated the number of factories to be more than 8,000 (Winterbottom and Baumann-Pauly 2017).
10

> We estimate that there are approximately 3,800 of these factories, which includes a mix of formal, registered subcontractors and informal, unregistered subcontractors. These factories tend to be smaller than direct exporters and operate on much tighter profit margins. They are less familiar with international labor standards and have fewer discretionary resources to invest in safety or efficiency improvements. This part of the sector has remained largely invisible to the international community until now. Few resources or inspections are directed towards subcontracting factories or towards ensuring that workers in these factories enjoy minimum standards of safety and workers' rights.
>
> (Stein 2016)

11 Exceptions include Oxfam International (2004), Clean Clothes Campaign (2008), and Raworth and Kidder (2009).
12 See Baumann-Pauly et al. (2015) for an analysis of the legitimacy of both initiatives:

> Overall, however, both initiatives fall short in important legitimacy criteria on the input dimension, which in turn limits their legitimacy on the output dimension. Weak representation and buy-in of key local actors undermines the implementation process and threatens its sustainability. Moreover, the narrow framework of the initiatives in terms of efficacy (fire and building safety exclusively) and in terms of coverage (only official suppliers of Accord and Alliance brands) fails to acknowledge the scale and complexity of establishing a safe and sustainable garment sector in Bangladesh… The Accord and the Alliance were never intended to address the full range of challenges, but their effectiveness and legitimacy even within the narrow scope they seek to address will be limited because of the linkages among these complex issues. Ultimately, it is clear that the Accord and the Alliance do not address the full scope of the problems and that both have key shortcomings when it comes to input and output legitimacy.
>
> (p. 18)

13 Schüßler and Lohmeyer (2017) find in their study that several firms in the German garment industry are planning to pursue direct supplier relationships in order to facilitate closer contact and greater transparency and developing long-term relationships with suppliers was a strategic goal.

Works cited

Ali, M. (2006, November). "Rise of the Readymade Garments Industry in Bangladesh: Entrepreneurial Ingenuity or Public Policy." Paper presented at the Workshop on Governance and Development. Dhaka: Bangladesh Institute for Development Studies.

Anner, M. (2018). *Binding Power: The Sourcing Squeeze, Workers' Rights, and Building Safety in Bangladesh since Rana Plaza*. Research Report. Penn State: Center for Global Workers' Rights (CGWR).

Ashraf, H. (2017). "Beyond Building Safety: An Ethnographic Account of Health and Well-Being on the Bangladesh Garment Shop Floor." In Prentice, R. and De Neve, G., Eds. *Unmaking the Global Sweatshop: Health and Safety of the World's Garment Workers*. Philadelphia, PA: University of Pennsylvania Press.

Bair, J., Anner, M. and Blasi, J. (2017). "Sweatshops and the Search for Solutions, Yesterday and Today." In Prentice, R. and De Neve, G., Eds. *Unmaking the Global Sweatshop: Health and Safety of the World's Garment Workers*. Philadelphia, PA: University of Pennsylvania Press.

Barrientos, S., Gereffi, G. and Rossi, A. (2012). "Economic and Social Upgrading in Global Production Networks: A New Paradigm for a Changing World." *International Labour Review*, Vol. 150, No. 3–4, pp. 319–340.

Barrientos, S. and Smith, S. (2007). "Do Workers Benefit from Ethical Trade? Assessing Codes of Labour Practice in Global Production Systems." *Third World Quarterly*, Vol. 28, No. 4, pp. 713–729.

Bartley, T. (2005). "Corporate Accountability and the Privatization of Labor Standards: Struggles over Codes of Conduct in the Apparel Industry." *Research in Political Sociology*, Vol. 14, pp. 211–44.

Baumann-Pauly, D., Labowitz, S. and Banerjee, N. (2015). "Closing Governance Gaps in Bangladesh's Garment Industry – The Power and Limitations of Private Governance Schemes." Available at SSRN: https://ssrn.com/abstract=2577535 or doi:10.2139/ssrn.2577535.

Belal, A.R., Cooper, S.M. and Khan, N.A. (2015). "Corporate Environmental Responsibility and Accountability: What Chance in Vulnerable Bangladesh?" *Critical Perspectives on Accounting*, Vol. 33, December, pp. 44–58. doi:10.1016/j.cpa.2015.01.005.

Belal, A.R. and Roberts, R.W. (2010). "Stakeholders' Perceptions of Corporate Social Reporting in Bangladesh." *Journal of Business Ethics*, Vol. 97, No. 2, pp. 311–324.

Clean Clothes Campaign. (2008). *Cashing In: Giant Retailers, Purchasing Practices, and Working Conditions in the Garment Industry*. Available at www.cleanclothes.org.

Egels-Zanden, N. (2007). "Suppliers' Compliance with MNC's Codes of Conduct: Behind the Scenes at Chinese Toy Suppliers." *Journal of Business Ethics*, Vol. 75, pp. 45–62.

Gearhart, J. (2016). "Global Supply Chains: Time for a New Deal?" *Open Democracy*. www.opendemocracy.net/beyondslavery/ilc/judy-gearhart/global-supply-chains-time-for-new-deal.

Khan, S.R. (2009). *Export Success and Industrial Linkages: The Case of Readymade Garments in South Asia*. New York: Palgrave Macmillan.

Korovkin, T. and Sanmiguel-Valderrama, O. (2007). "Labor Standards, Global Markets and Non-State Initiatives: Columbia's and Ecuador's Flower Industries in Comparative Perspectives." *Third World Quarterly*, Vol. 28, No. 1, pp. 117–135.

Labowitz, S. and Baumann-Pauly, D. (2014). *Business as Usual Is Not an Option: Supply Chains and Sourcing after Rana Plaza*. New York: NYU Stern Center for Business and Human Rights.

Labowitz, S. and Baumann-Pauly, D. (2015). *Beyond the Tip of the Iceberg: Bangladesh's Forgotten Apparel Workers*. New York: NYU Stern Center for Business and Human Rights.

Locke, R.M. (2013). *The Promise and Limits of Private Power: Promoting Labor Standards in a Global Economy*. New York: Cambridge University Press.

Lund-Thomsen, P. (2008). "The Global Sourcing and Codes of Conduct Debate: Five Myths and Five Recommendations." *Development & Change*, Vol. 39, No. 6, pp. 1005–1018.

Nadvi, K., Lund-Thomsen, P., Xue, H. and Khara, N. (2011). "Playing Against China: Global Value Chains and Labour Standards in the International Sports Good Industry." *Global Networks*, Vol. 11, No. 3, pp. 334–354.

Nadvi, K. and Waltring, F. (2004). "Making Sense of Global Standards." In Schmitz, H., Ed. *Local Enterprises in the Global Economy: Issues of Governance and Upgrading* (pp. 53–94). Northampton: Edward Elgar.

Oxfam International. (2004). *Trading Away Our Rights: Women Working in Global Supply Chains*.

Piore, M. (1997). "The Economics of Sweatshops." In Ross, A., Ed. *No Sweat: Fashion, Free Trade, and the Rights of Garment Workers*. New York: Verso.

Prentice, R. and De Neve, G. (2017). "Five Years after Deadly Factory Fire, Bangladesh's Garment Workers Are Still Vulnerable." *The Conversation*. Available at https://theconversation.com/five-years-after-deadly-factory-fire-bangladeshs-garment-workers-are-still-vulnerable-88027?utm_source=facebook&utm_medium=facebookbutton.

Prentice, R. and De Neve, G., Eds. (2017). *Unmaking the Global Sweatshop: Health and Safety of the World's Garment Workers.* Philadelphia, PA: University of Pennsylvania Press.

Raworth, K. & Kidder, T. (2009). "Mimicking 'Lean' in Global Value Chains: It's the Workers Who Get Leaned On." In Bair, J., Ed. *Frontiers of Commodity Chain Research* (pp. 165–189). Stanford, CA: Stanford University Press.

Reinecke, J. and Donaghey, J. (2015). "After Rana Plaza: Building Coalitional Power for Labour Rights between Unions and (Consumption-Based) Social Movement Organisations." *Organization*, Vol. 22, No. 5, pp. 720–774.

Rubenstein, J. (2007), "Accountability in an Unequal World," *The Journal of Politics*, Vol. 69, No. 3, pp. 616–632.

Ruggie, J.G. (2003). "Taking Embedded Liberalism Global: The Corporate Connection." In Held, D. and Koenig-Archibugi, M., Eds., *Taming Globalization: Frontiers of Governance.* Cambridge: Polity Press.

Saxena, S. (2007). "Competition or Complacency? Can the Phase-Out of the Multi-Fiber Arrangement Spur Domestic Policy Reform in Asian Countries." *Pacific Rim Report* 46. San Francisco, CA: University of San Francisco.

Saxena, S. (2014). *Made in Bangladesh, Cambodia, and Sri Lanka: The Labor Behind the Global Garments and Textiles Industries.* New York: Cambria Press.

Schüßler, E. and Lohmeyer, N. (2017). "Changing Governance for Labour: Germany's Garment Supply Chains." Garment Supply Chain Governance Discussion Paper Series. Berlin: Garment Supply Chain Governance Project.

Schüßler, E., Frenkel, S., Ashwin, S., Kabeer, N., Egels-Zanden, N., Huq, L., Alexander, R., Oka, C., Lohmeyer, N., Rahman, S. and Rahman, K.M. (2018). "Changes in the Governance of Garment Global Production Networks: Lead Firm, Supplier and Institutional Responses to the Rana Plaza Disaster." Interim Report. Berlin: Garment Supply Chain Governance Project.

Shakya, M. (2013). "Behind the Garment Disaster in Bangladesh." *Global Dialogue*, Vol. 3, No. 4. http://isa-global-dialogue.net/volume-3-issue-4/.

Siddiqi, D. (2017). "Afterword: Politics after Rana Plaza." In Prentice, R. and De Neve, G., Eds. *Unmaking the Global Sweatshop: Health and Safety of the World's Garment Workers.* Philadelphia, PA: University of Pennsylvania Press.

Sinkovics, N., Sinkovics, R.R. and Hoque, S.F. (2016)." Rana Plaza Collapse Aftermath: Are CSR Compliance and Auditing Pressures Effective?" *Accounting, Auditing & Accountability Journal*, Vol. 29, No. 4, pp. 617–649.

Sinkovics, N., Sinkovics, R.R. and Yamin, M. (2014), "The Role of Social Value Creation in Business Model Formulation at the Bottom of the Pyramid – Implications for MNEs?" *International Business Review*, Vol. 23, No. 4, pp. 692–707.

Stein, N. (2016). Research Brief. *Foreign Funding Commitments for Bangladesh's Garment Sector.* New York: NYU Stern. Center for Business and Human Rights.

Vogel, D., (2008). "Private Global Business Regulation." *Annual Review of Political Science*, Vol. 11, pp. 261–282.

Winterbottom, M. and Baumann-Pauly, D. (2017). *Estimating the True Cost of Remediating the Ready-Made Garment Industry in Bangladesh.* New York: NYU Stern. Center for Business and Human Rights.

Winterbottom, M., Rosen, Z. and Baumann-Pauly, D. (2017). Research Brief. *Bangladesh Factory Safety-Four Years after Rana Plaza.* New York: NYU Stern. Center for Business and Human Rights.

Yu, X.M. (2008). "Impacts of Corporate Codes of Conduct on Labor Standards: A Case Study of Reebok's Athletic Footwear Supplier Factory in China." *Journal of Business Ethics*, Vol. 81, pp. 513–529.

Part I

Leading to the disaster

2 The longue durée and the promise of export-led development

Readymade garment manufacturing in Bangladesh

Shelley Feldman and Jakir Hossain

Introduction

The Rana Plaza disaster of April 24, 2013, in Savar Upazila in the Dhaka district of Bangladesh, is considered one of the deadliest industrial failures of the contemporary moment. The building collapse cost the loss of more than 1,100 lives and has left thousands more injured leading global trade unions to refer to it as "mass industrial homicide" (The Guardian 2016). As the country's worst industrial disaster, Rana Plaza garnered international outrage and led, almost immediately, to calls for reform of the Bangladesh readymade garment (RMG) sector, one that has been producing garments for the world market since the mid-1970s. This tragedy, however, was not an isolated incident, but, rather, part of RMG history that has been plagued by factory fires,[1] lock-ins, shop floor violence, and failures to resolve ongoing struggles between workers and management. Yet, it took more than 40 years for European and North American buyers to acknowledge the cost to Bangladeshi workers of cheap garment production, and to propose two international interventions, the Accord on Fire and Building Safety, and the Alliance for Worker Safety each, if differently, demanding safety checks by companies buying clothing from the world's second largest producer. These agreements have given factories until the summer of 2018 to improve the sector's physical infrastructure and working conditions, with noncompliance of agreed upon standards risking losses to some of the world's largest brands.

The horror of Rana Plaza comes on the heels of spectacular garment sector growth when, between 1978 and 1999, the RMG sector earned $26 billion. Today, despite the end of the Multi-Fibre Arrangement (MFA)[2] in 2005, the 2008–2009 global financial crisis and recession, political instability, poor infrastructure, and corruption, Bangladesh's export sector has remained robust, sustaining a 6% annual growth rate since 1996. The value-added component for the period 1978–1999 was US$7.6 billion or 29% of the sector's earning, and continues to remain modest. While the Bangladesh Garment Manufacturers and Exporters Association (BGMEA) and the Bangladesh

Knitwear Manufacturers and Exporters Association (BKMEA) recognize the sector's failure to produce higher-end products able to increase value addition, many firms have yet to improve infrastructure, provide training, or enhance capacity building to enable exporting higher value-added products. The slow growth in backward linkages, on the other hand, can, perhaps, partially be explained by the country's inability to mobilize its weak textile base. Although one estimate suggests that 80% of garment accessories were locally produced, valued at $0.5 billion a year (Rahman and Bhattacharya 2000 in Hossain et al. 2017), what was evident in the 1980s was that all of the materials for RMG were imported, including fabric, buttons, thread, and all of the packaging. Consequently, such heavy dependence upon imports meant that the total value addition from this sector was only 23% of gross exports (Hossain et al. 2017). More recently, there has been a growth of modern textile industries producing yarn and fabric, increasing total value addition from about 37% at the end of 1990s to approximately 45% (Rahman et al. 2008 in Hossain et al. 2017). According to the International Monetary Fund (IMF), in 2016 the Bangladesh economy was the second fastest growing major economy, with 7.11% GDP, up from 6.12% in 2015. The contribution of industry to the GDP was 28.1%, with RMG contributing the largest part.

This growth has come in the context of the absence of an entrepreneurial elite as well as of a low-wage labor force since women held broadly to notions of *purdah* and female seclusion. The construction of an entrepreneurial elite recognizes a shift among elite and upper middle-class Muslim family expectations from sons, and some daughters, securing employment in the professions – as doctors, engineers, and lawyers, or in the military or civil service – to become central figures in industry, including in the RMG sector. Kochanek (1996: 708) highlights this point, "Bengal were controlled by Bengali Hindu, Marwari, and British traders...there was not a single large-scale industrial enterprise in East Bengal controlled by a Bengali Muslim nor were they present in the jute trade, tea or inland water transport." Moreover, for Bengali Muslims after Partition, this "pattern of ownership in trade, commerce, and industry did not change significantly." Further, entry into the business community was limited by their "lack of capital, a preference for investment in land, and the absence of a business vacuum comparable to the one that developed in West Pakistan...[which, according to Kochanek (1996: 708)], resulted in both apathy toward trade and industry and a lack of opportunity." For workers, declines in the sustainability of small-scale agriculture and opportunities offered by entrepreneurial kin helped to change rural family expectations for daughters. This change included the belief that a daughter's status was premised on their family's ability to refuse their participation in the labor market, to a view of young women as wage earners and contributors to family status. Given these changes, what has been the character of the sector over time? And, what can we learn from this changing context to better understand the conditions that have shaped the rapid expansion of the RMG sector, the disasters that have followed in its wake, including Rana Plaza, and responses to the Accord and Alliance, two efforts to improve the sector in accordance with global labor standards?

This chapter offers an overview of the RMG sector, identifying key policies guiding production and export, and showcasing the building of an industrial labor force so as to historicize the Accord and Alliance agreements. A long view of the sector helps to situate Bangladesh manufacturing in the global economy and draws attention to its changing structure, organization, and conditions of production identifying some of the conditions that likely contributed to the Rana Plaza disaster. This long view will contribute to explaining the failure of some RMG firms to comply with recognized global regulations. We also briefly explore the histories and understandings of primarily first-generation rural, and subsequently urban, women workers. Significantly, a failure to monitor physical infrastructural, build capacity, or consider the working conditions of a primarily female labor force have characterized the RMG sector since its inception. Exploring these changes in relation to each other will expose the contradictory consequences of dramatic economic growth and the securing of export production for the world market for the quality of the worksite, worker safety, the right to organize, and the economic security that such employment provides its workers.

The emergence of the RMG export sector: policy, political regimes, and law

The export-oriented garment manufacturing sector in Bangladesh began in the late 1970s following the new MFA (1974–2004)[3] that led the Asian Tigers – Singapore, Hong Kong, South Korea, and Taiwan – to secure subcontracting arrangements and partnerships with quota-free, labor surplus economies in the region.[4] The rising costs of production in East Asia, the emergence of a militant union movement in countries such as South Korea (Ogle 1990), and ethnic unrest in Sri Lanka (Chowdhury 1987) also contributed to the relocation of garment manufacturing to Bangladesh. The opportunity offered by "quota-hopping" in search of sites for export garment manufacturing coincided with IMF and World Bank demands to shift from a national development policy of import substitution to policies emphasizing export-led growth. This shift included the denationalization of state enterprises and the allocation of resources away from agriculture and toward urban industrial development, establishing the basis for the country's incorporation as a site of cheap labor into the world economy and as an important player in the global value chain of garment production. This shift grounded the neoliberal orthodoxy that has guided the country's development strategy since then.

This export-led strategy included the promotion of private investment, the construction of a wage labor force, and the development of export processing zones. These changes supported the interests of the Asian Tigers as well as North American and European buyers to secure a site for the production of cheap apparel manufactured goods. Thus, Bangladesh's demand-driven integration into the global economy has shaped, and continues to shape and frame compromises between buyers and sellers at the cost of limiting spaces for worker's voices, the freedom to organize, and, strategically, to continue to justify low wages so as to remain competitive in the global marketplace.[5] Said differently, the marriage of buyer-driven interests and an aid regime demanding an export-led development agenda has set the parameters of the Bangladesh economy since the early 1980s. As Sobhan (2003) suggests, liberalization and structural adjustment policies in Bangladesh have shifted from a regime of aid-dependence to one of trade-dependence.

This shift began with Korean capital, training, and support from Daewoo, and sewing machines from the Korean producer Juki, opening a number of companies in Bangladesh to initiate garment manufacturing for the world market. What started in 1978 with fewer than 12 garment firms, by 1985, included 450 independent companies, and, by 2013, increased to more than 5,800 firms and subcontractors. Today, the industry includes 4,482 garment factories (BGMEA 2017), a slight decline since the two agreements were signed. Initially, production of RMG did not begin in designated export processing zones but, instead, began in unregulated "bonded warehouses" that were built where entrepreneurs rented or owned property. Government support for bonded warehouse facilities (BWF) were to encourage the rapid expansion of the sector, and included permission to import fabric under back-to-back letters of credit (L/C) which served as an incubator for new entrepreneurs as these measures limited the capital required to initiate production. Thus, entrepreneurs could enter the sector with the capital required to hire labor and underwrite related capital requirements, as raw materials (fabrics, buttons, thread, and packaging) could be procured against the master L/C that originated with the order placed by the buyer. Under the rules of the BWF, no customs duty had to be paid on imported fabrics and, further, entrepreneurs benefited from the duty-drawback facility which reimbursed them on imports for which BWF were not available.[6]

A number of policy initiatives were critical to enable Bangladesh to quickly open its markets to the global apparel trade. Martial Law Administrator and later President Ziaur Rahman (1975–1981) immediately denationalized public sector enterprises and encouraged private capital through incentives to dramatically increase investment. In 1983, garment manufacturers and exporters organized the BGMEA that began with 12 manufacturers and exporters, and now boasts a membership of about 4,300 (Saxena 2014). The Association continues to serve as the apex trade body representing export-oriented woven manufacturers and exporters, and has been recognized as such by its representation on the board of advisors of the Alliance for Bangladesh Workers Safety (http://bangladeshworkersafety.org/who-we-are/leadership/board-of-advisors). The Association was supported by the passage of the Bangladesh Export Processing Zones Authority Act,

1980, that was charged with the "creation, development, operation, management, and control of export processing zones and for matters connected therewith" (BEPZA 2016). A number of years later, in 1996, the BKMEA organized as a trade association to facilitate and promote the production of knitwear and to cater to the demand generated by the changing apparel global value chain.

Institutional changes to support an export-led development strategy were furthered by General Ershad's (1981–1990) introduction of the New Industrial Policy (NIP) in 1982 that included tax relief and the provisioning of industrial sites with roads, ports, and electric power to encourage private sector industrial participation. The NIP reflected an acceleration of the changes brought forward by the monetary reforms, denationalization initiatives, and ceilings on private investment, including a further relaxation of industrial sanctioning procedures and the liberalization of import controls and industrial import procedures initiated under Ziaur Rahman (ILO-ARTEP 1993). Together, these rapid and dramatic changes to business as usual were envisioned as necessary for meeting the structural adjustment requirements of the new aid regime (Feldman 1993; Rahman and Bhattarchya 2000; Ahmed 2001).

With the democratic transition against military rule in the 1990s, the NIP continued to garner the support of each subsequent regime in power. Revisions in industrial policy in 1986, 1991, 1999, 2005, 2009, and 2010 promoted the infrastructure and environment to support export production and trade, and reiterated the commitment of each regime to deregulation, privatization, and the development of a competitive export sector. During this period, the pace of reforms intensified as the government responded initially to the Structural Adjustment Facility (SAF) and the Enhanced Structural Adjustment Facility (ESAF) of the IMF and the World Bank. The 2005 Industrial Policy, for instance, envisioned that within a decade export manufacturing would account for 30%–35% of GDP, and 35% of the total employed workforce. Recent figures for export manufacturing indicate that by 2012 the country had already reached 20.16% of GDP with slight declines since then, despite the global recession of 2008.[7] Further, employment growth in the RMG sector has averaged about 8% per year and accounts for about 40% of total manufacturing employment, with an additional 0.2 million people employed in other industries linked to garment manufacturing (Khundker 2002 in Kabeer and Mahmud 2004b: 137).

Labor law in Bangladesh followed the Factories Act, 1934, operational during the British colonial period until 1965 under Pakistani rule when it was renamed the East Pakistan Factories Act, and remained in force through liberation in 1971. While a commission was established more than 20 years later to review these laws, in 1992, followed by a draft code that was available in 1994, the new labor law was adopted by Parliament as the Bangladesh Labor Act in 2006. This law regime followed almost two decades of export production and placed industrial workers, including garment worker, under its jurisdiction, but excluded workers in export processing zones (EPZs) until the 2004 EPZ Act (Hossain 2011).[8] Following the Rana Plaza disaster, however, and in response to international pressure and threats to suspend Bangladesh's trade preferences by the USA, a 2013 amendment to the Act led to some improvements in the workers' rights including freedom of association, collective bargaining, workplace safety, and changes in the registration process of unions (Greenhouse 2013; Hossain et al. 2017; Zajak 2017). Along with these amendments of the BLA, Labour Rules (2015) were issued to clarify the formation and activities of safety committees, as well as contributions to the worker welfare fund and provisions of festival bonuses (Hossain et al. 2017). A number of additional advances for labor include provisions for the creation of Health and Safety Committees in factories with more than 50 workers, the specification of collective bargaining rights, and support for the development of trade unions from international institutions, which were supported by both international donor agencies and trade unions.[9] This institutional support put labor conditions in Bangladesh, particularly in the export sector, in conversation with global standards and expectations, notwithstanding remaining problems with the implementation of these advances.

For example, unionization continues to suffer from low social recognition and fragmentation, witnessed by the 540 registered unions in the garment sector and the considerable competition among them (Independent 2017). Moreover, "formal and informal restrictions continue as do government harassment and employer resistance that take the form of intimidation, violent attacks, and the dismissal of workers" (Feldman 1992; ITUC et al. 2016 in Zajak 2017: 1011). Thus, although regulations of the sector have been introduced over the course of this long period, evidence suggests that policy proscriptions regarding infrastructure have been either nonexistent or weak, and oversight institutions to ensure worker safety are generally either ineffective or open to foul play, leaving questions of compliance open to negotiation.

However, there is little doubt that the labor policy environment came under serious review following Rana Plaza contributing to what Streeck and Theelen (2005 in Zajak 2017) refer to as "institutional layering," attaching new rules to extant ones as a way to strengthen weak national institutions. In addition, the post-Rana Plaza period witnessed the institutionalization of two other governance structures and national policy reform. The first agreement, the Accord on Fire and Building Safety, is a legally binding agreement between global brands, retailers, and trade unions designed to improve health and safety standards in RMG supplying factories and mandates independent safety inspections which involve both trade unions and local groups. The Accord was signed by two global unions, 180 apparel companies, NGOs, and seven Bangladeshi trade unions who agree to regular inspections of factory sites. A second institutional reform is the Alliance for Bangladesh Worker Safety that includes 28 North American buyers who refused to sign the Accord and is not a legally binding agreement but, like their Accord counterparts, aims to improve structural, fire, and electrical safety hazards in supplying firms. A third intervention is the creation of a National Plan of Action that likewise is committed to factory inspections, but these latter two do so excluding trade unions' representation or financial support for making these improvements (Zajak 2017).[10]

Despite what we learn from following the policy and legal context of the sector's unfolding, it provides only a partial understanding of the conditions that may have contributed to both the dramatic rise of RMG production in Bangladesh and the disasters that have plagued the industry since its inception, ending with its most horrific, Rana Plaza. To more fully apprehend the conditions leading to Rana Plaza, and the adequacy of responses to it, requires going beyond formal institutional changes to understanding of the character of the entrepreneurial elite and the workers who comprise the sector.

The contours of the sector: constructing an entrepreneurial elite and a female working class

Who were the earlier entrepreneurs who built the RMG sector? Interviews[11] that Shelley Feldman conducted with these innovators made immediately evident that a number of them had previously been in the upper echelons of the civil service, a cadre that represented the well-educated economic, social, and political elite. They were part of the rapid changes taking place in government, often charged with implementing the export-led growth requirements of the IMF and the World Bank, and thus able to take advantage of government support for the development of the private sector. Their positions enabled them to draw on their long-established networks in the service, and the deployment of familial and international connections since a number of them had been educated abroad. Other Bengali (now Bangladeshi) Muslims who could not engage in the traditional sectors – jute, cotton textiles, sugar, banking and insurance because these were nationalized by the Awami League government immediately following liberation – engaged instead in trade, real estate speculation, and construction (Kochanek 1996).

Those who entered the sector thereafter generally were from less affluent class positions, especially more recent entrants who more likely own subcontracting firms, be less educated, and often without personal international contacts. But, for those who first established the sector, discussions revealed their recent interest in business and limited private sector experience. Feldman's discussions frequently concluded with an invitation to visit their new factory which she was pleased to accept, only to find doing so excluded a tour of the shop floor. But, most evident during these factory visits was their location in residential areas of Dhaka city and in residential buildings rather than industrial sites able to accommodate the weight and working of machinery and a large number of workers.

In a number of cases, newly built factories were operational even before construction was complete. In one case, a visit during the rainy season in 1984 revealed that production was underway after the floors of a new factory were poured but when the exterior walls were still under constructed and electrical wiring had yet to be protected. The result was that passersby had a direct window on the whizzing of sewing machines and the oddity, at the time, of seeing hundreds of factory women visibly working from the street below (Feldman 2001). This lack of attention or awareness may, in part, be a consequence of the rapidity with which the sector was allowed to grow, and to the lag in government regulation that recognized the connection between the production needs of entrepreneurs and the need to also regulate the construction sector.[12]

By the early 1990s, however, rather than a scattered set of buildings that served as bonded warehouses located wherever owners had property, factories were built along Airport Road, a major artery of the city relatively close to the airport that was rapidly becoming a center for garment production. It would be 15 years after Reaz Garments and the Desh-Daewoo joint venture began, in 1993, before the opening of the Dhaka EPZ in Savar, 21 miles from the city center and 16 miles from the Hazrat Shahjalal International Airport. Today, garment factories within EPZs account for approximately 12% of the sector's employment and approximately 20% of both national exports and foreign direct investment. EPZ factories are generally larger than those outside the zone, operate with the most up-to-date machinery, have direct relations with international buyers, and backward linkages with the domestic textile sector. Such factories are in stark contrast to earlier producers with respect to value addition, backward linkages, and capital-intensive production.

Factories located outside the EPZ may have direct orders from buyers but more likely serve as subcontractors for larger firms and vary in size and profit margins. Their low wages result in significant turnover as workers regularly shift firms if they wish to increase their wages and build on their experience, as neither training nor mobility is available on site. Subcontracting firms, in particular, are also generally less likely to conform to international or nationally established employment regulations, minimum wages, or working conditions. During the period prior to Rana Plaza, and given the absence of government oversight or monitoring, a proportion of these firms operate akin to the unregulated informal sector (Kabeer and Mahmud 2004a). Moreover, the 92 inspectors hired by the Department of Inspection for Factories and Establishments, and responsible for inspecting more than 4,500 RMG factories and an additional 25,000 other establishments, have been far from adequate. In June 2013, following the Rana Plaza catastrophe, the number of inspectors increased to a total of 390, but this figure, too, is far below what is required to assess and monitor the RMG sector in accordance with global standards.

Notable about the factories operating outside the EPZs is the 2014 initiative to relocate RMG factories on 530 acres of land at Bausia, Barisal, as a "readymade garment palli" or village to consolidate those factories operating in an unplanned way at various localities of the capital (Financial Express 2014). With loans from the USA, Bausia village is expected to include more than 200 factories and contribute up to $50 billion in export value by doubling its exports by the year 2021 (Bain 2015). Recognition that most EPZ factories operate in "decrepit unsafe buildings" and do not comply with health and safety regulations, the argument is that relocation to Bausia can be better monitored. While it may assist in meeting global labor standards, it may also be a move to maintain low wages by providing employment to new rural entrants in areas without union presence or activity.

Currently, there are eight operational EPZs: Dhaka and Chittagong account for 75% of EPZ employment followed by Adamjee and Karnafuli which account for an additional 9%, and Khulna (Mongla), Comilla, Uttara, and Ishwardi account for the remaining employment generated by EPZ production. Employment in the EPZs generally indicates higher wages although turnover, like employment outside the EPZs, is characterized by a four-tier manufacturing chain. Orders from large brand and international retailers come through their sourcing offices (buyers) and are contracted with large manufacturers who, in turn, subcontract all or part of an item to medium-sized manufacturers who may subcontract the work to small manufacturers or to piece rate home-based workers. Under these subcontracting agreements, workers are at the mercy of brokers who determine production and compensation rules blurring the distinction between employer and worker and making it difficult for workers to know to whom they can claim their legitimate rights in the absence of labor standards. Global competition also has been used as a rationale to justify the unwillingness of the government to monitor conditions of employment, but also as the aversion of some employees to challenge poor working conditions and low wages since they depend on the EPZ employment for survival.

While early figures indicated that at least 253,825 workers, mostly female, were employed in more than 190 companies in the zones (BEPZA 2010), recent figures show that this increased to 450,000 workers employed in the eight EPZs, 65% of whom are women. This shift suggests that the better working conditions and more mechanized production in the zones, such as that which characterizes knitwear, are jobs that employ a significant proportion of male labor.[13] Thus, as Bangladesh moves toward relatively more capital and technology intensiveness, the once largely female labor force is likely to be replaced by male labor, while women remain in woven garments or in subcontracting firms. Combined with the failure of firms to provide job training, and the lower wages characteristic of woven production, the argument that garment production can, and should, target women as part of a poverty reduction strategy is called into question.

By the 1990s, women accounted for more than 90% of the almost four million garment workers and, today, their labor continues to fuel garment exports which, as of 2017, accounts for 81% of the country's total exports (BGMEA 2017). Further, with the shift from primary exports to manufactured goods, garment exports surpassed $28 billion in earnings by 2016 and it is the largest contributor to the country's sustained economic growth and rising foreign exchange reserves (BGMEA 2017). Even during the 1990s, the RMG sector grew at a compound rate of 15% per year (Rahman and Bhattacharya 2000) while total large-scale manufacturing grew at 7% annually, but only 4% when the garment sector was excluded (Kabeer 2004: 5). Foreign exchange earnings from garment exports likewise grew steadily from only 4% in the early 1980s, 41% in the 1990s, and 77% in 2001–2002, and, since the mid-2000s, they account for 80% of the country's total exports (Feldman 2015; BGMEA 2017). A recent figure suggests that garments are anticipated to comprise 82% of exports valued at $50 billion by 2021 (Bain 2015).

The sector includes both knitwear and woven products where the former increased from a negligible part of exports during the initial rise in export production in the late 1980s, to 25% of total exports by the early 2000s. According to their webpage, the knitwear industry has created 1.6 million direct jobs and 0.5 million indirect jobs (BKMEA n.d.);[14] in 2013–2014 its contribution to GDP was almost 7%. Its backward linkage has added an additional 2% to the country's GDP. As a significant part of the RMG sector, the BKMEA has garnered support from German Technical Cooperation (GTZ) and works closely with the Asian Development Bank, World Bank, JICA, UNIDO, BRAC, Ministry of Finance, and other national and international organization (BKMEA n.d.) and it recently begun to offer skill development, health and other services, as well as working toward green production.

These spectacular growth rates have been fueled by women's labor. Yet, while we now assume the availability of women's labor in Bangladesh, their absence from the labor market until the opening of the garment sector meant that a labor force had to be constituted by employers. Further, as first-generation workers, a status that for many continues today, women were generally inexperienced about institutions that could aid in securing their rights. In fact, early Bangladeshi women workers typified the iconic woman export worker: shy, hardworking, and with little time for organizing given their household obligations. Further, young female garment workers were fearful about speaking up for their interests as they lacked experience of public engagement or participation in collective actions or projects, and had few resources upon which to draw when their rights were violated, including penalties for violators of rules of contract (Kabeer 2005). In fact, for many, the paradox was that employment offered them an opportunity to avoid an arranged marriage or leave the constraints of a household, even as work in the garment sector reproduced gender inequality and gender subordination (Amin et al. 1998; Kibria 1995, 1998; Kabeer 2000; Kabeer and Mahmud 2004b). To appreciate the context leading women to rapidly become industrial laborers, I now turn to the conditions that supported urban migration, including a brief mention of the declining agrarian sector which contributed to changing both family subsistence needs and gender norms, thereby enabling households to respond to the demand for labor from a nascent RMG manufacturing sector.

The push and the pull: a changing agrarian context and the response to urban employment[15]

What is most interesting about the transition from import substitution to export-led growth is that the RMG sector began with neither an available labor force nor, as we have suggested, an established industrial elite which means that one cannot assume an extant labor force, a reserve army of labor, ready and available as need arises, to be incorporated into global capital formation (Feldman 1991). Instead, a pool of labor willing and able to work in garment manufacturing had to be constituted within the constraints of the structural and normative relations that shaped life in the country at the time (Feldman 1992, 2001). The construction of a labor force, and the creative ways that women were included, offers a window on the making of Bangladesh as the second largest exporter of apparel wear in the world, second only to China.

To appreciate the creation of an urban[16] working class, it is crucial to understand the demand for wage work as coterminous with the erosion of material and social resources and networks among a growing proportion of the rural population. The transformation of the agrarian production structure is exemplified by the loss of agricultural subsidies and infrastructure and decreasing land security and fragmentation, coupled with the changing character of patriarchal control and authority (Feldman 1993, 2001). For example, of a sample population of first-generation women workers, 45% came from landless families and, for those whose families owned land, most were from small and marginally producing households with limited opportunities to expand their production. Less than 7% came from surplus-producing households. Only 9% of first-generation men came from landless households while 30% were sons of surplus-producing families. Thus, male and female workers represent different segments of the rural population, and likely maintain different linkages to their village home once employed. And, unsurprisingly, men faced different forms of structural inequality than women in the labor market confirming Elson and Pearson (1981a, 1982b; Pearson 1996, 1998), among others, who argue that employment often leads to an intensification of women's exploitation and subordination, even as it provides new opportunities for them.

While the census has generally failed to provide data on rural female employment, arguably because their work was usually household based, considered part-time, and often paid in kind, by the mid-1970s poor women were becoming increasingly visible in various informal employment relations, including, but not limited to, field cultivation for wages. These wage relations complemented the declining demand for household laborers, in response to changes invoked by the introduction of rice mills and declines in family-based workers in cottage industries. Middle-class rural women, too, witnessed a change in their work opportunities as they found employment in the growing government and NGO health and education sectors. Significantly, too, the introduction of microcredit schemes for rural women signaled new values tied to the control of money and to the increasing legitimacy of labor as a commodity.

In combination, these changes exposed an increasing dependence on more than one family member required to secure employment to meet family subsistence needs, leading some families to take girls out of school to work in RMG, envisioned to enable them to be responsible for their own subsistence or, on some occasions, to support a sibling's education. In the early 1980s, given low wages, some women workers also depended on support from their families to make ends meet. For the extremely poor and for female-headed households such demands were not new. But, for others, these changes led to women's increasing demand for work and the willingness of parents to allow daughters to participate in wage work (Feldman 1993). For these reasons, among others, the stigma associated with young women's employment has declined over time (Amin et al. 1998: 188) and, for those able to secure work in garment manufacturing, their employment has led to their increasing value as marriage partners given their networks and the status associated with urban employment (Adnan 1989; Kibria 1998).

Such normative changes – from status premised on a family's ability to keep daughters out of the labor market, legitimized by popular notions of *purdah* and women's seclusion – would, by the 1990s, expose modern sector work as a resource to be negotiated in marriage arrangements (Feldman 1993: 230, 2009; Adnan 1989; Kibria 1995, 1998; Amin 1997; Kabeer 2000).[17] But, these figures mask how individual entrepreneurs sought to constitute a labor pool that would enable them to build a globally competitive labor market and export sector, a set of practices to which I now turn.

This predominantly rural context, with more than 80% of the population engaged in agriculture, and women's labor almost invisible on both the rural and especially the urban landscape, became the bases for an emergent industrial elite to construct a class of export production workers. And, in the absence of an effective labor market, first-generation entrepreneurs were forced to build a labor pool through connections with their rural kin, enabled because many retained close relations with their village homes. For instance, it was not surprising when entrepreneurs were asked where they were from (apnar desh kotai?), they would claim that they "hail from Noakhali, Chittagong or Comilla." This identification, and ongoing relations with their rural kin, was central to their building and maintaining family status that would often be marked by investments in small rural schools or mosques in their village of origin. Other entrepreneurs maintained rural connections and property by regularly accessing rice for their daily consumption.

Thus, when faced with the need for labor, these entrepreneurs turned to their rural networks and sought support from their poor rural kin with the promise that they would take care of, and serve as guardian for, their daughters by employing them in their own factories. For inexperienced rural dwellers, this was interpreted as employment in a familial context, confirmed when they learned that male and female workers referred to each other as *bhai or bon* (brother and sister). And, when a family had relatives in Dhaka who could provide accommodation for their daughters, these networks offered additional security, as well as lines of communication, between rural families and their daughters. This construction of employment as familial enabled families who previously kept their daughters from employment – as a sign of family status – to sustain their normative understanding of appropriate female behavior. It also enabled labor recruitment to work within the context of a changing labor market, but also to not radically alter interpreting female propriety as under male guardianship and patriarchal control (Feldman 1993). As Amin and her colleagues (2008: 194) note, "many women portray their workplace as a protected environment," even as evidence clearly shows that there was a stigma associated with young women's employment. But this stigma, too, would change as women themselves explained their own notions of respectability.

Once hired, however, women would arrive in Dhaka fearing they would lose their way home from work or confused by life in the city (Feldman 1993; Amin et al. 2008: 191). Moreover, at this time, the physical infrastructure to support them was nonexistent: women could not readily find accommodation as apartment owners would not rent to single women or to groups of women, only a few women had relatives able to provide a place to stay, and employers did not provide factory accommodation. Some employers would eventually do so, but only 1.1% of female workers in 1990 and 0.6% in 1997 lived in such accommodations (Zohir and Paul-Majumder 1996). Further, public transportation was limited, and it took some years before *tempos* (small mini-vehicles accommodating six to ten travelers and offering cheap travel) were popularized, leaving most women to choose to walk to work in order to save money.

To be sure, labor recruitment would change dramatically with the rapidly expanding scale of production and the massive influx of migrants in search of employment. This reduced employers' dependence on their personal networks, as workers expanded their own rural networks and built new ones in the densely populated slums where they built accommodation. This shift is confirmed by the absence of formal recruitment practices, even as newspapers and posters are sometimes employed to publicize available jobs (Amin et al. 1998). Transportation options, too, would expand and increase worker's options as public buses increased in number, as have tempos offering workers greater transportation choices.

Discussion of the extraordinarily low wages of Bangladesh garment workers has been well documented. For example, Sajeda Amin and her colleagues (1998: 192) capture the strategies women deploy to raise their monthly wages: "I began with a monthly wage of Tk.250 [$6]. Twenty days later I went to another factory where they offered me Tk.800 [$19]. Nine months later, I went to a third factory where I got Tk. 1200 [$28]." Remaining in the last factory for three or four years without a noticeable increase, this worker moved again to increase her wages to Tk.1600 [$37] including wages, transport expenses, and a holiday bonus. The practice of moving "between factories is related not only to wage level but also to regularity of payment, amount of overtime, personal relationships with management, and attitudes of families" (Amin et al. 1998: 192).

This example showcases women's strategic practices, often beginning in individual action in response to their personal needs, but who are increasingly open to collective forms of organizing, despite the fear of personal as well as generalized retribution and the loss of income (Feldman 2015).[18] The example also reveals the growing autonomy and political consciousness of women workers who increasingly are likely to struggle for improved physical infrastructure, working conditions, and contractual rights. By the 1990s, accidents and fires at individual factories would provoke a collective response and, by the 2000s, strikes and walkouts became more frequent and more generalized across the sector. By 2009, protests also became more violent as when police opened fire killing three workers and wounding many others (ITUC 2010). Again, in June 2010, more than 50,000 garment workers organized in Ashulia to force the closing of at least 100 factories as protests over low wages turned deadly. This growing coordination among workers across factories, and the increased use of the police, presaged what was to come in the months that led to worker responses to the government's announcement of the new minimum wage in 2011.

Together, these struggles reveal a growing worker consciousness and collective identification, particularly concerning the lack of formal contracts, irregularities in pay and benefits, failure to acknowledge entitled maternity leave, and noncompliance with overtime rules and allowances. They also reveal the growing significance of labor rights organizations, especially during the struggle over a new minimum wage where the government actually acknowledged that RMG wages are "inhuman."[19] Yet, the sustained unrest and disruption in the industry throughout 2010 worried local suppliers and foreign buyers alike and, when coupled with the country's dependence on a single export to maintain export earnings, led the government to move very slowly to address wage demands. Its slow movement reveals the contradictions for government when politicians from both parties – the Awami League and the Bangladesh Nationalist Party – invest in the garment sector and maintain a significant voice in industrial policy reform and, significantly, in its implementation. Ironically, even the recognition of unions can be interpreted as a compromise, since labor union formalities and bureaucratic procedures may be more easily controlled than the episodic strikes and *hartals* (demonstrations) that have characterized workers' response to poor working conditions and low wages.

Significantly, too, has been the unwillingness of the government to take adequate action to protect a population central to its position in the global economy and foreign exchange earnings. For instance, its relationship to entrepreneurs with whom they maintain strong connections or who are party members has led to ignoring government rules and to the turning of a blind-eye to the creative use of loopholes to enable illegal forms of accumulation. In these ways, the weak enforcement of national labor laws, building codes, and city zoning laws has meant that factory owners are unaccountable for providing safe working environments. This is in addition to the failure of the government to monitor and/or sanction the construction industry, a sector notable for its corruption, the 10% rule, that require them to build toward specification (Personal communication).

The failure to monitor working conditions and meet, or at least approximate, ILO standards, including appropriate infrastructure and minimum wage standards, are those who argue that wages reflect low productivity thereby blaming workers rather than their working conditions. This argument may be descriptively apt, but there has been very limited effort by the industry to upgrade workers or to improve conditions that promote productivity. Instead, entrepreneurs continue to argue, as they did more than 30 years ago, that they are trapped between the buyer-driven demands of a global industry and a domestic environment that demands increasing compliance with international standards. While a few factories have upgraded their infrastructure accordingly, most have yet to comply with labor laws, setting the context for a sector plagued by ongoing disaster, the most devastating of which was Rana Plaza in 2013.

Concluding reflections: what does this account suggest for post-Rana Plaza efforts at reform?

In this chapter we have outlined dramatic changes in the Bangladesh economy since the introduction of export garment manufacturing in the 1970s, when quota restrictions on the Asian Tigers, coupled with new structural adjustment policies of the IMF and the World Bank, reshaped trade in RMG production between Asian economies and those in North American and Europe. As we emphasized, with the transition from an import substitution to an export-led growth strategy led by international donor demand and a new national focus, the government established new incentive structures to encourage direct foreign as well as domestic investment, primarily in the RMG sector. They did so by building institutional and infrastructural capacity – including the Bangladesh Export Processing Zones Authority, support for BWF, tax holidays, and permission to import fabric under back-to-back L/C – and began discussions to build EPZs. These supports served as an incubator for new entrepreneurs to quickly enter the sector and included, as well, labor laws that were envisioned to limit mobilization and the development of labor union representation. Today, despite the ending of the

MFA in 2005, and global economic crises and a recession soon thereafter, the garment sector continues to be Bangladesh's largest export and income source with clothing exports currently estimated to be more than quarter of a billion dollars annually.

Given these critical changes, we have paid special attention to the absence of both an established industrial elite and a female labor force necessary to enable the quick integration of Bangladesh's RMG production into the global economy. We have suggested that the inexperience of an entrepreneurial elite more interested in short-term profits rather than long-term investment, and a dependence on inexperienced, first-generation, young, migrant, rural women set the stage for the working conditions which have not dramatically changed as the sector matured. We argued that forms of recruitment and patronage relations shaped the construction of the workforce and their dependence on wage income, where the flexibilization and informalization of employment created continued uncertainty and vulnerability among workers. Yet, despite being plagued by inexperience, workers have become increasingly outspoken in their struggle to improve working conditions and rights.

In the industry, the failure of many to view the RMG sector as part of a long-term investment strategy has resulted in an unwillingness to upgrade infrastructure or provide training to workers to enable them to compete for the production of more value-added products. Instead, the logic animating employer-worker relations is low wages, high turnover, and a failure to conform to contractual agreements. Further, hazardous working environments have led to the death of numerous factory workers throughout the 1970s–2005 period, with little government response or monitoring of the industry. In a single incident, Tazreen Fashions fire, as many as 125 workers lost their lives, yet these tragedies were not only ignored by government, but also by international brands. The fire also failed to forewarn the international community of consumers, who had previously organized against child labor decades earlier, of what this incident signaled for future disasters; nor did the government sanction individual factory owners with closure if they failed to meet even minimal national standards. In other words, Rana Plaza was an accident waiting to happen given the absence of a monitoring and inspection system that held to even a minimal standard of acceptable working conditions. It would be three decades after the Tazreen Fire before labor demands for improved wages and working conditions would challenge the industry as a whole. Yet, wage demands were only partially realized, as the employers' associations argued that if Bangladesh were to remain competitive it could not meet the demanded increase: a decision that was buttressed by the government's unwillingness to set a higher minimum wage, even as exports from Bangladesh continued to exceed expectations.

Now, almost five years after Rana Plaza, what can we learn from these long-term conditions of sectoral growth? How can understanding these conditions of economic exploitation, breaches of contract, and hazardous working conditions continue to characterize the industry? Moreover, how might we better respond to the lack of transparency and responsibility as an industrial norm (Telesur 2017)? One response to Rana Plaza has been the suspension of the privileged market access offered by the US Generalized System of Preferences (GSP).[20] In effect since 1976, the GSP provides preferential duty-free entry into the US market for some products based on adherence to workers' rights provisions. These provisions are: (1) right of association, (2) right to organize and bargain collectively, (3) prohibition of forced or compulsory labor, (4) minimum age for the employment of children, and (5) acceptable conditions of work with respect to minimum wages, hours of work, and safety and health. It took two major industrial disasters – Tazreen Fashions fire and the Rana Plaza building collapse – before the US GSP was suspended, in 2013, citing serious shortcomings in labor rights and workplace safety.

It is worth emphasizing again that the noncompliance of international workers' rights is currently the single most important issue for Bangladesh to continue to receive market access benefits under the EU-Everything But Arms (EBA) initiative. The European Union already has warned Bangladesh of suspending trade preferences unless the country makes progress in the implementation of workers' rights. Three bodies of the European Commission in a March 18, 2017 joint communiqué said that it was essential that Bangladesh implement four recommendations made by an ILO committee or risk being excluded from the GSP they had previously enjoyed. The ILO's Committee of Experts on the Application of Conventions and Recommendations (CEACR) (1) asked for amendments to the 2013 Labour Act; (2) asked for workers within export processing zones be allowed to form trade unions and associate with other, outside, trade unions; (3) argued for urgent legal action against anti-union activities and remedies for victims of such actions; and (4) sought ensurance that the government would not arbitrarily dismiss trade union applications.

Yet, in an assessment undertaken two years after Rana Plaza, Labowitz and Baumann-Pauly (2014, also White 2015) found that of 3,425 inspections carried out, only eight factories met the standards set by the Accord. Moreover, the total list of factories found on the Accord and Alliance lists summed only 1,800, leaving most of the highest risk, often unregistered factories of subcontractors outside the purview of both agreements. Further, the government appears rather mixed in their willingness to sustain support for the Accord and Alliance that are expected to end in May and June respectively. In a recent article in a Bangladesh daily newspaper, *Jugantor*, one entrepreneur argued that despite his claim that his factory met the requirements of the Accord, an inspection revealed otherwise, and found that the factory needed to include fire doors, fire hydrants, an automatic alarm or detection system, and a fire sprinkler system. The demand for such improvements was not only viewed as unreasonable and likely to "create an unstable situation by encouraging unemployed and agitated workers to move against owners," but also, according to this entrepreneur, can lead to falsely informing buyers and thereby undermine the country's garment sector, a position reportedly shared by the BGMEA and the Commerce Minister of Bangladesh. Sadly, without GOB support for regular inspections and monitoring of the conditions of work, and a willingness to uphold the standards outlined in the Accord and Alliance after their five-year agreements have ended, leaves little hope for improving the working conditions in the RMG sector in Bangladesh.

Postscript

The current Accord was set to expire in May 2018 but was initially renewed until May 2021 by more than 45 international brands including Kmart Australia, Target Australia, Primark, H&M, Inditex, C&A, Otto, KiK, Aldi South, Aldi North, Lidl, Tchibo, LC Waikiki, and Helly Hansen as well as trade unions. The renewal stipulated that a commitment to ensure workers' rights to freedom of association be added to the safety inspection and remediation program and the safety committee and safety training program. Requiring a commitment to the right of workers to organize and join unions as fundamental in assuring workplace safety led Bangladeshi employers' associations to denounce the extension of the Accord premised on a requirement of external monitoring.[21] Instead, the BGMEA proposed a workplace safety platform, *"Shonman"* (Respect), whose steering committee would include representatives of government (commerce and labor), employers (BGMEA and BKMEA), trade unions, brands, and the ILO. In April 2018, however, a restraining order was issued by the High Court on what eventually became the Transition Accord, the result of which led to the end of the Accord after 30th November 2018.

The GOB agreed that there is no need to extend the Accord and its required inspections and monitoring for another three years, but agreed to a six-month extension to approve a Remediation Coordination Cell (RCC) as part of the Ministry of Labour and Employment who are charged with monitoring the sector after the term of the Accord. However, the fate of the renewed Accord remains an open question as, in mid-October, the High Court halted the extension following a writ petition filed by a leader of an organization of garment workers and employees. The petition sought a response to the legality of the extension of "the agreement without permission from the government, owners and workers," claiming that it should be declared illegal (https://bdnews24.com/business/2017/10/16/high-court-halts-new-bangladesh-accord-on-garment-factory-fire-building-safety). Since then, a hearing on the petition filed by the Accord challenging the High Court directive and asking it to end all activities in Bangladesh on 30 November has been adjourned seven times (https://www.just-style.com/news/bangladesh-accord-court-hearing-delayed-for-seventh-time_id135949.aspx). Since then, the Supreme Court of Bangladesh gave another short-term extension to the

Bangladesh Accord, scheduling the next hearing to determine the safety programme's fate on 19 May 2019 (http://industriall-union.org/bangladesh-unions-call-for-accord-to-continue-on-6th-anniversary-of-rana-plaza).

Notes

1 For a list of industrial accidents just since 2005, see Major industrial accidents in Bangladesh in recent years, Reuters 3 July 2017. Accessed at www.reuters.com/article/us-bangladesh-blast-accidents-factbox/factbox-major-industrial-accidents-in-bangladesh-in-recent-years-idUSKBN19P0JN.

2 The MFA regulated textiles and clothing exports by limiting the rate of export growth of exporting countries and an exception to the GATT principle of non-discrimination by allowing importing countries to impose quotas on large and efficient suppliers (Hossain 2012).

3 Despite being negotiated as a temporary measure, the MFA continued until 1994, was incorporated into the WTO Agreement on Textiles and Clothing (ATC) in 1995, and phased out ten years later, in 2005.

4 This strategy enabled the Asian Tigers to "move up" the value chain to higher value-added activities and more capital-intensive industries (Gereffi 1999; also Appelbaum and Gereffi 1994; Frederick and Gereffi 2011; Gereffi and Memedovic 2003).

5 A 1990 report indicated that wages in the garment industry were as low as US$ 0.09 per hour (Gray 1990: 15, in Feldman 1993: 234). After years of struggle, in 2013 wages were raised to BDT5300 (US$68), still below the then national poverty line of BDT6336 (US$78). In ongoing protests in 2017 workers were unsuccessful in their demand to increase the monthly minimum wage to BDT15000 (US$187). Using the threat that production would move to China with a wage increase, evidence instead suggests that as China increases its economic footprint globally, it is likely to move up the value chain and outsource low-end garment manufacturing to places where labor is cheaper, thus securing Bangladesh's place in the RMG global market (Feldman 2015: 28).

6 Over-invoicing and other illicit practices were widespread at the time (Feldman 1984).

7 Manufacturing employment accounts for 19% and female employment 15% of total employment (https://data.worldbank.org/indicator/SL.IND.EMPL.ZS).

8 Export Processing Zones Workers Association and the Industrial Relations Act, 2004 prohibited trade unions from organizing in EPZs.

9 These include the International Labour Organization (ILO), German development agency (GIZ), Friedrich-Ebert Foundation, and international trade unions including IndustriALL and UNI Global Union (Zajak 2017).

10 A 2016 analysis revealed considerable delays in repairing safety defects in supplying member companies of the Alliance and concern about overstating the progress of the Alliance (Clean Clothes Campaign 2017, accessed at https://cleanclothes.org/news/2016/11/21/alliance-for-bangladesh-worker-safety-overstates-progress-while-workers-lives-remain-at-risk). Oversight by the Clean Clothes Campaign signals the significance of consumers in improving the production environment, a point that cannot be developed here but see the Harkin Bill on child labor (proposed US Child Labor Deterrence Act 1993) for a similar consumer-led initiative.

11 Interviews with entrepreneurs and workers were carried out between March and November 1984 (Fulbright Grant Number 83-006-IC) and again in 1988.

12 Institutions responsible for monitoring industrial buildings include the Department of Inspection for Factories and Establishments entrusted with implementing the BLA 2006, and the Bangladesh National Building Code 2006 establishing

minimum standards for the design and construction for all buildings. Despite such laws, monitoring and enforcing safety in construction remains confusing about who is authorized to enforce standards, a shortage of manpower, and an absence of a national safety certification and licensing system for engineers, contractors, and workers (The Daily Star, 12 October 2017).

13 www.bepza.gov.bd/activities/view/57a17a5c-e8f4-40fe-9f4c-48a2c0b99bee.

14 www.bkmea.com/contribution-knitwear.html.

15 This section draws on Feldman 1993 that was based on a referred sample of unstructured, intensive interviews with workers and employers. Information was also gathered from members of the Planning Commission, the Ministries of Labour, Industries and Social Welfare, and the Export Processing Zone Authority, as well as from the donor community who financed and provided technical assistance to help realize policy changes and the country's new industrialization strategy.

16 Rural migration led to an urban crisis given extant urban infrastructural capacity and the rapid doubling of the population, from 6 to 12 million people between 1990 and 2005. In the greater Dhaka area, the population reached an estimated 18 million in 2017 with a density of 23,234 people per square kilometer: a 4.2% annual growth rate (http://worldpopulationreview.com/world-cities/dhaka-population/).

17 See also the work Kabeer and Mahmud (2004a) and Rahman and Islam (2013) for a demographic profile of women workers.

18 These paragraphs draw heavily on Feldman 2015: 25–31.

19 In a parliamentary speech, the prime minister recognized garment workers' wages as "not only insufficient but also inhuman," observing that "workers cannot even stay in Dhaka with the peanuts they get in wages." Raising the hopes of garment workers, the prime minister argued that owners should also give a portion of their profits to the workers for their survival (The New Age, July 22, 2010).

20 https://ustr.gov/issue-areas/trade-development/preference-programs/generalized-system-preference-gsp.

21 See *The Daily Star*, "Garment makers oppose Accord's time extension" July 2, 2017. Available at www.thedailystar.net/business/garment-makers-oppose-accords-time-extension-1427134.

References

Adnan, S. 1989. Birds in a Cage: Institutional Change and Women's Position in Bangladesh. *ADAB News*, January–February.

Ahmed, N. 2001. *Trade Liberalisation in Bangladesh: An Investigation into Trends*, Dhaka: University Press Limited.

Amin, S. 1997. The Poverty-Purdah Trap in Rural Bangladesh: Implications for Women's Roles in the Family. *Development and Change*, 28: 213–233.

Amin, S., Diamond, I., Naved, R. T., and Newby, M. 1998. Transition to Adulthood of Female Factory Workers in Bangladesh. *Studies in Family Planning*, 29(2): 185–200.

Appelbaum, R. P., and Gereffi, G. 1994. Power and Profits in the Apparel Commodity Chain, in E. Bonacich, L. Cheng, N. Chinchilla, N. Hamilton, and P. Ong, eds., *Global Production: The Apparel Industry in the Pacific Rim* (pp. 41–62). Philadelphia: Temple University Press.

Bain, M. 2015. Quartz, Bangladesh is building "garment villages" to double its already-huge clothing exports, https://qz.com/477915/bangladesh-is-building-garment-villages-to-double-its-already-huge-clothing-exports/. Accessed December 2017.

Bangladesh Export Processing Zones Authority (BEPZA). 2016. Commencement of NARI Project Training Program in EPZ. www.bepza.gov.bd/activities/view/57a17a5c-e8f4-40fe-9f4c-48a2c0b99bee. Accessed 13 November 1971.

Bangladesh Garment Manufacturers and Exporters Association (BGMEA). 2017. 14 November 2017. www.bgmea.com.bd/home/pages/tradeinformation. Accessed December 2017.

Bangladesh Knitwear Manufacturing and Export Association. n.d. BKMEA: An Innovative and Creative Organization. www.bkmea.com/BKMEA-at-a-glance.html. Accessed January 2017.

Chowdhury, J. A. 1987. Garment Industry in Bangladesh: Its Problems and Prospects, *Journal of Business Administration*, 13(3): 348–368.

Daily Star, The. 2010. Garment workers' minimum wage fixed at Tk 3,000. July 29.

Daily Star, The. 2017. Ensuring construction safety in Bangladesh. 12 October. www.thedailystar.net/round-tables/ensuring-construction-safety-bangladesh-1475314.

Elson, D., and Pearson, R. 1981a. 'Nimble Fingers Make Cheap Laborers': An Analysis of Women's Employment in Third World Export Manufacturing. *Feminist Review*, 7(Spring), 87–107.

Elson, D., and Pearson, R. 1981b. The Subordination of Women and the Internationalization of Factory Production, in K. Young, C. Wolkowitz, and R. McCullagh, eds., *Of Marriage and the Market*. London: Conference of Socialist Economists.

Feldman, S. 1991. Rural Industrialization: The Shaping of 'Class' Relations in Bangladesh, in S. G. McNall, R. F. Levine, and R. Fantasia, eds., *Bringing Class Back In: Contemporary and Historical Perspectives* (pp. 119–138). Boulder: Westview Press.

Feldman, S. 1992. Crisis, Islam, and Gender in Bangladesh: The Social Construction of a Female Labor Force, in L. Beneria and S. Feldman, eds., *Unequal Burden: Economic Crises, Persistent Poverty, and Women's Work*. Boulder: Westview Press.

Feldman, S. 1993. Contradictions of Gender Inequality: Urban Class Formation in Contemporary Bangladesh, in A. Clark, ed., *Gender and Political Economy: Explorations of South Asian Systems* (pp. 215–245). Delhi: Oxford University Press.

Feldman, S. 2001. Exploring Theories of Patriarchy: A Perspective from Contemporary Bangladesh. *SIGNS*, 26(4): 1097–1127.

Feldman, S. 2009. Historicizing Garment Manufacturing in Bangladesh: Gender, Generation, and New Regulatory Regimes. *Journal of International Women's Studies*, 11(1): 268–288.

Feldman, S. 2015. "Just 6p on a T-shirt, or 12p on a Pair of Jeans": Bangladeshi Garment Workers Fight for a Living Wage, in H. A. Ghosh, ed., *Asian Muslim Women: Globalization and Local Realities* (pp. 21–38). Albany: State University of New York Press.

Financial Express, The. 2014. Tofail Urges Admin to Ready Garment Palli in 3 Years. *The Financial Express*, 10 July.

Frederick, S., and Gereffi, G. 2011. Upgrading and Restructuring in the Global Apparel Value Chain: Why China and Asia are Outperforming Mexico and Central America. *International Journal Technological Learning, Innovation, and Development*, 4(1/2/3): 67–95.

Gereffi, G. 1999. International Trade and Industrial Upgrading in the Apparel Commodity Chain. *Journal of International Economics*, 48(1): 37–70.

Gereffi, G., and Memdovic, O. 2003. *The Global Apparel Value Chain: What Prospects for Upgrading by Developing Countries* (pp. 1–46). Vienna: United Nations Industrial Development Organization.

Gray, C. D. 1990. Protection or Protectionism. *Far Eastern Economic Review,* 13 September: 15.

Greenhouse, S. 2013. Under Pressure, Bangladesh Adopts New Labor Law, *New York Times.* 16 July.

Guardian, The. 2016. www.theguardian.com/.../rana-plaza-collapse-murder-charges-garment-factory. 18 July.Hossain, J. 2012. *Economic Security for the Working Poor? Trade-Linked Labor Standards, Workers' Rights and the Politics of Representation of Bangladesh's Garment Workers*, PhD Dissertation, University of Trento, Italy, April 2012. Available at http://eprints-phd.biblio.unitn.it/755/1/PhD.

Hossain, N. 2011. *Exports, Equity and Empowerment: The Effects of Readymade Garments Manufacturing on Gender Equality in Bangladesh*, World Development Report 2012. Background Paper. Washington DC: The World Bank.

Hossain, J. M. A., and Sharif, J. H. 2017. Linkages of trade and labour standards in global supply chains in Bangladesh. Available at http://library.fes.de/pdf-files/bueros/singapur/13430.pdf with a synopsis as part of who benefits from trade? Findings on the link between trade and labour standards in the garment, footwear, and electronics industries in Bangladesh, Cambodia, Pakistan, and Vietnam Singapore. www.fes-asia.org/news/who-benefits-from-trade/.

ILO-ARTEP. 1993. Social Dimensions of Economic Reforms in Bangladesh. *Proceedings of the National Tripartite Workshop Held in Dhaka*, Bangladesh, 18–20 May, 1993. New Delhi: International Labour Organisation, Asian Regional Team for Employment Promotion.

Independent, The. 2017. RMG sector has 540 registered trade unions. 3 February.

International Trade Union Confederation (ITUC). 2010. Bangladesh: Three Workers Killed During a Peaceful Protest, 14 December, Available at www.ituc-csi.org/bangladesh.html. Accessed 30 December 2011.

ITUC, UNI Global, IndustriALL. 2016. Evaluation of the Bangladesh Sustainability Compact, Available at http://admin.industriall-union.org/sites/default/files/uploads/documents/Bangladesh/ituc-iauni_evaulation_of_the_bangladesh_sustainability_compact_january_2016_final.pdf.

Kabeer, N. 2000. *The Power to Choose: Bangladeshi Women and Labour Market Decision in London and Dhaka*. London and New York: Verso.

Kabeer, N. 2004. Globalization, Labor Standards, and Women's Rights: Dilemmas of Collective (In)action in an Interdependent World. *Feminist Economics, 10*(1): 3–35.

Kabeer, N. 2005. Gender Equality and Women's Empowerment: A Critical Analysis of the Third Millennium Development Goal 1. *Gender & Development*, 13(1): 13–24.

Kabeer, N., and Mahmud, S. 2004a. Globalization, Gender and Poverty: Bangladeshi Women Workers in Export and Local Markets. *Journal of International Development*, 16(1): 93–109.

Kabeer, N., and Mahmud, S. 2004b. Rags, Riches and Women Workers: Export-Oriented Garment Manufacturing in Bangladesh, in M. Carr, ed., *Chains of Fortune: Linking Women Producers and Workers with Global Markets* (pp. 133–162). London: Commonwealth Secretariat.

Khundker, N. 2002. Globalisation, Competitiveness and Job Quality in the Garment Industry in Bangladesh, Chapter 3 in Muqtada, M. et al., eds., *Bangladesh: Economic and Social Challenges of Globalisation*. Dhaka: University Press Limited.

Kibria, N. 1995. Culture, Social Class, and Income Control in the Lives of Women Garment Workers in Bangladesh. *Gender and Society*, 9: 289–309.

Kibria, N. 1998. Becoming a Garments Worker: The Mobilization of Women into the Garments Factories of Bangladesh, in C. Miller and J. Vivian, eds., *Women's Employment in the Textile Manufacturing Sectors of Bangladesh and Morocco* (pp. 151–177). Geneva: UNRISD/UNDP.

Kochanek, S. A. 1996. The Rise of Interest Politics in Bangladesh. *Asian Survey*, 38(7): 704–722.

Labowitz, S., and Baumann-Pauly, D. 2014. *Business as Usual Is Not an Option: Supply Chains and Sourcing after Rana Plaza*. New York. Center for Business and Human Rights, Report of the NYU Leonard N. Stern School of Business.

Mahmud, S., and Kabeer, N. 2003. Compliance versus Accountability: Struggles for Dignity and Daily Bread in the Bangladesh Garment Industry, *Bangladesh Development Studies*, 29(3–4): 21–46.

Ogle, G. E. 1990. *South Korea: Dissent within the Economic Miracle*. London: Zed Books.

Pearson, R. 1996. Industrialization and Women's Subordination: A Reappraisal, in V. M. Moghadam, ed., *Patriarchy and Economic Development: Women's Positions at the End of the Twentieth Century* (pp. 169–183). Oxford: Clarendon Press.

Pearson, R. 1998. Nimble Fingers Revisited: Reflections on Women and Third World Industrialization in the Late Twentieth Century, in C. Jackson and R. Pearson, eds., *Feminist Visions of Development: Research, Analysis and Policy* (pp. 171–188). London: Routledge.

Rahman, M. and Bhattarchya, D. 2000. 'Bangladesh experience with trade and investment liberalization: a perspective on poverty alleviating implications', Country Paper: *Bangladesh in Liberalization and Poverty: Is There a Virtuous Circle?* Chapter 5, Consumer Unity and Trust (CUTS) Centre for International Trade, Economics and Environment, Jaipur.

Rahman, M., Bhattacharya, D., and Moazzem, K. G. 2008. *Bangladesh Apparel Sector in Post MFA Era: A Study on the Ongoing Restructuring Process*. Dhaka: Centre for Policy Dialogue.

Rahman, R. I., and Islam, R. 2013. *Female Labour Force Participation in Bangladesh: Trends, Drivers, and Barriers*. International Labour Organization, New Delhi: ILO DWT for South Asia and Country Office for India.

Saxena, S. B. 2014. *Made in Bangladesh, Cambodia, and Sri Lanka: The Labor Behind the Global Garments and Textiles Industries*. Amherst; New York: Cambria Press.

Sobhan, R. 2003. The Shift from Aid Dependence to Trade Dependence, *Weekly Holiday*, 31 October (39th Anniversary Edition).

Streeck, W., and Thelen, K. 2005. *Beyond Continuity: Institutional Change in Advanced Political Economies*. Oxford: Oxford University Press.

Telesur. 2017. 4 Years after Bangladesh Rana Plaza Disaster, Workers Unsafe, 24 April. Available at www.telesurtv.net/english/news/4-Years-After-Bangladesh-Rana-Plaza-Disaster-Workers-Unsafe-20170424-0024.html.

White, G. B. 2015. Are Factories in Bangladesh Any Safer Now? *The Atlantic*. 17 December.

Zajak, S. 2017. International Allies, Institutional Layering and Power in the Making of Labour in Bangladesh. *Development and Change*, 48(5): 1007–1030.

Zohir, S. C., and Paul-Majumder, P. 1996. Garment Workers in Bangladesh: Economic, Social and Health Condition, Research Monograph: 18, Bangladesh Institute of Development Studies.

3 Off the radar

Subcontracting in Bangladesh's RMG industry

Sanchita Banerjee Saxena and
Dorothee Baumann-Pauly

Introduction[1]

After the factory collapse that killed almost 1,200 workers at Rana Plaza in a suburb of Dhaka, the tragedy was a wake-up call to the global fashion industry and those who benefit from it: consumers in the United States and Europe who have never been able to buy more clothes more cheaply than they can today; the fashion brands that are some of the biggest companies in the world; and leaders within Bangladesh, whose economy is deeply dependent on the continued growth of garment manufacturing. Rana Plaza was a symbol of a larger uncomfortable truth about the global apparel supply chain: low-wage garment work can come at almost unimaginable costs.

After the Rana Plaza disaster, the NYU Stern Center for Business and Human Rights started a two-year-long study looking at the actual size of the garment industry in Bangladesh, concluding that there are more than 7,000 garment factories producing for the export market. The NYU report (2015) revealed that the industry relies on thousands of previously unacknowledged subcontracting factories. In a country with chronic factory safety concerns even for the biggest factories that directly work with foreign brands, this finding is deeply concerning and shows that the road to remediating the safety concerns in Bangladesh's garment industry is more difficult and complex than most stakeholders acknowledge. A follow-up study from the BRAC University's Centre for Entrepreneurship Development in Dhaka confirmed the NYU Stern Center's findings. Using a similar methodology that combines analysis of several online databases and field research, the BRAC University Center found over 8,000 garment factories in Bangladesh.

Why does the actual size of the industry matter so much? Defining adequate solutions requires a proper definition of the problem. Without better knowledge about the size of the industry and the scope of the problem (how prevalent are fire safety and building integrity issues in all levels of the supply chain), approaches designed to address these issues will not be able solve the problem comprehensively. It is even questionable that current approaches, which involve inspecting the direct suppliers of

Western brands, solve the issue partially. NYU's research has shown that Bangladesh's garment industry operates as a production network with intertwined levels of productions sites: some of which are working directly with brands, some operate off the radar to accommodate the ever-increasing demands for lower prices and shorter lead times in an industry with high seasonal fluctuations. Partial solutions in an environment with interconnected production sites are likely not to render the industry as a whole safer.

The findings in this chapter highlight that even today as many as three million workers are employed in workplaces that fall outside the scope of any current monitoring or remediation mechanisms that were set up after Rana Paza. While many local suppliers say the industry has consolidated since 2015, the findings of these two parallel studies make clear that a significant number of subcontracting factories continue to produce garments. These factories remain outside the scope of the most important international factory safety initiatives that were created in the aftermath of the 2013 Rana Plaza tragedy. Understanding the true scope of the problem could also move the discussion beyond remediating individual factories to addressing systemic issues including infrastructure challenges.[2]

The research highlighted in this chapter is an important step in gaining greater understanding of the true size and complexity of the apparel supply chain in Bangladesh. It is incontrovertible that the supply chain is bigger, more complex, and contains greater risk for more workers than previously imagined. New ways of thinking and acting are needed to ensure that all factories provide employment in safe conditions and with the dignity of work for all workers.

Indirect sourcing

Indirect sourcing relies on the routine practice of subcontracting, often through purchasing agents and in a manner that is not transparent to buyers, to increase margins and boost production capacity while keeping costs low. As orders are subcontracted and in some cases re-subcontracted, production moves into facilities that are outside the scope of current regulation and often are "noncompliant" with minimum standards for safety and workers' rights. Indirect sourcing is an essential, though poorly understood, feature of the business models of global buyers and national-level suppliers in Bangladesh. Acknowledging these relationships is key to understanding the real scope of the factory safety challenges in Bangladesh. It also is essential for developing comprehensive policy responses that both will protect workers throughout the sector and will ensure the sustained growth of Bangladesh's export economy.

The findings in this chapter portray a widening gap between direct and indirect suppliers. Direct suppliers – those factories that global fashion brands acknowledge – are subject to increasing oversight of working conditions and elevated standards for fire and building safety. But these factories are just the tip of the iceberg. For every facility where labor conditions are improving, there are many more factories where workers toil in conditions that present risk of serious harm and abuse of labor rights. Factories that indirectly supply the export market operate below the surface. These factories are vital to Bangladesh's ability to produce high volumes of low-cost clothing in response to fluctuating seasonal demand. But they operate in the shadows.

Small factory owners that rely mostly on subcontracts benefit in the indirect sourcing model, as well. The international financing systems for sourcing garments are complex. The capital investment and sophistication of the relationships required to make this financing work create barriers to entry for smaller factories. Subcontracting can be appealing because, as one small owner said, there is "no banking problem, no transport problem" as there is in international, credit-based orders taken by larger "mother" factories.

Factories that take direct orders from international buyers assume all responsibility for every aspect of production from procuring materials, to cutting, sewing, finishing, packaging, and transport. This requires significant investment of capital, sophisticated international relationships, and capacity to withstand production delays due to late delivery of materials or other factors. Subcontracting is therefore an attractive business model for those in the middle and lower end of the supply chain. Policy solutions must take into account the high barriers to entry for direct relationships with international buyers and the needs of small business owners in the supply chain.

Western buyers also are profiting from the indirect system of sourcing. Despite strong language in their policies about nontransparent subcontracting, factory owners report that many buyers devote little time and attention to understanding the nature and scope of this practice. As one mid-sized owner described, "[Some] brands want to ignore subcontractors. They have their targets, too – 98% on-time shipment – and they don't care how they get the products." Another owner recounted how customers will sometimes subtly suggest the use of a subcontractor, asking the factory owner if he has an "alternative source" to complete production.

Our assessment is that the government's efforts and other efforts by brands to eradicate 'unauthorized' subcontracting will not be successful until they acknowledge and address the role of indirect sourcing strategies as a key driver for the prevalence of risky, unregistered factories.

If the indirect sourcing model was conducted within an effective regulatory framework and efficient markets, it could allocate and reallocate production according to the competitive advantages of each actor in the supply chain. The absence of those conditions, however, has resulted in a supply chain driven by pursuit of the lowest nominal costs. This has undermined wages and working conditions, investment in technology and training, and improvements in productivity and quality.

How prevalent is informal subcontracting?

Informal factories are a subset of indirect suppliers. They do not register with the government, the trade associations, or foreign brands and rely on subcontracts with other, larger factories to fill their production lines. In the June 2015 survey of two subdistricts of Dhaka, 32% of the 479 factories surveyed were informal subcontractors producing at least partly for the export market. They are characterized by their small size – on average, they employ 55 workers; among all factories on the official list, the average number of workers per factory is 650. Informal subcontractors tend to focus on a single production process, such as sewing, washing, dyeing, or printing. The top three barriers to enhance productivity for informal factories were limited electricity, fluctuating order volumes, and political instability.

Workers in this part of the sector are especially vulnerable because they are invisible to regulators and their employers operate on such slim margins that they cannot invest in even basic safety equipment or procedures. Small, under-resourced factories must rely on labor-intensive production methods rather than making capital investments in machines and processes that improve efficiency. They also undercut larger, more compliant factories on price. Informal factories do not pay taxes, submit to regulation, or bear the costs of labor rights compliance.

We are not aware of any inspections of informal subcontracting factories and visibility into this part of the sector remains very limited. This survey is the first attempt to begin a systemic assessment of informal subcontracting. But the combination of survey data, anecdotal reporting, and journalistic accounts reinforce a view of informal factories as being subject to almost no regulation or oversight, where even basic standards of safety, health, and labor rights are not enforced. As profit margins tighten through repeated subcontracting, labor is the only flexible cost component. Machinery, electricity, gas, and rent are fixed costs; managers operating on hair-thin margins seek to reduce overall costs by squeezing workers through low wages and long hours, or by employing children.

Though some academics have disputed this view of informal subcontracting, the growing body of research into the true nature of the apparel supply chain suggests that these factories are as, if not more, dangerous than the regulated factories at the top of the sector.[3] Moreover, the survey results show that informal subcontracting continues to be a prominent mode of production, as almost a third of factories in the survey areas were informal subcontracting factories.

What the data tell us and why it is important

The research reveals five key findings:

1   We estimate that there are more than 7,000 factories producing garments for the export market in Bangladesh, divided between direct and

indirect sourcing factories. Previous estimates of the size of the sector accounted for 4,000–4,500 factories. The study shows that the universe of factories producing for export is much larger than previously understood, and that indirect sourcing factories are a significant driver of production and employment. From 2013 to 2015, while the number of direct exporters remained constant, total apparel export volumes fluctuated substantially. This can be explained in one of two ways: either each direct exporter is able to dramatically increase and decrease its production in response to shifting demand, or the thousands of small factories that comprise the indirect sector enable direct exporters to accommodate significant shifts.

2   In a June 2015 survey of two subdistricts of Dhaka, 32% of the 479 factories surveyed were informal subcontractors. Ninety-one percent of informal factories produced at least partly for export. Informal factories are a subset of indirect suppliers. They do not register with the government, either of the two national trade associations of apparel manufacturers, or foreign brands. Workers in this part of the sector are especially vulnerable because they are invisible to regulators and their employers operate on such slim margins that they cannot invest in even basic safety equipment or procedures. This kind of subcontracting also artificially depresses prices because it does not account for the full cost of producing in accordance with minimum labor standards.

3   The Bangladesh Accord for Fire and Building Safety (Accord) and the Alliance for Bangladesh Worker Safety (Alliance) – two factory safety programs initiated by more than 200 foreign brands – encompass only 27% of factories in Bangladesh. The programs have received significant public attention and have announced a commitment to spend up to US$100 million over five years to improve factory safety, but they are narrowly focused on a subset of direct suppliers. Almost three million workers are not covered by these programs.

4   Despite thousands of inspections, fixing factories proofed to be difficult. While all factories that directly work with Accord or Alliance brands were eventually inspected, the process of remediation was much slower than expected. After five years of inspections and remediation, Accord and Alliance both report that manufacturer fixed over 80% of the remediation issues that inspectors had identified. Yet, the number of factories that have completed 100% of the inspection items remains low. For example, after five years (April 2018), only 142 factories in the Accord had fully completed the Corrective Action Plans.[4]

This chapter does not examine why factory remediation has been so slow, but it is clear that something does not add up.

5   In 2015, more than US$280 million in commitments have been announced for the garment sector in Bangladesh since Rana Plaza. While it is significant that foreign governments, development organizations, philanthropies, and foreign brands are announcing large commitments,

it is not yet clear how many of these resources are being spent or if any of this money is being applied to remediate factories. It is clear that resources are not being directed toward the thousands of indirect suppliers that remain in the shadows. There is not yet a clear understanding of what it will take to ensure that workers in these factories are safe and enjoy basic labor rights.

Based on employment information from the official factory list, there are 5.1 million workers in the garment sector. The ILO estimates that there are 4.2 million workers. Given that our research shows that the number of factories is significantly larger than previous estimates, it is not surprising to see that there also are almost a million more workers in the sector than previously understood.

Limitations of compliance models

Achieving a safe and sustainable apparel supply chain in Bangladesh will require a shift in mind-set about which entities are responsible for fixing factories. Since the mid-1990s, the international community's primary response to well-documented labor rights problems in the apparel supply chain has been to deputize private companies to ensure workers' rights. Bangladesh is a stark illustration of the limits of this model. On the one hand, private compliance efforts by individual companies have resulted in improvements in some factories. At the high end of the supply chain, brand-sensitive multinationals work closely with their primary suppliers in relationships undergirded by standardized, professional business practices.

But most factories in Bangladesh are not this kind of modern, formal enterprise. Approximately half of the factories in Bangladesh are indirect suppliers that do not maintain relationships with foreign buyers. Because they operate on slim margins and often lack sophisticated business experience, they do not use modern business methods and are unfamiliar with international standards for labor rights. Factories that indirectly supply global brands are not included in private compliance initiatives.[5] To be sure, brands have a responsibility toward workers in factories beyond their first-tier suppliers. All brands benefit when subcontracting factories are in compliance with minimum standards. A systemic approach is needed that enlists a wider array of actors to elevate standards in the entire RMG sector.

The Accord and Alliance and incompleteness of monitoring regimes

The two factory safety programs initiated by foreign brands encompass only 27% of factories, which tend to be larger and better resourced than all other factories. Because they are in the largest factories, the two initiatives encompass 45% of workers though more than three million workers remain outside their purview.

While global fashion brands had been unwilling to take large-scale, collective action on factory safety prior to April 2013, Rana Plaza was a catalyst for brands to come together to develop common standards and approaches to improve fire and building safety. The Accord includes global and local unions and more than 200 brands, while the Alliance encompasses 27 North American brands. The programs have received significant public attention and have committed to spend up to US$100 million over five years to improve factory safety. But they are narrowly focused on a subset of direct suppliers.

Much attention has been devoted to parsing differences between these two initiatives. Our analysis concludes that the Accord and the Alliance are fundamentally similar and that in key aspects, both are insufficient.[6] Neither the Accord nor the Alliance addresses the role of indirect sourcing practices in their members' supply chains. Both are prioritizing rapid inspection of those factories that maintain direct relationships with their member brands, but neither initiative has yet developed a coordinated and clear system for financing remediation efforts based on the results of their inspections.

There are significant differences between Accord and Alliance factories and other factories. Accord/Alliance factories tend to be large, with a median factory size of 1,200 workers. Among all factories on the official list, the median factory size is of 650 workers, and in our survey, informal factories were even smaller, with a median size of 55 workers. On the whole, Accord and Alliance brands are concentrated in the largest factories, while outside of this top tier of the sector, factories are mostly small- and medium-sized enterprises.

As earlier research identified, factories that are the primary suppliers of Accord and Alliance brands tend to have greater access to capital, stand-alone facilities not in mixed-use buildings, and more sophisticated foreign relationships with buyers and suppliers of key inputs (such as fabric, accessories, and packaging material). Developing such a large factory requires access to capital, relationships with foreign buyers and suppliers, dedicated land, and sufficient electricity to run many machines. These factories can be highly sophisticated, efficient, profitable, and even sustainable. For example, Viyellatex Group was recognized in 2013 as the recipient of PVH's global sustainability award and is now going green in its operations.[7]

While it is significant that almost half the workforce is covered by the extensive fire and building safety programs run by the Accord and the Alliance, the data show that 2.8 million workers do not enjoy these benefits. This means that there is a risk of a widening gap between those factories that maintain relationships with American and European brands and those that are either indirect suppliers or supply brands from other parts of the world. All workers in Bangladesh are entitled to minimum standards of safety and dignity at work.

Fixing factories

Making serious accidents less likely, factory owners are fixing many individual safety problems. The Accord reports that 84% of such issues have been resolved in the 1,631 active factories it is overseeing; the Alliance cites 88% (April 2018).[8]

The data reveal that the most improvement has been made on electrical issues, followed by fire hazards, and then structural problems. Accord records show that 96% of factories with unsafe dust on electrical equipment have removed it; 84% that had inadequate protection and support for electrical cables have remedied the problem; and 82% with deficient circuit breakers have done the same. Significant variation crops up within each category. Accord fire statistics show that 96% of factories with lockable gates have removed them, but only 41% that had inadequate fire detection and alarm systems have installed and verified suitable replacements.

Why are so few factories successfully being fixed? There are two reasons. First, the most essential upgrades to make factories safer, such as electrical improvements and moving to purpose-built facilities, are expensive. The Alliance estimates that the average cost of remediation is US$250,000–$350,000 per factory and it would require 1.2 billion to update the rest of the sector.

Second, it appears that the position of the brands in the Accord and the Alliance is that the significant cost of factory repairs is the responsibility of their suppliers. By their own accounts, factory improvements have only been completed in a small percentage of Accord and Alliance factories. The situation is now at something of a stalemate over burden sharing for factory improvements. Factory owners apparently are not making the investments identified as necessary in Accord and Alliance inspections, and brands are unwilling to underwrite the costs themselves.

An alternative model: direct, strategic sourcing

Indirect sourcing increases risk by reducing control and transparency in the supply chain. While this is the most prevalent sourcing model in Bangladesh, an alternative model is beginning to emerge. A small group of leading buyers and suppliers are starting to practice a more direct, transparent sourcing model in which the buyer works with partner suppliers on a long-term basis. We discuss the elements of this more direct and transparent sourcing strategy as an important alternative to indirect sourcing.

The elements of this model include the following:

- Long-term-order forecasting: the buyer provides the supplier with a multiyear perspective on expected order volumes. The buyer and supplier agree on quality, delivery, and price expectations over this period. (Contracts have clauses that allow the buyer to revise order volumes if market conditions so require.)

- Investment in technology, training, and facilities: the longer-term time horizon gives the supplier the security to invest in new technology and training to improve efficiency, reducing nonlabor costs.
- Purpose-driven compliance monitoring: suppliers audit their own performance against social and environmental metrics, which are spot-checked by the buyer. Remediation is viewed as collaborative exercise in problem-solving, not a "gotcha" exercise.
- Trust-based negotiation around unexpected challenges: when problems arise – production delays, cost overruns, social or environmental noncompliance – the buyer and the supplier communicate transparently about the problem and take steps to remediate the root cause of the problem, including adjusting sourcing practices by the buyer.
- Business incentives for high performance on working conditions: buyers offer business incentives for the outcomes they want, by rewarding high-performing suppliers with longer-term contracts, higher order volumes, and favorable pricing.

The direct sourcing model is increasingly common in footwear production and is now spreading into the apparel sector, as well. A growing body of research concludes that this long-term, trust-based, business-driven model also produces better outcomes with respect to working conditions and code of conduct compliance. This approach may not completely eliminate nontransparent subcontracting, but it significantly changes the incentives for obfuscation.

In the broader supply chain, buyers adopting this approach tend to be those that are most concerned with brand reputation, quality, research and development, and stability in their supply chains, such as Nike and Uniqlo. It is often the most price-sensitive brands that employ short-term sourcing relationships in which they have little leverage to demand higher standards of labor compliance from suppliers they may not work with in the future. But there are notable examples of low-price retailers that are working to better understand and consolidate their supply chains and to forge deeper partnerships with their suppliers.[9]

Subcontracting can be a healthy part of this model, as long as it is transparent and conducted with oversight from a combination of the "mother" factory, the buyer, and the government.

Some of the biggest, most progressive Bangladeshi manufacturers we spoke to point out that they would prefer to work only with trusted and approved subcontractors and would assume responsibility for ensuring that they meet the labor standards expectations of their buyers.

The sheer volume of orders going to Bangladesh, however, coupled with decreasing prices and increasing costs has overwhelmed them and led them to resort to wider and wider networks of subcontractors. Manufacturers argue that buyers need to make longer-term sourcing commitments and offer fairer prices in order to equip manufacturers to make the investments develop their capacity to achieve higher standards for safety and working conditions.

What needs to be done

Acknowledge the full scale and complexity of indirect sourcing

Achieving visibility over the full supply chain at a systemic level, rather than in the context of each individual foreign brand, is a precondition for more completely fulfilling the rights of all of Bangladesh's apparel workers. *To foreign brands*: reverse the incentives for primary business partners away from a punitive system that punishes subcontracting to one that rewards transparency about the practice. Prioritize understanding where product actually is being produced. Brands can play an important role in legitimizing indirect suppliers as an important source of productive capacity, but one that requires new approaches for oversight and compliance with labor standards. This does not mean that brands bear sole responsibility for remediating or even monitoring conditions in indirect suppliers. But brands can and should lead in setting a new tone about indirect sourcing that creates space for other stakeholders to take action. *To local manufacturers*: increase transparency about the practice of indirect sourcing and its role in the production process. *To the government of Bangladesh and the trade associations*: make information available about regulatory systems that apply to direct and indirect suppliers. *To foreign governments and international organizations*: put indirect sourcing on the global agenda about supply chains, including the G-7 agenda, the ILO's meeting on supply chains in 2016, the World Economic Forum, and the OECD's guidance efforts for companies in the apparel and footwear sectors.

Identify the true size of Bangladesh's export garment sector

The mapping of 7,000 factories and the survey of two subdistricts in Dhaka presented in this research and the accompanying map (see Appendix 1 for details on the methodology) are an important first step in identifying the full scale of garment production in Bangladesh. But more and better data are required to identify the full extent of the sector. *To the ILO, in cooperation with the trade associations, unions, and the government of Bangladesh*: conduct a comprehensive survey of direct and indirect sourcing in Dhaka and Chittagong. The ILO should allocate personnel and financial resources under its existing RMG program to underwrite a comprehensive survey. The government and the trade associations should authorize and fully endorse the survey to encourage openness on the part of all factories, especially informal and indirect suppliers. In our comprehensive survey of Tongi and Rampura, it took six surveyors three full days to identify almost 500 factories, working in three teams. With the same small team, it would take about 42 work days to identify all garment factories in Bangladesh, or just over two months.

Currently underway is a mapping project by BRAC University. They have adopted NYU's mapping methodology and are working with a technology partner (Sourcemap) to digitally map all garment factories in Bangladesh. First results of this project and an interactive map are expected in early 2019. It remains to be seen if this mapping exercise will systematically include subcontracting facilities, including facilities that officially produce only for the domestic market but, according to NYU research, regularly accept orders for export as well.[10]

Regulate and create incentives to formalize indirect factories

A dynamic, sustainable garment sector would fairly distribute the costs of labor rights compliance across all firms in the sector, not just those that maintain direct relationships with foreign brands that demand compliance as part of the price of doing business. *To the government of Bangladesh*: improve enforcement in the indirect exporting part of the sector. Raising the odds of inspection and even prosecution for labor rights and safety violations (in addition to other regulatory obligations, such as taxation and business registration) among indirect suppliers would discourage firms from remaining informal and encourage factories to meet minimum standards of labor rights and worker protection.

To direct suppliers: help indirect exporters formalize through a "buddy system." Working through a buddy system, direct suppliers could transfer knowledge and potentially resources to help small- and medium-sized subcontracting factories achieve minimum standards for labor rights and safety compliance. Rubana Huq, managing director of Mohammadi Group, suggested such a system in a 2014 *Wall Street Journal* op-ed: "Every stronger factory should assume responsibility for boosting the industry's reputation by helping smaller factories comply with new standards. If 250 responsible manufacturers could each monitor and mentor 10 smaller factories on compliance issues, that would then alter the reality for 2,500 factories."

To international financial institutions and the government of Bangladesh: undertake infrastructure development in electricity, transportation, and gas. Indirect suppliers rely on the underdeveloped public infrastructure grid, leaving them especially vulnerable to electrical fires. Corruption at the highest levels of government prevented Bangladesh from receiving World Bank funding for a major bridge project in 2012. Since then, the World Bank has pulled back from funding the kind of large-scale infrastructure projects that would help lower costs across all factories in Bangladesh. The government should investigate and prosecute corruption allegations to restore confidence among international lenders, in addition to fulfilling its commitment to spend fully wire residential electrical infrastructure. International lenders should reconsider policies that restrict financing for infrastructure projects.

To private-sector lenders and Bangladeshi banks: improve access to capital for small- and medium-sized enterprises. Limited access to capital remains a significant barrier for indirect exporters to make necessary improvements, such as acquiring land for a purpose-built facility, investing in electrical and fire safety systems, or even simply meeting payroll on a regular basis. While significant loan commitments have been made by international lenders and brands, these generally target direct exporters and are made available in dollars, not in the local currency in which indirect exporters conduct business. Working together, international lenders and local banks should develop targeted financing facilities for indirect factories, including an expanded pool of loans available in Bangladeshi Taka. *To the ILO*: expand the scope of existing RMG initiatives to include indirect factories and strategies for formalizing this part of the sector.

Make the case for continued investment in Bangladesh

Foreign brands made five-year commitments to stay in Bangladesh through the Accord and the Alliance in 2013. With the five-year mark on the horizon, coupled with a worsening security situation and slow progress on labor rights reforms, there is an urgent need for Bangladeshi leaders and factory owners to demonstrate that Bangladesh continues to be a good investment for the global fashion industry. *To the government of Bangladesh*: strengthen the climate for mature industrial relations, in which independent unions can thrive. The government should lead in strengthening protections for trade unionists, including by investigating and prosecuting crimes against union organizers, and creating space for the union movement to advance.

To Bangladeshi leaders and factory owners: take ownership of an international effort organized around the concept of "shared responsibility" to realize a vision for a safe and sustainable garment sector. A new model is emerging for tackling the most entrenched governance problems in global supply chains through a shared responsibility approach. Leaders within Bangladesh should embrace this model, generating a mandate to address labor and safety issues in all factories and inviting all relevant stakeholders to join the effort. Shared responsibility for improving the overall system of garment production is an ambitious objective; leaders should approach it as a matter of vital importance for the future viability of the industry and the country's economic development.

Convene a taskforce

Given the scale of the challenge presented by the large universe of indirect sourcing factories (in addition to well-known problems among direct sourcing factories), a new structure will be required to organize ambitious action among the key stakeholders. *To private philanthropies and/or governments*: with a mandate from Bangladeshi leaders and buy-in from the international community, underwrite an entity or secretariat to organize a taskforce with a mission to develop a roadmap for a safe and sustainable garment sector in Bangladesh. The taskforce will require senior leadership from within Bangladesh, as well as international stakeholders. It should work over the course of 12–18 months to develop a comprehensive and specific roadmap to upgrade the entire export garment sector. The roadmap should include the wide-ranging set of policy tools, financial resources, and regulatory incentives that will be required to achieve a garment sector that delivers on the promise of expanded economic opportunity and the dignity of work for all workers. It should attach a cost to these improvements.

To the taskforce secretariat: convene all actors with a stake in a more safe and sustainable garment sector, including foreign brands, local manufacturers (both direct and indirect suppliers), unions, governments, international financial institutions, and the Accord and the Alliance. The taskforce must be supported by strong administrative functioning – regular meetings, transparent processes for considering and deciding on key issues, clear communication, and engaging appropriate experts.

Share costs and responsibilities

No single actor can underwrite the significant costs of upgrading Bangladesh's garment sector. Local and international participants should share the costs. *To brands, leading local manufacturers, the government of Bangladesh, foreign governments, development organizations, international financial institutions, private philanthropies, the Accord, the Alliance, the ILO, and unions*: share responsibility for the costs of upgrading the garment sector to make it safe and sustainable for the long term.

In a shared responsibility model, there is no set approach that would dictate the size of each stakeholder's financial responsibility. Working through the taskforce, all stakeholders should develop a formula for sharing costs that is fair and transparent. A formula is likely to result in proportional sharing of costs among stakeholder groups and individual actors. For example, governments of consuming countries may collectively assume responsibility for a portion of the total cost, which could be divided based on level of imports from Bangladesh. Of course, strict oversight will be required to ensure that funds are used for their intended purpose.

Conclusion

Global buyers and national-level suppliers in Bangladesh benefit from an indirect sourcing model that relies on the routine practice of subcontracting, often through agents and in a manner that is not transparent to buyers and regulators. The purpose of this strategy is to increase margins and boost production capacity while keeping costs low. Indirect sourcing has been an essential, though poorly understood, feature of the garment sector in Bangladesh and is likely to continue to be important in the future given the nature of the industry and the reluctance of brands to reflect on their purchasing practices that set incentives for subcontracting. Indirect sourcing is a root cause of many of the problems associated with poor working conditions and lack of factory safety in Bangladesh.

The two major private initiatives created in 2013 by global brands and retailers – the Accord and the Alliance – represent an unprecedented collaboration among global brands to address structural weaknesses collectively and they achieved substantive progress in some parts of the industry. But these two initiatives were set up for five years and are about to phase out. Both initiatives also never systematically included subcontracting facilities (unless brands investigated and put them on the list of suppliers) which caused a bifurcation of the industry with direct suppliers becoming bigger and better and subcontractors remaining off the radar, despite their critical role for the timely and cheap production of garments in Bangladesh.

The departure of Accord and Alliance by 2019 raises the question for how to ensure factory safety for all garment-producing facilities in Bangladesh in the future. From our analysis of business models it is clear that a future approach that includes smaller subcontracting facilities in Bangladesh's production network cannot rely only on these manufacturers to pay for factory safety upgrades. Smaller facilities will not have the resources to do so and thus different approaches need to be explored. A taskforce run by local stakeholders and supported by international stakeholders would be best positioned to come up with a strategic plan that works for the entire RMG sector.

Foreign governments and international financial institutions also need to play an important role in sharing the burden of filling governance gaps. At present, most foreign funding is focused on investments in Better Work Bangladesh, worker empowerment and skill development programs, food security, labor inspections, and combatting human trafficking. Foreign governments and international financial institutions have not focused sufficient attention and funding on the underlying problems, for example the infrastructure failings that exacerbate risks to factory and worker safety.

Appendix 1: methodology for the study

Prior to 2014, there was little publicly available, reliable information about the number of garment factories in Bangladesh. Before Rana Plaza, most estimates put the number of factories at 4,000–4,500. The government of Bangladesh launched its own factory database, the two trade associations updated their websites and factory registries, and the Accord and the Alliance began to publish monthly lists of factories that supply their members. These lists contain rich information about factory location, types of production (sweaters, tops, children's, etc.), annual production volume, number of sewing machines, and numbers of male and female workers. The five sources of data presented a unique opportunity to quantitatively analyze information about the factories and workers that comprise the country's powerful garment sector.

In October and November 2014, the NYU Stern School team collected all of the data from the five source lists, which resulted in more than 11,000 factory records. Through a painstaking process of manual de-duplication, a team of Stern MBAs combined records that represented the same factory, eliminating more than 3,800 duplicates. The de-duplication was completed in August 2015. They call the resulting list of 7,179 factories the "official list" of factories in Bangladesh because factories on these lists have registered with one of the five entities that maintain factory data. The cleaned up, comprehensive list is available on the website, www.stern.nyu.edu/ bangladesh-factory-map, where it is accompanied by a factory map. The map presents the first comprehensive view of any country's apparel manufacturing sector at a national level. It includes interactive information about the 7,000 factories on the official list, in addition to factory information in 65 neighborhoods.

As rich as the official data are, they do not tell a complete or accurate story of how garments are produced and the workers who are producing them. The official data contain only that – factories that are officially registered either with the government, one of the trade associations, or with one of the foreign initiatives. The earlier research indicates clearly that there is a wide network of informal factories that remain unregistered and where workers are invisible to regulators, inspectors, and buyers. We also know that the official lists, particularly BGMEA and BKMEA, include factories that do not physically exist or exist in name only. This means that the official data are inflated by factories that do not exist and exclude factories that do exist. To test the validity of the official list and the prevalence of informal factories, they conducted a comprehensive survey of two subdistricts in Dhaka – Tongi and Rampura – in June 2015.

They use the official list to determine the subdistricts with the highest concentration of garment facilities and selected Tongi (#6) and Rampura (#12) as survey areas. The selected subdistricts are geographical hubs for garment production. Tongi and Rampura are not only areas of high factory concentration themselves, but they are also surrounded by other areas where subcontracting is prevalent. Tongi, for example, in the northern part of Dhaka City, borders Uttara (#8) and is close to Gazipur (#2). Rampura on the south-east part of the city is closer to the old town (Fatullah #1), where garment production originally started before production moved to the outskirts of Dhaka. While Tongi is one of the districts with the highest concentration of Accord/Alliance production (39%), Rampura is one of the districts with the smallest percentage (9%). The local assessment team also judged Tongi and Rampura as most suitable in terms of their accessibility and size.

Four assessment teams, each comprised of two local survey experts, walked every street in Tongi and Rampura over three full days in June 2015. Their objective was to identify every facility involved in the garment business in these areas. The facilities they identified included larger factories that cut, sew, and package finished products, but also facilities that produce accessories (zippers, buttons, etc.), or only perform individual production steps, such as printing or washing.

The teams accessed over 90% of the garment facilities on the official list in the two areas. They surveyed management staff on a set of business-related questions, including information about current business challenges, as well as where the factory fits in the regulatory landscape.

They were able to assess whether a factory was a direct exporter, a registered subcontractor, or an unregistered subcontractor by asking factory managers about their membership in the trade associations, whether they "take UD" (the formal import/export permit issued by the trade associations on behalf of the government), and whether they were producing for export.

A factory can be a member of the trade association, but not take UD (official subcontractor) or be an unregistered factory that produces for export (informal subcontractor). Informal subcontractors do not maintain direct relationships with foreign buyers, take UD, belong to a trade association, or register with a government entity.

Notes

1 This chapter draws on sections from previously published reports by the New York Stern Center for Business and Human Rights (listed in the Works Cited), which have been reprinted for this chapter with the permission of the authors and the Stern Center.
2 Baumann-Pauly, D. (2017). *Assessing the true size of the garment industry in Bangladesh and why it matters.* NYU Stern Center for Business and Human Rights.
3 See https://bhr.stern.nyu.edu/statement/cgwr-response-ii.
   https://bhr.stern.nyu.edu/statement/2016/2/12/cgwr-bangladesh-response.
   https://bhr.stern.nyu.edu/statement/2017/8/28/mmmc8twv3rlo9lnfvrk6ozkkf4lptt.
4 http://bangladeshaccord.org/wp-content/uploads/Accord_Quarterly_Aggregate_Report.
5 This is described in greater detail in Chapter 1.
6 This is also detailed in Chapter 4.
7 Viyellatex Group, "Awards and Achievements," http://viyellatexgroup.com/index.php?option=com_k2&view=item&layout=item&id=6&Itemid=47.
8 http://bangladeshaccord.org/progress/.
9 One noteworthy example is H&M, a Swedish retailer specializing in low-cost fast fashion. The company sources clothing from 300 factories in Bangladesh, which comprise a significant portion of its global supply chain.
   Interviews with H&M's Dhaka office and several of its suppliers (that we identified independently of the company) suggest that H&M is endeavoring to establish a different kind of relationship with its suppliers. Consistent with H&M's official policy, factory owners report that H&M permits subcontracting, as long as the

factory is inspected. H&M and its suppliers say that they work together find an approved subcontractor if one is required. H&M issues a warning the first time production is discovered in an unapproved facility, and cuts the contract the second time. H&M also offers business incentives for better working conditions. H&M includes social compliance factors in its supplier relationships management system, rewarding strategic suppliers who demonstrate high performance. As one experienced agent-turned-supplier (who does not source for H&M) said, "The easiest way to get compliance is through the business relationship."

10 www.sourcemap.com/blog/2018/3/6/sourcemap-travels-to-dhaka-to-launch-massive-digital-mapping-of-bangladeshi-garment-factories.

Works cited

Barrett, P. M., Baumann-Pauly, D., and Gu, A. (2018). *Five Years after Rana Plaza: The Way Forward*. New York: NYU Stern Center for Business and Human Rights.

Baumann-Pauly, D. (2017). *Assessing the True Size of the Garment Industry in Bangladesh and Why It Matters*. New York: NYU Stern Center for Business and Human Rights.

Labowitz, S., and Baumann-Pauly, D. (2014). *Business as Usual Is Not an Option: Supply Chains and Sourcing after Rana Plaza*. New York: NYU Stern Center for Business and Human Rights.

Labowitz, S., and Baumann-Pauly, D. (2015). *Beyond the Tip of the Iceberg: Bangladesh's Forgotten Apparel Workers*. New York: NYU Stern Center for Business and Human Rights.

Part II
Dealing with the aftermath

4 Opportunities and limitations of the Accord

Need for a worker organizing model

Chaumtoli Huq

Introduction

On April 24, 2013, the world witnessed one of the most horrific workplace accidents in industrial history when the Rana Plaza building collapsed resulting in the death of 1,134 garment workers, and injuring of thousands more. The public tragedy visually unfurling on social media and television as the number of deaths escalated by the hour demanded a dramatic, substantive, public legal response mirroring the scale of injustice.

What resulted was the formation of two international factory safety and inspections agreements funded by global brands that produce their garments in Bangladesh. These agreements, the Accord on Fire and Building Safety in Bangladesh ("Accord") and Alliance for Bangladesh Worker Safety ("Alliance"), were aimed at addressing structural and fire safety based on a private-market approach. While these agreements were historic in that there had not been a unified effort by global brands to address factory safety issues, they were in the end not a radical departure from the existing legal framework of corporate social responsibility programs by global brands that audited factory conditions. The Accord does distinguish itself in that it is a binding agreement between global brands, unions, and NGOs allowing for some union participation, but it is limited in its scope by its sole focus on factory inspections, which is further limited to fire and building safety.

Five years later, we still read stories of factory fires, unsafe conditions, and we have not seen marked material changes in the lives of workers in terms of wages, benefits, and their ability to self-organize to form trade unions. This chapter will focus on the opportunities and limitations of the Accord. I focus on the Accord because it is heralded as the pro-labor agreement, and covers more of the factories, though some of the points can be applied to the Alliance. I discuss how the Accord functions more like a business service agreement than a labor agreement, is narrowly tailored to structural safety concerns and fails to address additional safety concerns impacting a female majority workforce, maintains the business model of garment production that keeps wages low and discourages organizing, and does not fundamentally change the socioeconomic relationships between worker, supplier, and global brands.

Further, I argue that without a broader labor rights focus to these safety programs, binding global brands through agreement to follow and be liable for labor rights in their business practices and change their business model, the impact of the Accord and similar agreements will remain limited. The Accord relies on private market approaches to address workplace safety and labor rights which its proponents concede. As such, they reflect the dominant neoliberal approaches, similar to past corporate social accountability efforts, to address human rights violations by corporate actors which have proven to be ineffective.

However, there still exist opportunities to redirect the focus of these agreements toward building the capacity of workers to demand better working conditions and supporting organizing. I suggest strengthening its effectiveness by creating a worker organizing model. We already have begun to see some promising changes in the extended 2018 Accord as they are instructed to develop protocols for freedom of association complaints. Yet again, the addition of this protocol does not have the necessary specificity and remedial mechanisms in place to make it effective, but its inclusion signals a right direction.

Background of the Accord

The Accord on Fire and Building Safety in Bangladesh (otherwise known the "Bangladesh Accord" or the "Accord") was formally signed by more than 40 apparel companies, two global trade unions, IndustriALL and UNI Global, and eight Bangladeshi trade unions on May 23, 2013. Clean Clothes Campaign (CCC), Worker Rights Consortium (WRC), International Labor Rights Forum (ILRF), and Maquila Solidarity Network are nongovernmental organizational (NGO) witnesses to the agreement. By October 2013, additional brands joined the Accord bringing its total to over 190 apparel companies from over 20 European, North American, and Asian countries, and Australia.

The Accord covers 1,400 factories, whereas the Alliance covers 600, and the remaining factories are inspected in collaboration with the International Labour Organization (ILO) and the Bangladeshi government. In addition to these factories that produce garments for export, a vast majority of them produce garments for local and regional markets. Conservative estimates from the Bangladesh Garment Manufacturers and Exporters Association (BGMEA) indicate that there are 5,000 factories in Bangladesh with a four million-person workforce, and other estimates show factories including subcontractors to be 7,000.

The Accord creates a system where signatory global brands fund a factory inspection program specific to fire and building safety. Examples of safety issues include installation of certified fire doors, automatic fire alarm systems, unobstructed fire exits, and electrical wiring. The program is monitored by a steering committee of brands and unions. The global brands commit to continue sourcing garment from suppliers while they undergo any remediation and to assist in funding for remediation.

The development of the Accord preceded the Rana Plaza disaster back to 2010 in the wake of a fire at the Garib & Garib Sweater Factory in Dhaka, which killed 21 workers. Human rights NGOs like WRC, ILRF, and CCC that focused on eliminating sweatshops in factories proposed safety proposals with brands; these proposals became the basis for the Accord. These human rights NGOs had a direct role in the drafting and the negotiation of the Accord between brands and unions, becoming witness signatories. The provisions of the Accord took substantial shape before Rana Plaza and did not take into consideration the changed circumstances after Rana Plaza and the urgent need to push for the inclusion of labor rights protections. ILRF, as one of the groups advocating for the Accord, received 47% of their funding from foundations (not trade unions) and 47% from the US government in 2012–2013 during this period of negotiation. Workers' Rights Consortium is primarily governed by US-based student and university administrators. The funding and governance structures of NGOs that were the drivers of the conceptual and drafting of the Accord is important to understanding that the proposals that formed the basis for the Accord was not a grassroots process.

European-based global trade union federation IndustriaALL was a signatory to the Accord but they did not form until 2012, well after the drafting of proposals that formed the basis for Accord, and they describe their work related to the Accord as leading "the drive in pushing more than 200 global fashion brands to *sign* the legally-binding Bangladesh Accord on Fire and Building Safety." It took the horrific tragedy of the Tazreen factory fire and Rana Plaza to galvanize support and pressure for global brands to sign on to the Accord as conceived and drafted, but it was not a catalyst to push for expanded labor rights.

In *Thinking beyond Accord and Alliance*, Professor Nafisa Tanjeem questions the claim that the Accord is representative of all unions and worker groups in Bangladesh. She writes: "signatories of Accord or members of various boards of Alliance are usually the ones that speak English, are well-connected with transnational activist networks, or receive transnational funds and sponsorships for labour organising initiatives." So, while some Bangladeshi unions were "included" in the discussions and as signatories, funding and other governance structures in terms of which unions are affiliated with European-based global unions meant it was primarily directed by organizations outside of union and civil society spaces of Bangladesh.

Given the world's attention on the Bangladeshi garment industry, this was a moment to push for a more robust global labor agreement inclusive of core labor rights, inclusive of freedom of association. If Bangladeshi unions led these discussions on the Accord compared to externally funded human rights NGOs, we may have seen a greater understanding of the need to include labor rights, at least freedom of association rights in it from the outset.

This awareness came five years later in the 2018 Accord, which extended the application of the Accord to 2021, and added that the Steering Committee of the Accord will develop "a training and complaints protocol to ensure that workers' rights to Freedom of Association are respected *in relation to protecting their own safety* under the scope of this agreement" (2018 Accord). Even still, the exercise of the freedom of association rights is only limited to safety concerns.

Limitations of the Accord's effectiveness

On the surface, a joint agreement signed by global brands, unions, and NGOs to address factory safety is momentous. A closer examination reveals some limitations based on its scope, function, and operation within the context of the global garment industry. Specifically, the Accord functions more like a business-service agreement than a labor agreement. It is narrowly tailored to structural safety concerns, fails to address additional safety issues impacting a female majority workforce, and maintains the business model of garment production that keeps wages low and does not fundamentally change the socioeconomic relationships between worker, owner, and global brand.

The Accord functions like a private business for services agreement rather than a labor agreement

The Accord is promoted as a pro-labor agreement comparing it to a collective bargaining agreement which is generally defined as a legally enforceable contract for a specified period between the management of an organization and its employees represented by a union which sets down terms and conditions of its employment. A month after the collapse, the *New York Times* editorial board reasoned that the tragedy would be a catalyst for change in the industry in Bangladesh just as the Triangle Shirtwaist fire in New York that ushered in a new wave of labor legislation. On its own website, the Accord simply describes itself as a "legally binding agreement."

The Accord has also been compared to a specific type of labor agreement that existed in garment factories in the United States called a jobber agreement where the company and its subcontractors agree to hire subcontractors who were unionized or agreed to other terms and conditions of employment to address widespread abuse in subcontracting. A jobber does not manufacture garments in his own shop, but subcontracts them. These agreements differ from traditional collective bargaining agreements because they cover conditions in supplier factories not directly owned by the company. Since the Accord is an agreement between brands and worker groups, it is often compared to a jobber agreement. Scholars have pointed out that the Accord is limited in its scope to only safety whereas a jobber's agreement contracted with suppliers on a wide range of issues including wages.

At its essence, it is a private agreement for services between brands and unions to conduct safety inspections, and if owners do not comply, brands will not purchase from the owner. The agreement is limited to inspection and remediation, but not to wages and organizing which are central issues for workers. Less a collective bargaining agreement, it functions more like a business or service contract invoking the coercive power of the economy to remediate safety issues in the factories.

Proponents highlight the Accord as a binding agreement and therefore labor friendly in part because there is a legal process within it for any dispute arising under terms of the agreement. If a brand fails to comply with any part of the agreement, a signatory can bring a complaint within a nonjudicial administrative dispute resolution process. The disputes are limited to the scope of the agreement which involve factory inspections. That there is a dispute provision in the agreement does not make it a labor friendly agreement. This point misunderstands contracts and agreements. All properly executed agreements are binding on the parties that sign it. The terms of the Alliance are binding on their signatories. The Alliance is just not binding between union and brands. The Alliance does not have a dispute process if there is a violation, but that does not make it nonbinding. It makes it unenforceable if either party does not abide by the terms of the agreement in a legal process be it judicial or administrative. Further, having a mechanism in the Accord to enforce the agreement is limited to its terms which here are about factory inspections, not a full range of labor rights. The arbitration mechanism does not allow workers to leverage it for greater rights. In fact, some garment owners have resisted it and closed factories, leaving workers without a job.

In a heralded arbitral win under this clause, the claim against the brands was that they failed to require suppliers to remediate facilities within the mandatory deadlines imposed by the Accord and failed to negotiate commercial terms to make it financially feasible for their suppliers to cover the costs of remediation. Even there, the issue did not involve a workers' rights issue but a commercial issue. Further, the arbitration tribunal held not to make public the name of the brand such that worker groups would know who violated the Accord, thereby taking away any power of transparency and accountability or leveraging the decision for organizing.

Even if we view the Accord as a workers' agreement, simply focusing on the fact the unions are signatories, and there is a mechanism for the parties to address breaches of the narrow scope of the agreement which involves fire and building safety issues, does not make this a good contract to protect labor interests. It is true that global brands, unions, and NGOs are signatories to the agreement, but these parties alone do not convert it to a labor or workers' rights agreement or make it beneficial to advance workers' interests or rights.

Even though well-meaning and intentioned, because of the funding and governance structure of human rights NGOs and the relationship of international unions with local unions connected to transnational networks, as discussed above, they are not accountable or answerable to the vast segment of workers. It is not surprising that trade unionists like Amirul Haque Amin, National Garment Workers Federation, have said that the "Accord provides limited scope for unionization, and participation of workers." A 2015 survey by Bangladesh Garment Worker Unity Forum, a grassroots labor group, found that 98% of garment workers have never heard of the Accord or Alliance. This has been my own experience conducting worker interviews in Bangladesh. An agreement that is not known by the vast majority of the workforce cannot be said to be representative of their interests.

Given this context, Bangladeshi unions have been pushing for more freedom of association rights, stating from the beginning that had there been a trade union at Rana Plaza, we would not have seen the high number of deaths. "Union rights are so important. We need the freedom of association. If the garment workers don't get this, Rana Plaza will happen time and time again" says labor leader Nazma Akter. Cracks in the building were shown the day before the building collapsed, and the police ordered evacuation of the building, but the building owner ignored the order and pressured workers to continue working. Bank workers in a lower floor were told to evacuate. Garment workers were required to go on and work. Thus, it is union protection, not building safety that relies on professionalized engineers and technocratic approaches, that could have saved workers' lives. This protection was noticeably absent in the Accord. While freedom of association is referenced in the 2018 Accord, the agreement does not lay out specific mechanisms to ensuring its enforcement.

I also note that the Accord was not passed through the legislative process of Bangladesh, any democratic law-making process or any referendum process involving workers, or even in the international sphere whereby they could be able to directly comment on its usefulness or applicability. This relates to my earlier point that the Accord cannot be said to be a worker-representative agreement. Contrast the signing of the Accord a private, market agreement with the long consultation process from 2014 to pass a binding treaty to regulate the business activities of transnational corporations. As discussed further below, global brands have been resisting any agreement that binds them to additional rights and obligations. It is easier to sign agreements to fund inspections which they have been doing than commit to any additional labor rights.

Beyond the scope of this piece, the Accord as a private, transnational agreement that has repercussions on workers that has not been vetted through any democratic process raises additional questions about the nature of these transnational agreements that bypass the state. As weak and dominated by garment owners' interest as the Bangladesh state may be, this supranational, private market approach to safety does not create space for workers to exercise any power within state apparatus to advocate for their rights. This explains why there has been a vibrant-worker led movement that operates in parallel to the negotiations for the Accord. The Accord also has been sued in the Bangladesh courts, and the High Court has ruled on its suspension. An appeal of this decision by Accord is pending. With its goal to turn over the administration of the Accord to the government in 2021, it is not clear what efforts, if any, the Accord is taking to build the capacity of state and civil society actors to take on this task.

The Accord is not proven to be effective to address safety and labor rights in the female majority garment industry

In assessing any agreement or contract, we have to ask: what rights are created, risks allocated, and to what responsibilities do corporations obligate themselves? How does this agreement fit within the larger context of the industry? What do workers get in this bargain? Does it create the socioeconomic conditions for expansion of rights?

When the Accord is evaluated with these questions in mind as a contract, we see that it is limited to inspection, training for health and safety committees. In addition, companies are not obligated to fund factories for remediation, and workers do not get any direct benefits in terms of wages, or severance where the factories close. The 2018 Accord addresses some of these problems with the first Accord such as requiring the payment of severance to workers who lose employment as a result of factory closures due to safety or to maintain their employment if a factory decides to relocate. For suppliers, the new Accord requires brand to work with them to provide financing to remediate safety issues.

Even if we were to evaluate the contract in its limited scope, it also has not safeguarded safety because there have been fires and safety issues. In 2015, there was a fire in an Accord inspected factory. In addition, in 2017, a boiler explosion at a garment factory inspected by the Accord killed ten and injured dozens. Boiler inspections are currently not covered under the Accord's fire and safety inspections. As a result, even though the factory in question had been inspected by Accord engineers in October 2016, the boiler itself had not been checked.

Hasan Ashraf, an anthropologist who conducted six months of fieldwork in a Dhaka knitwear factory, writes about the long list of everyday health threats he witnessed: from dust and smoke inhalation, noise, lack of ventilation, eyestrain, musculoskeletal pain, stress, and exposure to lights, electric wires, and chemical adhesives. Ashraf discovered that workers are having to make a trade-off between earning a living and caring for their health, which can rapidly depreciate during their working lives, undermining their long-term physical and mental well-being. The Accord creates health committees, but it does not allow for right to organize when we know that employers consistently obstruct and thwart this right. Health committees cannot be a substitute for true worker-led organization.

Here, I note the uncritical and technocratic use of the term "safety" used by the Accord and its proponents. Reports evaluating the Accord five years later state that worker safety has improved, based on the number of factories inspected and violations found. As Anner finds, there has been an increase of workers' rights violations since Rana Plaza. How can it be said that workers are "safe" when worker rights violations have increased? The ILO, which sets international labor standards, has noted that one of the trends in employment has been the increase in precarious, uncertain, and unpredictable working conditions. Precarious labor has been defined by

> uncertainty as to the duration of employment, multiple possible employers or a disguised or ambiguous employment relationship, a lack of access to social protection and benefits usually associated with employment, low pay, and substantial legal and practical obstacles to joining a trade union and bargaining collectively.

When we evaluate worker safety through the discussions of precarity as it relates to workers' status from ILO, we see that workers have in fact not been made "safer" by the Accord.

Further, when we understand that the majority of the workforce is female, and the Accord does not address health and safety issues such as sexual harassment and assault, denial of maternal leave benefits resulting in poor health, the idea that workers are "safer" is divorced from the reality of women workers' lives on the ground. Jennifer Rosenbaum, US director of Global Labor Justice, said:

> We must understand gender-based violence as an outcome of the global supply chain structure. H&M's and Gap's fast fashion supply chain models create unreasonable production targets and underbid contracts, resulting in women working unpaid overtime and working very fast under extreme pressure.

In my own piece, *Workers Rights through a Gender Lens*, I argued that the Accord is "limited in addressing key issues impacting the workplace safety of women workers and their overall rights" because they fail to recognize the specific ways that women workers' health and safety are impacted by the supply chain structure, social norms and familial relationships, and lack of enforcement of local laws such as maternity leave. For example, in the summer of 2013, I interviewed survivors of the Rana Plaza tragedy and learned from medical professionals that pelvis fractures, injuries to reproductive organs, and urinary tracts were common due to the building collapsing on their bodies, yet advocacy focused on campaigns for prosthetics versus any effort for reproductive or mental health services. An emphasis on building and fire does not get to these health and safety concerns that are unique to the female majority workforce.

The safety standard for Accord is zero deaths, which is of course what we all want. However, zero deaths cannot be the sole aspiration for a labor agreement for workers in the twenty-first century. Should not the standard be a right to live with dignity with the full range of labor rights guaranteed at the minimum by the ILO? We create a false dichotomy when we say workers are safe due to inspections; when in fact substantial evidence shows that workers experience more workers' rights violations and precarious employment, especially women workers. The discussion of worker safety as structural and not the full range of ways workers' lives are precarious (or, stated, unsafe) reveals that the Accord is limited even in its core mission of achieving workplace safety. We must raise the questions: what purpose does the uncritical, technocratic use of the word "safe" or "safety" serve and whom does it benefit. This notion of safety, as defined by the Accord as being the number of factories inspected, allows for market promotion as part of corporate responsibility program rather than actual holistic health and safety from workers' perspective or norms set by ILO. When viewed from the norms established by ILO that discuss workers' rights and evidence on workers' actual working conditions, workers have not been made "safer."

The Accord does not alter the socioeconomic power relationships between parties or change the business model in the global garment industry

When we examine the rights and responsibilities the Accord creates on the signatories, we see additional limitations. It does not change the relationship between buyer and owner to increase prices which would allow owners to pay for higher wages and even nonwage benefits. In fact, the Corporate Social Responsibility (CSR) and purchasing units of multinational brands work separately. Mark Anner, in his report, *Binding Power: The Sourcing Squeeze, Workers' Rights, and Building Safety in Bangladesh since Rana Plaza*, makes this precise point. His research has found that the hypercompetitive structure of the global supply chains has contributed to a sourcing squeeze where buyers seek a lower price from suppliers which impacts workers' rights. He writes: "The price squeeze has contributed to the declining real wages and *an increase in workers' rights violations* since Rana Plaza." This finding is significant given all the attention workers' rights have been given since Rana Plaza. One would expect a decrease in workers' rights violations. This contradiction exists because of the inherent nature of the business model of the garment industry, which drives prices and wages down to make a profit. An agreement that does not acknowledge this economic reality is doomed to be limited in its success.

In 2013 Nobel laureate and economist Muhammed Yunus suggested either an international wage for garments set by buyers or a 50 cent surcharge on each piece of clothing and to create a Garment Worker Welfare Trust which could provide for garment workers physical safety, pensions, health care, and retirement, among other benefits. He notes that the extra surcharge may reduce the company's profit margins, but he argues that the company can make that up by marketing an ethical product. Leaving aside the mechanics of this proposal, and valid critique that he suggested an NGO not labor organization to administer the trust which counters efforts to empower workers, his proposal does acknowledge the price pressure that leads to worker rights violations. His proposal highlights that the global brands need to be responsible in wage setting, and that only increased wages will help with safety. Not surprising, his proposal was rejected quickly in part because such a proposal would alter the pricing of the industry and cut into the profits of the global brands. To obligate themselves to an international wage would change their business practice and affect their profit margins, then the lump sum financing of a factory inspections program. Each brand is required to pay a set amount based on their size and revenues to support the governance of the Accord.

In a different context, I, too, have argued the link between wages and safety in my piece, *Wages and Safety: Two Sides of the Same Coin*, where workers interviewed shared that they continue to enter unsafe factories because they fear the factory will close and they will lose their wages entirely. Wages incentivize workers to make different choices around safety. If they know their wages are guaranteed or jobs secure, they will be more likely to raise safety issues. I wrote: "As long as the wage-safety equation tilts towards a need for wages, safety decisions will not be paramount for workers."

As such, the Accord does not change the socioeconomic relationship between the parties in the supply chain that creates the conditions for these unsafe workplace conditions in the first place, or the business model that keeps wages low, or provides an infrastructure that allows for workers to organize. It is given that employers must provide a safe workplace, but what additional rights or explicit tangible benefits do workers obtain here, as they would in a collective bargaining. The goal of a collective bargaining agreement is to level the economic bargaining powers of workers and management.

The Accord does not directly create new legal rights or benefits for workers. As discussed below, any new rights such as an increase of the minimum wage were obtained through organizing. The central issue that Bangladeshi workers have repeatedly called for is higher wages, and if that is their central labor demand, the Accord does not address it. Workers can neither leverage the Accord to push for higher wages nor unionization.

Labor rights since Rana Plaza obtained through organizing by Bangladeshi workers

Six years later, Bangladesh minimum wage remains the world's lowest in the global garment industry. The 2013 and 2018 changes to the minimum wage in Bangladesh and continued struggle for increased workers' wages were due to workers mobilizing. In August 2014, a vibrant campaign for wages was underway by workers of Tuba Group, which was owned by Delwar Hossain, the same owner of Tazreen Fashions where a fire resulted in the death of at least 112 workers in November 2012. Again, in 2015, workers from another factory, Swan Jeans, mobilized for wages owed after the factory abruptly closed. In December 2016, there was a mass movement for wages and labor organizers were arrested. After Rana Plaza, the wage board increased the minimum wage to 5300 taka ($66) but that amount had not changed despite rising living costs. Finally, in January 2018, the government set a wage board to set up a new wage structure for garment workers. In March 2018, Bangladeshi labor unions with the support of international allies demanded a wage increase to 16,000 taka ($192). The wage was only increased to 8000 taka ($100) from 5300 taka ($63) which was woefully inadequate to meet the needs of workers and their families. Nonetheless, it was labor mobilizing and support from allies that led to this increase.

It seems that there are two parallel advocacy worlds: the demands garment workers are making at the grassroots level and externally funded human rights NGOs. All of this worker organizing and mobilizing occurring alongside, almost in a parallel advocacy universe, to the work of the Accord underscores how removed it is from workers' immediate concerns.

The crackdown by the Government of Bangladesh in December 2016 reveals the dire circumstances that labor organizers experience in organizing. Garment workers and labor leaders experienced unfair or fabricated criminal cases in Bangladesh after wage strikes in December 2016. Since the strikes, labor organizers have reported, "regular police visits to their offices, vandalism and destruction of union offices, police raids on training programs and activities and continuous police surveillance of union offices." The *New York Times* editorial board recently reported on this crackdown: "The crackdown is clearly intended to intimidate workers and keep Bangladesh a low-wage country, thus protecting an industry that accounts for some 80 percent of export earnings." Human rights organizations urged the Government of Bangladesh to stop persecuting organizers. Human Rights Watch (HRW) has been monitoring the persecution of labor organizers since Aminul Islam's death in 2012, and has repeatedly urged the government to stop harassment of organizers. In 2014, HRW urged the government to investigate the threats to labor organizers. Those threats continue to this day. It is not possible to view Accord as a labor success when these crackdowns on labor organizers are happening alongside factory inspections.

Even today, workers and unions are mobilizing for increased labor rights.

This vibrant labor mobilizing for wages is operating outside of the sphere of the administration of the Accord, and raises the question of how the Accord is functioning to support broader labor rights. We know that increased wages and the right to unionization are directly linked to safety and working conditions. While the Accord requiring global brands to require building and fire safety inspections and to bind themselves to this agreement is important, it cannot be said to improve worker safety when we see increased precarity of workers' conditions. The workers' rights agreement does not cover wages and unionization, and statistics have shown the conditions for workers have deteriorated.

The Accord is similar to prior corporate social responsibility approaches considered to be ineffective

In order to understand the limitations of the Accord and its essentially business nature, we must view the Accord in the context of other CSR programs. In this regard, having an international agreement that binds global brands to some obligation is helpful, and illustrates that at least on one issue, inspections, governance is possible. It would have to go further in scope.

There are similar examples of using market approaches to address labor rights. The UN Global Compact supports voluntary socially responsible behavior of corporations by encouraging them to integrate ten principles into their strategies and operations. The Guiding Principles for Business and Human Rights seeks to provide an authoritative standard for preventing and addressing the risk of adverse human rights impacts linked to nonbinding business activity. The Organization for Economic Cooperation and Development Guidelines for Multinational Enterprises are nonbinding principles and standards for responsible business conduct in a global context. Many other bodies and industry groups have devised sectoral codes of conduct. So far these have failed to prevent continued abuses of corporate power. However, within these debates, countries from the Global South are demanding more binding corporate accountability agreements.

These limitations exist because corporations do not want to change the business model of the industry which creates price squeezes on suppliers to increase their profits and because they simply do not want to be regulated or obligated. Most of the corporate guidelines/approaches have taken a voluntary, self-governance, policy approach and have not been effective. As Florence Palpacuer details in *Voluntary versus Binding Forms of Regulation in Global Production Networks: Exploring the Paradoxes of Partnership in the European Anti-Sweatshop Movement* activists have adapted a market-based approach to their activism compared to the more confrontational approaches earlier in the movement which make it easier for corporations to respond to activist demands without providing any mechanism to account for social outcomes.

In years past, the idea that voluntary compliance is more effective has held some influence, but with time, evidence has shown that voluntary agreements are not effective, and corporations do not comply even when governments do pass mandatory auditing laws. Unless corporations are held accountable to human rights abuses, these voluntary approaches will continue to be ineffective. Two examples demonstrate this: the Corporate Human Rights Benchmark (CHRB) results and the Modern Slavery Act.

The CHRB ranked 98 of the world's largest publicly traded companies from three at-risk sectors, on human rights performance. The CHRB is a unique collaboration led by investors and civil society organizations dedicated to creating the first open and public benchmark of corporate human rights performance. The study found that on the whole, companies perform better on policy commitments and governance. Performance drops off when it comes to acting on those risks, tracking responses and remediating harms. The study compared company practices to the UN Guiding Principles on Business and Human Rights and other international standards, and ranked the companies based on their implementation of the internationally recognized standards. The results of the study were that only six of the 98 major companies had implemented more than 50% of the benchmark standards. The average score of all 98 companies was only 28.7% implementation of the benchmark standards.

Reports under the UK Modern Slavery Act also show lack of compliance. Under the Act any company with a turnover of at least £36 million (approx. 46.8 million) operating in the UK is required to report on the steps they are taking to eliminate slavery and human trafficking from their operations and supply chains. The Business & Human Rights Resource Centre launched its UK Modern Slavery Act Registry in February 2016. The Resource Centre actively monitors the release of company statements and adds them to its free and open Registry to allow comparison and benchmarking of companies' policies and practices. Of the 1,700 statements tracked so far, only 15% fulfill all three minimum requirements of the Act (however, this is a 6% improvement from six months ago). Many companies failed to provide any information on the action they are taking or be open about where the risks lie in their supply chain. Even where the brands are required to provide compliance, their responses to reveal steps to eliminate trafficking are poor.

The finding that companies perform better on policy commitments or governance issues rather than any effort to change substantively workers' rights or remediate harms is echoed in a study by Stephanie Barrientos and Sally Smith in *Do Workers Benefit from Ethical Trade? Assessing Codes of Labor Practice in Global Production Systems*. They found labor codes had "little or no change in freedom of association, the right to collective bargaining or discrimination." The impact on the codes on income was mixed. "There was no instance of codes having led to wage increases through a collective bargaining agreement." They conclude that there is a disjuncture between a compliance approach and a worker empowerment approach.

These examples directly relate to the Accord, which is more a business and governance type of agreement than an agreement that confers rights on workers. It is thus not surprising that brands are open to signing the Accord as a factory inspection program than agree to be bound or obligated to additional labor rights. And from Barrientos and Smith's study it shows that such agreements like the Accord have not had any beneficial impact on broader labor rights. We have seen that workers' rights violations have increased since Rana Plaza. Thus, the Accord is not a radical departure from the existing CSR programs, even if it has NGO and brand signatories and a dispute mechanism.

The Accord has been extended to 2021 and in light of these critiques has made some changes to its agreement such as acknowledging the importance of freedom of association rights for workers. However, this inclusion is limited to trainings on freedom of associational rights, and workers can bring freedom of association complaints through its dispute process as it only relates to safety. Again, the scope of freedom of association rights is limited, despite the overwhelming critique that freedom of association rights is critical to improving workers' employment conditions. We have seen that some brands have not continued to sign on to the Accord again, reflecting the view that at the end of the day the global brands do not want to be obligated to uphold labor rights.

Toward an organizing model for global labor agreements

The organizing opportunity to hold global brands accountable for labor rights violations was when the whole world's attention was on the horrifying Rana Plaza images. It lay bare what happens when global brands are not regulated. At that moment, advocates should have pushed for a comprehensive labor rights agreement, which recognized the pressures in the industry to keep wages down, and the importance of trade unions. This would have followed an organizing model for labor agreement, which centered on improving the working conditions of workers, and creating opportunities for workers to form unions.

In the labor movement context, the organizing model is a broad concept that refers to how social movement organizations should prioritize and configure their work which is centered on building power for workers in contrast to a business/service model which is based on delivery of services to members and reinforces member reliance on the formal organization of unions. The Accord follows a business/service model in contrast to an organizing model, which has the potential for workers to push for additional labor rights. As such, and discussed above, we have seen its limitations.

It has been consistently said that had there been a trade union in Rana Plaza, we would not have had the level of deaths as we did because workers would not have been pressured to work even after they say cracks in the building. With the continued absence of a trade union, we are still seeing labor rights violations and obstructions to organizing. However, it can still be revived as a path forward if workers are actively involved and organizing is supported.

There are some encouraging developments in the formation of global agreements that may provide some avenues for greater labor rights such as the H&M Global Framework Agreement and the Freedom of Association Protocol in Indonesia. The H&M agreement includes setting up national monitoring committees, initially planned for countries such as Cambodia, Bangladesh, Myanmar, and Turkey to safeguard the implementation of the agreement from the factory floor upward, and to facilitate a dialogue between the parties on the labor market. The Protocol details obligations on supplier and brands to ensure freedom of associational rights. Both are still voluntary and provide some administrative nonjudicial process, but at least reflect an explicit and directed effort to address freedom of association rights for which workers in Bangladesh have been calling.

These are improvements, and do encourage support of trade union rights, but they do not provide a clear mechanism when violations occur. They function through monitoring committees. They do not bind companies to remediate for human rights abuses. They fall into the nonbinding trap that we have seen to be ineffective. Unless these global agreements bind global brands to be accountable labor rights and provide a mechanism to redress harm, and integrate an organizing model into their conception of the agreement, sadly we will continue to see limits on our progress for full labor rights.

Conclusion

The Accord and Alliance have no doubt improved structural safety in factories. Because the agreements do not alter the economic relationships between the brands, suppliers, and workers, the conditions that create unsafe working conditions remain, and their effectiveness is limited. Their adoption of a business and service contract concept to labor rights in contrast to an organizing model minimizes their impact on broader labor rights. Without pushing brands to commit to further rights, obligating them to remedy violations, we will continue to have noncompliance. We need an agreement that will require brands to do more – that is what workers are demanding, and we need to fashion our legal strategies based on their demands.

Note

This chapter is based on research conducted from 2014 to 2015 in Bangladesh, as a Senior Research Fellow with American Institute for Bangladesh Studies (AIBS) interviewing various stakeholders to assess effectiveness of Accord. Dhaka University LLM Students Farhan Hoque and Zulkarnine Mim assisted me in the field research. I have returned to Bangladesh in the summers of 2016 and 2017 to continue my research. I also draw from a series of articles written for *The Daily Star*, which can be found at www.thedailystar.net/author/chaumtoli-huq during my time in Bangladesh, as well as a full-length documentary, the first of its kind to document the lives of garment workers, that I researched and produced. A short trailer can be found through the following link http://lawatthemargins.com/video-sramik-awaaz-workers-voices-documentary-short/.

Bibliography

4 Years after Rana Plaza: Increased Worker Repression. www.solidaritycenter.org/4-years-rana-plaza-increased-worker-repression/#sthash.tCrS036G.dpuf.

Accord on Fire and Building Safety in Bangladesh. 2013. http://bangladeshaccord.org/. Statement on 2015 Fire at Dignity Textile Mills Limited. http://bangladeshaccord.org/2015/06/accord-statement-on-fire-at-dignity-textile-mills-limited-natun-bazaar-sreepur-gazipur/.

Accord on Fire and Building Safety in Bangladesh: May 2018. https://bangladeshaccord.org/wp-content/uploads/2018-Accord-full-text.pdf.

Alliance for Bangladesh Worker Safety. 2013. www.bangladeshworkersafety.org/.

Amao, Olufemi. 2011. *Corporate Social Responsibility, Human Rights and the Law: Multinational Corporations in Developing Countries*. Routledge. ISBN: 978-0-415-59785-2.

Anner, Mark. March 22, 2018. *Binding Power: The Sourcing Squeeze, Workers Rights, Building Safety in Bangladesh since Rana Plaza*. Penn State. Center for Global Workers Rights (CGWR). https://ler.la.psu.edu/gwr/documents/CGWR 2017ResearchReportBindingPower.pdf

Ashraf, Hasan. 2017. Beyond Building Safety: An Ethnographic Account of Health and Well Being on the Bangladesh Garment Shop Floor, *in Unmaking the Global Sweatshop: Health and Safety of the World's Garment Workers*. Philadelphia: University of Pennsylvania.

Bangladesh Garment Manufacturers and Exporters Association (BGMEA). www.bgmea.com.bd/home/pages/tradeinformation.

Bangladesh garment workers call for increased minimum wage. www.industriall-union.org/bangladesh-garment-workers-call-for-increased-minimum-wage, May 3, 2018.

Barrientos, Stephanie, and Sally Smith. 2007. Do Workers Benefit from Ethical Trade? Assessing Codes of Labor Practice in Global Production Systems, *Third World Quarterly*, Vol. 28, No. 4, Beyond Corporate Social Responsibility? Business, Poverty and Social Justice (2007).

Brands that have not signed the 2018 Accord. June 29, 2018. www.industriall-union.org/brands-that-have-not-signed-the-2018-accord.

Business and Human Rights Center. Binding Treaty. www.business-humanrights.org/en/binding-treaty.

Clean Clothes Campaign
Freedom of Association Protocol Indonesia. https://cleanclothes.org/resources/recommended-reading/freedom-of-association-protocol-indonesia/view.
History of Bangladesh Accord https://cleanclothes.org/resources/background/history-bangladesh-safety-accord/view.

Corporate Benchmark. 2017 Results. www.corporatebenchmark.org/.

Dhaka Tribune. June 1, 2018. High Court extends Accord's inspection for a period for 6 more months. www.dhakatribune.com/bangladesh/court/2018/06/01/high-court-extends-accord-s-inspection-period-for-6-more-months.

Evans, Benjamin. Accord on Fire and Building Safety in Bangladesh: An International Response to Bangladesh Labor Conditions, 40 N.C.J. Int'l L. & Com. Reg. 597 (2015).

Florence Palpacuer details in Voluntary versus Binding Forms of Regulation in Global Production Networks: Exploring the Paradoxes of Partnership in the European Anti-Sweatshop Movement, in Unmaking the Global Sweatshop. 2017. University of Pennsylvania Press.

Global Nonviolent Action Database. 2012–2013. Bangladesh factory workers protest for wages and better working conditions. https://nvdatabase.swarthmore.edu/content/bangladesh-factory-workers-protest-higher-wages-and-better-working-conditions-2013.

Human Rights Watch. Bangladesh Reports.
2013. Tragedy Shows Urgency of Worker Protections. www.hrw.org/news/2013/04/25/bangladesh-tragedy-shows-urgency-worker-protections.
2014. Protect Garment Workers. www.hrw.org/news/2014/02/06/bangladesh-protect-garment-workers-rights.
2017. Stop Persecuting Unions, Garment Workers, Human Rights Watch. www.hrw.org/news/2017/02/15/bangladesh-stop-persecuting-unions-garment-workers.

H&M. Global Frameworks Agreement. www.industriall-union.org/industriall-global-union-and-hm-sign-global-framework-agreement, March 11, 2015.

Huq, Chaumtoli. November 18, 2014. Wages and Safety: Two Sides of the Same Coin, *The Daily Star*, March 8, 2015. www.thedailystar.net/wages-and-safety-two-sides-of-the-same-coin-50818.
Workers Rights through a Gender Lens. March 25, 2015. www.thedailystar.net/op-ed/workers-rights-through-gender-lens-73562.
The State and Legal System Fails Bangladesh Workers Time and Time Again. 2016. http://lawatthemargins.com/state-and-the-legal-system-fails-bangladesh-workers-time-and-time-again/.

IndustriALL. 2017. Bangladesh Accord's binding process scores legal win. www.industriall-union.org/bangladesh-accords-binding-arbitration-process-scores-legal-win.

IndustriALL celebrates 5 years. www.industriall-union.org/industriall-celebrates-5-years, June 20, 2017.

International Labor Organizations (ILO). 2011. Policies and Regulations to Combat Precarious Employment. www.ilo.org/wcmsp5/groups/public/---ed_dialogue/---actrav/documents/meetingdocument/wcms_164286.pdf.

International Labor Rights Forum. Bi-Annual Report. 2012–2013. https://laborrights.org/sites/default/files/publications/ILRF%20Bi-Annual%20Report%202012-2013.pdf, September 2014.

ILO. Improving Working Conditions in the Ready Made Garment Sector Programme in Bangladesh. www.ilo.org/dhaka/Whatwedo/Projects/safer-garment-industry-in-bangladesh/WCMS_226530/lang--en/index.htm.

Kazmin, Amy. April 23, 2018. Rana Plaza five years on – safety is greater but not guaranteed. Financial Times. www.ft.com/content/7ec413ec-46e6-11e8-8ee8-cae73aab7ccb.

Monitoring Workers Rights: The Limits of Voluntary Social Compliance in Labor Repressive Regimes. May 25, 2017. *Global Policy*, Vol. 8, No. 3. https://onlinelibrary. wiley.com/doi/full/10.1111/1758-5899.12385.

New York Times Editorial Board.
   Bangladesh's Crackdown on Labor. www.nytimes.com/2017/02/01/opinion/ bangladeshs-crackdown-on-labor.html, February 1, 2017.
   Worker Safety in Bangladesh and Beyond. May 2013. www.nytimes. com/2013/05/05/opinion/sunday/worker-safety-in-bangladesh-and-beyond.html.

November 27, 2017. Five Years after Deadly Fire, Bangladesh's garment workers are still vulnerable. https://thewire.in/external-affairs/five-years-deadly-factory-fire-bangladeshs-garment-workers-still-vulnerable.

Organization for Economic Cooperation and Development (OECD). 2011. Guidelines for Multinational Enterprises. http://mneguidelines.oecd.org/.

Ovi, Ibrahim Hossain. January 14, 2018. Government forms new wage board for RMG Sector, *Dhaka Tribune*. www.dhakatribune.com/labour/2018/01/14/ rmg-workers-get-fourth-wage-board.

Paul, Ruma. July 3, 2017. Blast in Bangladesh garment factory kills 10, investigation underway, Reuters. www.reuters.com/article/us-bangladesh-blast/blast-in-bangladesh-garment-factory-kills-10-investigation-underway-idUSKBN19P0A0?il=0.

Permanent Court of Arbitration. 2017. Arbitrations under the Accord on fire and building safety in Bangladesh between Industriall Global Union and Uni Global union (as claimants) and two global fashion brands (as respondents). https:// pcacases.com/web/sendAttach/2238.

Prentice, Rebecca and Geert De Neve. 2017. *Unmaking the Global Sweatshop.* Philadelphia: University of Pennsylvania Press.

Sam Lazaro, Fred. April 9, 2014. Questions Linger a year after Bangladesh's garment factory collapse, PBS News. www.pbs.org/newshour/world/questions-linger-after-bangladeshs-garment-factory-collapse.

Solidarity Center, AFL-CIO. September 13, 2013. Bangladesh Accord is a Game Changer. www.solidaritycenter.org/experts-bangladesh-accord-is-a-game-changer/.

Tanjeem, Nafisa. April 21, 2017. Thinking Beyond Accord and Alliance, in Rana Plaza Special, *The Daily Star*. www.thedailystar.net/star-weekend/ thinking-beyond-accord-and-alliance-1393888.

Transparency in Supply Chains (TISC). April 1, 2018. UK Modern Slavery Act Non Compliance: Half of UK Organizations are Over 12 Months Due. https:// pressreleases.responsesource.com/news/95317/uk-modern-slavery-act-non-compliance-half-of-uk-organisations-are/.

Tuttle, Nicole. 2015. Human Rights Council Resolutions 26/9 and 26/22: Towards Corporate Accountability. www.asil.org/insights/volume/19/issue/20/human-rights-council-resolutions-269-and-2622-towards-corporate.

United Nations Global Impact. www.unglobalcompact.org/what-is-gc/mission/ principles.

United Nations, Office of the High Commissioner of Human Rights (OHCR). 2011. Guiding Principles on Business and Human Rights. www.ohchr.org/Documents/ Publications/GuidingPrinciplesBusinessHR_EN.pdf.

White, Gillian. May 3, 2017. What's Changed since More Than 1110 People Died in Bangladesh Factory Collapse? The Atlantic. www.theatlantic.com/business/ archive/2017/05/rana-plaza-four-years-later/525252/.

Yardley, James. Bangladesh Takes Step to Increase Lowest Pay. November 4, 2013. www.nytimes.com/2013/11/05/world/asia/bangladesh-takes-step-toward-raising-38-a-month-minimum-wage.html.

Young, Holly. April 24, 2014. Without stronger unions, Rana Plaza will happen time and time again, *The Guardian.* www.theguardian.com/global-development-professionals-network/2014/apr/24/rana-plaza-garment-workers-bangladesh.

5 Does third-party monitoring improve labor rights? The case of Cambodia

Kristy Ward

Introduction

Globalisation has shaped labor markets in many ways. How and where work is performed, and how it is regulated are increasingly influenced by international interests. The shift of economic production from the Global North to the Global South is an important dimension of this transition as emerging labor regimes in low-income countries tend to mean lower wages and a more compliant workforce. This has resulted in non-state, or third-party, regulation driven by pressure from transnational stakeholders. Non-binding regulatory regimes have had mixed outcomes leading to a debate about whether alternative forms of 'regulation' detract from state compliance responsibilities and sideline worker representation.

The response of local and international trade union movement stakeholders and apparel brands to the tragedy of the Bangladesh Rana Plaza collapse in 2013 that killed 1,129 workers – including a legally binding multi-stakeholder accord, a trade union alliance and implementation of several International Labour Organisation initiatives – demonstrates the persistence of alternative labor regulation in global production networks. This chapter argues that the focus on factory-level breaches and remediation within third-party monitoring programmes diverts attention from the underlying causes of labor law violations: buyer practices and substantive constraints on the ability of workers and their representatives to organise. A key question, therefore, is whether alternative 'regulation' strengthens state and international brand legitimacy without corresponding gains for workers.

To answer this question the chapter first considers debates about the role and effectiveness of third-party monitoring. It then examines the successes and challenges of the Better Factories Cambodia (BFC) programme drawing on interviews with union and labor NGO representatives in Cambodia conducted in August 2018. Importantly the chapter also includes the views of garment factory workers[1] which are often absent from discussions about third-party monitoring in global supply chains in Cambodia and elsewhere. The final section then identifies the limitations of third-party monitoring arguing that improved factory performance in some areas is limited by the de-politicisation of wider struggles for labor rights. The chapter concludes by exploring the implications of third-party monitoring for improved labor governance in the ready-made garment sector.

Labor regulation and global production networks

The challenge of how to regulate labor rights in global production networks is an area of ongoing concern for scholars, policymakers and labor activists. Central to this debate is how to regulate the complexity of actors and interactions in production networks which extend beyond national borders. These issues are made more complex by the failing of state regulation in many countries involved in textile and footwear manufacturing. In the absence of effective state regulation and enforcement, alternative mechanisms have emerged. Alternative 'regulation' is often driven by transnational interests and actors, is non-binding and operates parallel to state mechanisms. It may involve corporate codes of conduct established by major apparel brands, certification systems and compliance auditing. Third-party monitoring, as discussed throughout this chapter, involves actors other than the state – usually apparel brands or the International Labour Organization (ILO) – setting standards for employment conditions and auditing compliance to those standards.

To date, the analysis of third-party monitoring has largely focused on the effectiveness of methods and processes, or interactions with other forms of regulation. While these are important considerations, they divert attention from important questions like what drives labor rights violations in the first instance and what are the best mechanisms for redistributing economic and political power among actors to improve labor rights. These questions are important in contexts like Cambodia where regulation and enforcement are strong on paper but weak on implementation.

Labor rights activists and scholars have for some time raised concerns over the effectiveness of third-party monitoring. Criticisms include the focus on policing and monitoring (Saxena, 2018), lack of transparency in monitoring processes (Oka, 2016; Barrientos and Smith, 2007; Shea et al., 2010), the inability of point in time auditing methods to identify breaches of freedom of association and other enabling rights (Egels-Zanden and Merk, 2014), and diverse and conflicting interests among key stakeholders (Locke, 2013). Third-party monitoring can also lead to the stagnation of state regulation and enforcement. Ahmed et al. (2014: 258), for example, argue that a deliberate withdrawal of the state from labor regulation can positively effect foreign direct investment as 'contexts with a stable, or predictable, mis-governance and a government that has incentives to not intervene can yield strong performance in exporting manufactured goods'. This might indicate, therefore, that third-party monitoring is favourable to states as it enables them to manage labor at critical tipping points through direct and confrontational means, leaving third parties to get on with the day-to-day management of labor relations.

On the other hand more optimistic accounts of third-party monitoring highlight improvements in factory floor working conditions; primarily occupational safety and health (OSH), wages and overtime (Rossi, 2015; Rossi and Robertson, 2011; Polaksi, 2006; Brown et al., 2014). Third-party monitoring and transnational regulation is also thought to improve state regulation. Bartley (2011) and Amengual and Chirot (2016), for example, suggest that codes can either overlap or reinforce national laws, go beyond national laws to extend protections, or influence public regulatory frameworks over time. In particular, Amengual and Chirot suggest that Better Work Indonesia led to reinforcement of state regulation in instances where there was strong union mobilisation and where district manpower offices (responsible for inspection and dispute settlement) were willing and able to enforce public regulation. However, where state enforcement is negligible and worker mobilisation has been undermined, the complementarity of third-party monitoring and state regulation is more questionable.

Less frequently considered are the mechanisms through which third-party monitoring effects change. Barrientos and Smith make the distinction between *outcomes* and *process* rights suggesting that 'at heart is a tension between a focus on codes as a technical tool to achieve social compliance based on outcome standards, and a focus on codes as a means of enhancing the process through which workers claim their rights' (2007: 724; see also Anner, 2012). For example non-binding private regulation mostly focuses on tangible and apolitical issues of OSH, wages and overtime. Yet substantive rights that enable workers to organise and mobilise to improve working conditions – including freedom of association and collective bargaining – are persistent areas of non-compliance (see BFC, 2017).

More specifically, then, what is it about the dynamics between industrial relations actors that prompts regulatory compliance through frameworks with no legal sanctioning power? Scheper (2017) argues, in the context of the Accord on Fire and Building Safety in Bangladesh, that supply chain management practices triggered improvements in factory working conditions. Following the Rana Plaza collapse transnational buying companies and international trade unions signed a legally binding agreement to improve workplace safety and implement compliance monitoring. This was the first time that transnational buying companies had agreed to be legally responsible for labor rights violations. Suppliers, however, were pressured to act through the collective power of buyers and global union federations, rather than workers or local unions (Reinecke and Donaghey, 2015).

A critical question, as Oka (2017) suggests, is who holds companies to account for labor law compliance? In alternative regulation models, it is ultimately consumers and civil society. No one wants to buy clothes made in sweatshops; and naming and shaming puts brands at reputational risk. As Oka (2017) identifies, however, brands will only advocate for labor regulation compliance where there is a threat to political stability that impacts production, either directly or through consumer boycotts. Oka shows that in Cambodia brands only felt compelled to act, by threatening to withdraw operations, after mass strikes and military violence in 2014 against workers. However, a new Trade Union Law that enabled substantive limitations to the registration and operation of independent unions was passed by the Government of Cambodia in April 2016 without objection from all but one major brand. Scheper (2017) and Locke (2013) also analyse the influence of brands in labor rights regulation and compliance, arguing that the practices of brands in global supply chains contradict and compromise the compliance standards they, and others, require factories to implement. Demands placed on factories by buyers to meet large orders within tight time frames are predicated on excessive worker overtime, long hours and limited breaks. Factories then apply downward pressure on employees, including strategies to quickly replace staff that underperform or complain.

Missing from these debates are important dimensions of worker agency and union representation. At a practical level, workers are often not included either in the development of codes or in auditing factory compliance (Egels-Zanden and Merk, 2014). Yet workers themselves have long fought for labor rights well before implementation of adequate labor laws, third-party monitoring programmes and corporate codes of conduct. As Siddiqi argues the struggles of Bangladeshi garment workers point to a 'rich history of resistance' (2016: 61) including widespread wildcat strikes led by workers in 2006, 2010 and 2016. Hughes (2007) also outlines the forms of protest initiated by Cambodian garment factory workers in the early years of export-oriented manufacturing, supported by a fledgling political opposition, trade unions and the ILO.

Given workers' willingness to engage in collective action for improved labor rights, a more pressing consideration, then, is the effect of third-party monitoring programmes and tripartite processes on contentious forms of worker agency and representation; the types of action that have shown to be highly effective in pressuring labor reform such as the minimum wage strikes in Cambodia in 2013 and 2014. Various scholars point to the overall trend of de-politicising worker struggles through new forms of participation and representation including those prevalent in models of alternative regulation (Anner, 2012; Hughes, 2007; Siddiqi, 2016; Egels-Zanden and Merk, 2014). Minimum wage committees, tripartite structures and factory-level committees of management and elected worker representatives – often initiated by international organisations – have depoliticised and atomised public collective action. This has the effect of taking negotiations between representative organisations and powerful stakeholders 'behind closed doors' (Hughes, 2007: 843). It also limits worker participation to spaces which are imbued with unequal power relations, giving workers limited room for manoeuvre and channelling contentious collective action through a handful of elected representatives.

How, then, are labor rights fought for and gained in hybrid regulatory environments? And what role does third-party monitoring play in progressing the full gamut of labor rights that improve workplace safety and wages, while also strengthening worker agency and representation as key drivers of those and other rights? The next section considers the background and context of BFC before discussing its operation and limitations as a form of third-party monitoring in the following section.

The Cambodian context

Cambodia is often identified as a labor rights success in the Global South. Progressive labor law, tripartite labor processes, a unique ILO-managed factory monitoring programme and high union density in the garment sector are identified as key contributing factors (Rossi, 2015; Polaski, 2006; DiCaprio, 2013). On paper Cambodia's system of labor regulation is comprehensive. The 1997 Labour Law, developed with assistance from the ILO, provides for freedom of association, collective bargaining, and non-discrimination. Various processes and institutions have been established for the resolution of labor disputes including Ministry of Labour and Vocational Training (MOLVT) mediation, an independent Arbitration Council, and the common courts.

As Barrientos and Smith (2007) point out, alternative regulation operates within a broader social and institutional environment that shapes its reach and effectiveness. The political environment in which these changes have taken place is critical to understanding the history of labor reform. Cambodia is a semi-authoritarian state and an electoral democracy with the current ruling party – the Cambodian People's Party – having held power since the withdrawal of Vietnamese occupation in 1989. National elections are held every five years and observed by independent international monitors. However widespread allegations of electoral fraud occur following almost every election (Morgenbesser, 2017). Moreover, neo-patrimonialism has consolidated the economic and political power of the ruling and business elite (Hughes and Un, 2011). It is within this context that the struggle for labor rights plays out, thus influencing the role and effectiveness of regulatory mechanisms.

The effectiveness of industrial relations institutions is hampered by a lack of judicial neutrality, weak rule of law and close relationships between business and government. Unions report that cases taken to the MOLVT for mediation are rarely decided in favour of workers and unions. Moreover, the Trade Union Law passed in 2016 has had a detrimental effect on the ability of unions to organise and represent workers. Unions and workers often take matters to global apparel brands for intervention once public dispute resolution processes have been exhausted. While tripartite structures – such as the Labour Advisory Committee – are in place, much of the debate among tripartite partners centres on working conditions in garment factories, and primarily minimum wage. Cambodia is therefore strong on regulation and weak on enforcement, meaning that the government does very little to enforce its own labor standards.

In Cambodia garment exports have been critical to economic growth. Factories are highly reliant on foreign brands for orders and garment exports make up 81.71% of overall exports (Oka, 2017). In 2017 the minimum wage for garment factory workers was US170 per month, and is reviewed annually. Despite minimum wage increases it has been argued that real wages in the sector have decreased given higher living costs and inflation (Ford and Gillan, 2018). Unlike many other countries with high local factory ownership, including Bangladesh, in Cambodia only 4% of ownership is domestic (BFC, 2017). The majority of factory owners in Cambodia are from China (36%) and Taiwan (20%) (BFC, 2017).

Cambodia's garment sector is heavily unionised with 3,166 local trade unions, 86 federations and 14 confederations registered with the MOLVT in 2015 (CAMFEBA, 2015). Union registration rose steadily after implementation of the 1997 Labour Law and growing international trade union support. The union movement is deeply embedded in national political struggles with close relationships between unions and political parties, particularly during national elections (Hughes, 2007; Arnold, 2017; Ward and Mouyly, 2016). Union affiliations have become increasingly divided. Employer and government sponsored unions have proliferated with only a small number of independent unions in operation. Seventy percent of factories monitored by BFC have at least one union (ILO, 2015). It is common for factories to have multiple unions at the enterprise level although as Oka (2016) shows this has a negative effect on labor rights compliance. Union registration at the plant level has declined significantly since implementation of the Trade Union Law in 2016. This has impacted on the registration and membership of trade union federations, which require the membership of seven locally registered unions.

Labor reforms have therefore enabled a higher density of unions, more competition among unions, the growth of pro-government and employer unions, and a dilution of collective power. The next section considers the primary third-party monitoring programme operating in Cambodia – BFC – within this landscape of local politics, including the internal and external pressures that have limited the programme's effectiveness.

Internal tensions

BFC is one form of non-state regulation based on core international labor standards and national labor laws. It is considered a multi-stakeholder initiative involving employers, the state, unions and brands/buyers. A detailed history of BFC has been outlined elsewhere and so will not be repeated here (see Marshall, 2017; Kolben, 2004; Arnold and Toh, 2010; Rossi, 2015). As a brief introduction, however, BFC started in 2001 as a unique experiment linking labor rights to trade. Established through the US-Cambodia Bilateral Textile Trade Agreement, the basic premise was straightforward. The United States would increase export quotas provided that labor rights iteratively improved. The Government of Cambodia lacked the resources and capacity to monitor and so the ILO initiated a multi-stakeholder third-party monitoring programme (BFC). The impetus for the programme to continue beyond the end of the trade agreement was to limit export licences to factories monitored by BFC.

Following the success of BFC in improving some working conditions in factories, the Better Work programme was developed in 2007 as a model for implementation in other countries including Haiti, Indonesia, Jordan, Vietnam, Nicaragua and Bangladesh. Participation in Better Work is mandatory for factories in only three of the seven country programmes, including Cambodia. Bair (2017), in her analysis of Better Work in Nicaragua, highlights the limitations of the programme as a result of optional participation including a high degree of difficulty in recruiting factories given the lack of incentives.

The aim of the BFC programme is to improve labor relations between parties and, in turn, strengthen labor rights. In recent years BFC has framed its mandate as a 'convenor, facilitator of dialogue and knowledge hub abound labour law' rather than a compliance monitor (BFC, 2017: 35). To this end a key strategy is to facilitate dialogue between factory managers, national policymakers and workers. A distinguishing feature of BFC when compared to other multi-stakeholder initiatives and corporate codes of conduct is a partnership approach with the State. BFC therefore goes beyond compliance auditing in an attempt to engage tripartite stakeholders to jointly developed strategies to improve labor rights. This includes factory assessments, an annual buyer forum for buyers, BFC staff and unions to share experiences, and training and advisory services for factory management and workers. Advisory services are provided on a fee-for-service arrangement which is an important source of income for the programme.

BFC is increasingly focused on knowledge transfer and advisory services as opposed to assessment and reporting. Training and advisory services are currently conducted in a range of areas including OSH, human resource management and labor law legislation (Rossi, 2015: 508; BFC, 2017). Social dialogue is also promoted at the factory level through the establishment of Performance Improvement Joint Consultative Committees, facilitated by BFC Enterprise Advisors (Merk, 2012). BFC therefore focuses on identifying breaches of national and international labor standards and then redressing compliance issues through a range of capacity building initiatives. As the 2017 BFC Annual Report shows however, compliance monitoring forms the bulk of BFC work with only 89 of 442 factories engaging BFCs advisory services, and 165 factories undertaking training (BFC, 2017). Assessments, on the other hand, were conducted in 395 factories between May 2016 and April 2017. Merk (2012) also identified issues with engagement of buyers, highlighting that discussions at the annual buyers' forum are non-binding and that many buyers choose not to participate.

The success of BFC as a model of third-party monitoring is premised on improved factory compliance with national and international labor standards (Brown et al., 2014). Independent monitoring has been central to BFC since its inception. BFC monitors compliance with labor laws in several areas including forced labor, child labor, discrimination and freedom of association, compensation, contracts and human resources, and OSH and work time (BFC, 2017). An extensive checklist to assess working conditions is drawn from the labor law and ILO conventions (BFC, 2017). BFC monitoring teams undertake unannounced site inspections up to three times per year which involve inspection of premises and interviews with workers and factory management. Each monitoring team comprises two people, and teams are rotated to avoid teams visiting the same factory twice (Rossi and Robertson, 2011). Independent assessments of working conditions at individual factories are conducted over several days and involve meetings with workers, employers and union officials (BFC, 2017).

The BFC public reporting database currently includes 480 factories, covering 85% of factories with export licences (BFC, 2017). When taking subcontracting factories into account the total percentage of factories covered is much lower. Publishing information about factory-level breaches has been found to have a direct and positive impact on improvement in labor rights (Brown, 2016). Factories producing for reputation-sensitive brands have higher levels of compliance when compared to other factories (Brown, 2016; Oka, 2010). Yet even factories without reputation-sensitive buyers showed compliance improvements. The decision to cease factory-level non-compliance reporting in 2006 resulted in a slowing and, in some cases, regression in compliance. Transparency reports were reinstated in 2014 with summary critical issue reports published online. This resulted in a 13% increase in compliance and a decrease in critical issue violations from 281 to 197 (BFC, 2017).

There is therefore an evident link between public disclosure and improved factory compliance. Workers and union representatives interviewed in August 2018, however, identified issues with the inspection process. They explained that factory management was skilled in concealing labor law breaches during factory inspections. Examples given by workers included factory management making monitoring teams wait at the front gates prior to conducting an inspection and coaching workers on how to respond to questions from monitoring officials. Workers often withheld information about working conditions during monitoring interviews for fear of contract termination. Some workers did inform monitors of the extent of labor rights violations at their workplace; however, they were subsequently fired or did not have their fixed duration contracts renewed. Many workers reported that factory management threatened that if the factory did not pass compliance monitoring they would no longer receive orders from large brands, which meant factory closure and job losses. Workers were also attuned to these realities. This is consistent with findings from Oka (2016) and Shea et al. (2010) who found that factories prepare in advance of inspections to conceal breaches. As BFC schedules inspections at the same time each year, factories prepare for inspections by hiding breaches and coaching workers to respond to auditor questions. Barrientos and Smith (2007) also note similar challenges in other countries where monitoring is undertaken by non-state actors including double book keeping, coaching workers and disguising non-compliance issues including child labor and hours worked.

Finally, without enforcement powers BFC is limited in the range of strategies it can deploy to redress compliance issues. Strategies for remediation of breaches focus on social dialogue. This approach, however, is void of politics and power relations. For example, plant-level committee meetings are facilitated by a BFC Enterprise Advisor with the aim of supporting parties to develop locally relevant solutions. Yet even the title of the joint management and worker committee – Performance Improvement Joint Consultative Committees – is cumbersome and potentially isolating for workers. The process of establishing invited spaces (Cornwall, 2004) for participation in discussions about improvements in labor rights takes contentious action away from workers and their representatives into a dynamic where workers have little bargaining power.

External pressures

It is evident, then, that the conduct of factory assessments and de-politicising approaches to social dialogue have limited the effectiveness of BFC in improving compliance with labor laws. Over a number of years BFC has taken measures to address these issues such as reinstating public reporting and supporting facilitated stakeholder dialogue. However the role of BFC as a comprehensive third-party monitoring mechanism has been most impacted by external pressures and politics, as this section shows.

Scholar and ILO claims of BFC success in improving labor rights require two qualifications. The first relates to the type of rights being addressed. Labor rights that are easy to fix and cost-effective have seen the most improvement as a result of BFC efforts. Whereas labor rights which go to the heart of power relations between capital and labor, and which may succeed in disrupting the control of factory management over workers, have either stagnated or regressed. An impact evaluation of BFC in Indonesia, Haiti, Jordan and Cambodia by Brown (2016) found almost no improvements in freedom of association and collective bargaining across a seven-year period. Similarly, the BFC 2017 Annual Report (BFC, 2017) acknowledges that freedom of association is an area that compliance has either stalled or declined. Harassment and intimidation of workers, anti-union violence, trumped up legal charges and court monitoring of union leaders, and union busting are commonplace as reported by both unions and workers.

Fixed duration contracts (FDCs) are a particularly successful strategy used by factories to undermine labor rights compliance. Of the workers interviewed only one was employed on an unlimited duration contract. Most employment contracts ranged from two to six months. Many workers had contracts of this length renewed for extended periods ranging from four to six years. While some workers felt that FDCs were beneficial as they were paid a 5% severance pay at the end of each contract, others were fearful of not having contracts renewed for a number of reasons. These included not meeting daily production targets on more than one occasion, joining or forming an independent union, discussing labor rights violations with external monitors during inspections or taking too many toilet breaks. The problematic use of FDCs has also been noted elsewhere (Human Rights Watch, 2015; Merck, 2012) and is clearly a tactic to ensure worker acquiescence to factory management pressure.

The second qualification is that BFC operates in a constantly changing political context. While improvements in some labor rights may be identified over time, the lack of attention to enabling process rights means that quick compliance wins can be easily undermined. Moreover, BFCs' ability to influence government and other stakeholders is impacted by these changing dynamics, with several union representatives commenting that BFC had 'more power' in the past. As Oka (2014) identifies, there are ongoing tensions between the Arbitration Council, BFC and the MOLVT over jurisdiction and legal interpretations. Since 2016 labor rights have been seriously undermined in Cambodia through strategies of containment deployed by the state, buyers and factory management. This is not to suggest that these issues are within the scope of BFC operations, but rather that social dialogue and compliance monitoring can only go so far when powerful actors seek to undermine non-binding regulation and the labor movement more broadly.

Subcontracting – the practice of larger factories registered for export outsourcing production to smaller unregistered factories – has increased considerably in recent years. In 2016 an additional 244 factories were registered with the National Social Security Fund[2] when compared to Ministry of Commerce records for officially registered factories with export licences; up from 106 factories in 2015 (ILO, 2017). The ILO reports that up to a quarter of all garment factories were subcontracting enterprises in 2016 and therefore not included in BFC monitoring. Union representatives interviewed also identified that subcontracting was an increasing problem for labor rights, with larger export factories establishing smaller factories in provincial areas to evade compliance monitoring from government bodies and third parties. Subcontracting factories have been shown to frequently violate labor rights with pressure to meet orders within tight deadlines (HRW, 2017), thus demonstrating that factories will continually find ways to circumvent monitoring and reporting to meet buyer production demands.

Since 2013 the government has also escalated efforts to undermine organised labor. The new Trade Union Law (passed in 2016) has substantively curtailed freedom of association by severely restricting the right of independent unions to register and operate. Moreover, only unions with Most Representative Status (30% or more of the total factory employees) can bring cases to the Arbitration Council. Consequently, the number of cases to the Arbitration Council has dropped dramatically since the trade union law came into effect in April 2016, down from 248 cases in 2016 to 50 cases in 2017 (Arbitration Council, 2017).

The new Universal Minimum Wage Law[3] will also undermine freedom of association. The law will establish a National Minimum Wage Council to set minimum wages across all sectors other than informal and domestic workers. Initially the council will focus on minimum wage in the garment sector. On the face of it this is a positive move as there is currently no minimum wage in Cambodia in any industry other than garment manufacturing. It is problematic, however, that proposed law will impose fines for criticising or protesting against annually adjusted wage setting. This government strategy appears to be an attempt to prevent a repeat of the widespread minimum wage strike action in 2014 that resulted in military confrontation with protesting workers and unions, and the death of four workers (Asia Monitor Resource Centre, 2014).

Does third-party monitoring work?

What, then, do we make of claims that third-party monitoring has substantively improved labor rights in Cambodia? And what lessons from the Cambodia experiment linking trade and labor rights are relevant in other contexts including Bangladesh? As Scheper (2017) argues, at the heart of the matter are power dynamics between labor and capital that are rooted in global supply chains. Yet third-party monitoring is often focused on factory-level breaches and remediation, with limited consideration for the factors that determine the ability of factories and labor to shape compliance or non-compliance in the first place: buyer practices and substantive constraints on the ability of workers and their representatives to organise.

Cambodia is a stable political environment for business that is weak on rights enforcement. This is no accident. Weak enforcement enables a competitive global advantage in keeping production costs low, while also enabling profits for local business and political elites either through direct investment or rent-seeking. The State has also shown a willingness to violently repress and contain labor mobilisation both for economic and political ends.

Third-party monitoring has clearly led to improvements in some working conditions. But as conditions have improved factories have found ways to circumvent these gains. Several key lessons from BFC are worth mentioning. First, as Bair (2017) argues, compulsory participation is critical. But what is the carrot, given there is no stick? In Cambodia factories are coalesced into compliance to avoid naming and shaming which impacts on buyer orders and factory profit margins. A tactical response has been to establish or outsource to subcontracting factories to maintain supply and volume, without the red tape of labor law compliance. Second, the accuracy of information collected during factory inspections has been called into question in Cambodia, and other contexts. If workers are risking dismissal by sharing accurate information about working conditions, then this suggests a highly unequal power dynamic that third-party monitoring in its current form cannot address. As Locke and Romis (2010) also highlight, however, focusing on the how inspections are conducted diverts attention from the higher order question of whether third-party monitoring is an effective method of guaranteeing both process and outcomes labor rights. I return to this point shortly.

A lack of BFC sanctioning authority when breaches are identified is also a key limitation. Who sanctions when the state refuses? In non-state regulatory frameworks there is a reliance on brands to sanction given their interest in mitigating reputational and economic risks. Yet this assumption is somewhat flawed. Oka (2017) has shown that brand concerns over their reputation will only prompt them to act when the issue is high profile (salient) and other international actors such as ILO mobilise. For example, brands responding swiftly and forcefully in the case of the violent crackdowns in 2014 when several workers were shot and killed and trade union leaders were unlawfully detained for over a month. Two years later the Trade Union Law, which severely restricts freedom of association and trade union formation (targeted at independent unions), elicited almost no response from brands. As Oka identifies 'brand leverage is not a panacea in the face of a government determined to stifle any countervailing power' (2017: 103).

What, then, is driving factories to improve conditions in response to third-party monitoring? First, concerns over brand reputation. This suggests, as others have argued (see Locke, 2013; Saxena, 2018), that third-party monitoring can only go so far in contexts where weak rule of law and intentional misgovernance benefit ruling and economic elites. While BFC was intended as a complementary mechanism to state regulation, in practice it has for the past two decades filled the void of state enforcement in Cambodia despite an operational regulatory architecture built around ILO labor standards. This is not to suggest that the state does not intervene in issues of labour relations. To continually attract investment States need to maintain a competitive advantage over other export-oriented manufacturing countries, primarily through low production costs. Economic bottom lines are compromised by volatile employment relations and workers demanding their rights prompting the State to intervene – often violently – when worker unrest reaches a potential tipping point.

Second, social dialogue initiatives act as a smokescreen for deeply embedded power relations in global production networks. BFC attempts to address some of the shortcomings in brand-led compliance and auditing by engaging the state as best it can, and by focusing on discussion and collaboration between stakeholders. BFC explains that 'In factories that receive advisory services, BFC helps set up bipartite committees and then supports these committees to start tackling the root causes of non-compliance' (BFC, 2017: 6). Yet at the heart of labor rights violations is a fundamental tension between the interests of workers, factories, brands and the state. Factory-level committees are a good start but to what extent will workers voice their concerns and suggestions knowing that their jobs are on the line?

Yet workers are not passive victims of employer tactics. The case of Cambodia has shown that even in an authoritarian regime which increasingly represses civil society activism workers frequently mobilise and strike on issues of minimum wages, unfair dismissal and freedom of association. They do this through union mobilisation, and without union involvement. Moreover, garment work has paved the way for women to lead more economically stable, independent and empowered lives in spite of the ongoing challenges faced in the workplace (see Siddiqi, 2016; Hughes, 2007; Derks, 2008). This seems rather at odds with the lines of accountability in third-party monitoring which privilege buyer, brand and transnational labor network power over the power that workers themselves regularly exercise.

Third-party monitoring, then, becomes a stand in for effective government regulation functioning primarily to enhance brand reputation and state legitimacy. While States might become more accountable and responsive to labor rights enforcement over time, the case of Cambodia has shown this not to be the case. As others have argued (see Scheper, 2017) supply chain continuity drives the fundamental premise of compliance monitoring and corporate codes. If the root causes of labor rights violations are supply chain practices driven by brands and a lack of worker agency and ability for collective action – which manifest as poor factory conditions – then focusing on factory-level remediation is a band-aid solution. Employment conditions are improved, but not to the extent that asymmetrical power relations between employers and workers, and brands and factories are disrupted.

Third-party monitoring in Cambodia has, however, gone some way to improving social dialogue between key actors by engaging buyers and creating semi-formal spaces for negotiation between workers and factory management. As Egels-Zanden and Merk (2014) argue, however, this parallel means of organising is a weak form of representation that undermines union mobilisation. In the context of Cambodia this is problematic as it has been shown that alternative regulation is most likely to reinforce state regulation when strong worker mobilisation is present (Amengual and Chirot, 2016). Therefore greater attention is required to enabling a range of opportunities for worker representation and engagement which challenge the decision-making status quo, and enable workers to claim greater representational and collective power to drive improvements in labor rights. Ultimately, however, different strategies – including pressure on the state to enforce its own labor laws – are needed to disrupt the enduring power dynamics between the state, global capital and labor. Otherwise third-party monitoring will continue to de-mobilise and depoliticise the efforts of organised labor to advance sustainable employment rights in global production networks.

Notes

1 Interviews and small focus groups were conducted with 19 workers (17 females and 2 males) from factories located in Phnom Penh and Kandal.
2 The National Social Security Fund registers enterprises with eight or more employees regardless of whether they are exporting or subcontracting (ILO, 2017).
3 At present the Labour Advisory Committee (LAC) make annual determinations regarding wages. The LAC comprises representatives from unions, employer associations and government. Only two LAC members are from independent unions.

References

Ahmed, F. Z., Greenleaf, A., and Sacks, A. 2014. The paradox of export growth in areas of weak governance: The case of the ready-made garment sector in Bangladesh. *World Development*, 56: 258–271.

Amengual, M., and Chirot, L. 2016. Reinforcing the state: Transnational and state labor regulation in Indonesia. *ILR Review*, 69(5): 1056–1080.

Anner, M. 2012. Corporate social responsibility and freedom of association rights: The precarious quest for legitimacy and control in global supply chains. *Politics & Society*, 40(4): 609–644.

Arbitration Council Foundation. 2017. *Annual Report 2017: Invest for the Future*. Phnom Penh: Arbitration Council Foundation.

Arnold, D., and Toh, H. S. 2010. A fair model of globalisation? Labour and global production in Cambodia. Journal of Contemporary Asia, 40(3): 401–424.

Arnold, D. 2017. Civil society, political society and politics of disorder in Cambodia. *Political Geography*, 60: 23–33.

Asia Monitor Resource Centre. 2014. *A Week that Shook Cambodia: The Hope, Anger and Despair of Cambodian Workers after the General Strike and Violent Crackdown*. Hong Kong: AMRC.

Bair, J. 2017. Contextualising compliance: Hybrid governance in global value chains. *New Political Economy*, 22(2): 169–185.

Barrientos, S., and Smith, S. 2007. Do workers benefit from ethical trade? Assessing codes of labour practice in global production systems. *Third World Quarterly*, 28(4): 713–729.

Bartley, T. 2011. Transnational governance as the layering of rules: Intersections of public and private standards. *Theoretical Inquiries in Law,* 12(2): 517–542.

Better Factories Cambodia. 2017. *Annual Report 2017*. Geneva: ILO & IFC.

Brown, D. 2016. The impact of better work: A joint program of the International Labour Organization and the International Finance Corporation. *Tufts University Labor Lab working paper.*

Brown, D., Dehejia, R., and Robertson, R. 2014. Factory decisions to become noncompliant with labour standards: Evidence from better factories Cambodia, in Arianna Rossi, Amy Luinstra, and John Pickles (eds) *Towards Better Work: Understanding Labour in Apparel Global Value Chains*. London: Springer, 232–250.

Cambodian Federation of Employers and Business Associations (CAMFEBA). 2015. *Cambodia's Trade Union Law. A Necessity. Employers' position paper.* Phnom Penh: CAMFEBA.

Cornwall, A. 2004. Introduction: New democratic spaces? The politics and dynamics of institutionalised participation. *IDS bulletin*, 35(2): 1–10.

Derks, A. 2008. *Khmer Women on the Move: Exploring Work and Life in Urban. Cambodia.* University of Hawaii Press.

DiCaprio, A. 2013. The demand side of social protection: Lessons from Cambodia's labor rights experience. *World Development*, 48: 108–119.

Egels-Zanden, N. and Merk, J. 2014. Private regulation and trade union rights: Why codes of conduct have limited impact on trade union rights, *Journal of Business Ethics*. 123: 461–473.

Ford, M., and Gillan, M. 2017. In search of a living wage in Southeast Asia. *Employee Relations*, 39(6): 903–914.

Hughes, C. 2007. Transnational networks, international organizations and political participation in Cambodia: Human rights, labour rights and common rights. *Democratization*, 14(5): 834–852.

Hughes, C., and Un, K. 2011. *Cambodia's Economic Transformation.* Copenhagen, Denmark: NIAS Press.

Human Rights Watch. 2015. Work faster or get out: Labour rights abuses in Cambodia's garment industry. Available at: www.hrw.org/sites/default/files/reports/cambodia0315_ForUpload.pdf.

ILO. 2017. Cambodian Garment and Footwear Sector Bulletin, Issue 6, May 2017.

Kolben, K. 2004. Trade, monitoring, and the ILO: Working to improve conditions in Cambodia's garment factories. *Yale Human Rights and Development Journal*, 7: 79.

Locke, R. M. 2013. *The Promise and Limits of Private Power: Promoting Labor Standards in a Global Economy.* Cambridge: Cambridge University Press.

Locke, R. M., and Romis, M. 2010. The promise and perils of private voluntary regulation: Labor standards and work organization in two Mexican garment factories. *Review of International Political Economy*, 17(1): 45–74.

Marshall, S. 2017. Using a historical institutionalist approach to assess the Cambodian better factories project, in John Howe, Anna Chapman and Ingrid Landau (eds) *The Evolving Project of Labour Law: Foundations, Development and Future Research Directions.* Sydney, Australia: Federation Press, 232–245.

Merk, J. 2012. *10 Years of the Better Factories Cambodia Project: A Critical Evaluation,* Community Legal Education Centre and Clean Clothes Campaign.

Morgenbesser, L. 2017. The failure of democratisation by elections in Cambodia. *Contemporary Politics*, 23(2): 135–155.

Oka, C. 2010. Accounting for the gaps in labour standard compliance: The role of reputation-conscious buyers in the Cambodian garment industry. *The European Journal of Development Research*, 22(1): 59–78.

Oka, C. 2014. Evaluating a promising model of non-state labour regulation: The case of Cambodia's apparel sector, in Deidre McCann, Sangheon Lee, Patrick Belser, Colin Fenwick, John Howe, and Malte Luebker (eds) *Creative Labour Regulation. Advances in Labour Studies.* London: Palgrave Macmillan.

Oka, C. 2016. Improving working conditions in garment supply chains: The role of unions in Cambodia. *British Journal of Industrial Relations*, 54(3): 647–672.

Oka, C. 2017. Brands as labour rights advocates? Potential and limits of brand advocacy in global supply chains. *Business Ethics: A European Review*, 00: 1–13.

Polaski, S. 2006. Combining global and local forces: The case of labor rights in Cambodia. *World Development*, 34(5): 919–932.

Reinecke, J., and Donaghey, J. 2015. After Rana Plaza: Building coalitional power for labour rights between unions and (consumption-based) social movement organisations. *Organization*, 22(5): 720–740.

Rossi, A. 2015. Better work: Harnessing incentives and influencing policy to strengthen labour standards compliance in global production networks. *Cambridge Journal of Regions, Economy and Society*, 8: 505–520.

Rossi, A., and Robertson, R. 2011. Better factories Cambodia: An instrument for improving industrial relations in a transnational context, in Papadakis, K. (ed), *Shaping Global Industrial Relations: The Impact of International Framework Agreements*. Basingstoke and Geneva: Palgrave Macmillan and ILO, 220–242.

Saxena, S. 2018. Beyond third-party monitoring Post-Rana plaza interventions. *Economic and Political Weekly*, LIII(16): 16–20.

Scheper, C. 2017. Labour networks under supply chain capitalism: The politics of the Bangladesh Accord. *Development and Change*, 48(5): 1069–1088.

Shea, A., Nakayama, M., and Heymann, J. 2010. Improving labour standards in clothing factories: Lessons from stakeholder views and monitoring results in Cambodia. *Global Social Policy*, 10(1): 85–110.

Siddiqi, D. 2009. Do Bangladeshi factory workers need saving? Sisterhood in the post-sweatshop era. *Feminist Review*, 91: 154–174.

Siddiqi, D. 2016. Before Rana Plaza: Towards a history of labour organizing in Bangladesh's garment industry, in Vicki Crinis and Adrian Vickers (eds) *Labour in the Clothing Industry in the Asia Pacific*. Oxon: Routledge, 60–79.

Toffel, M. W., Short, J. L., and Ouellet, M. 2015. Codes in context: How states, markets, and civil society shape adherence to global labor standards. *Regulation & Governance*, 9: 205–223.

Ward, K., and Mouyly, V. 2016. Employment relations and political transition in Cambodia. *Journal of Industrial Relations*, 58(2): 258–272.

6 Spaces of exception

National interest and the labor of sedition

Dina M. Siddiqi

Introduction

The Rana Plaza collapse is often represented as a moment of absolute rupture for Bangladesh's garment sector, signaling at the same time an imminent crisis in the global garment industry. The title of a report issued by the Center for Business and Human Rights at New York University, *Business as Usual is not an Option*, captures the general mood of those associated directly or indirectly with the industry, from buyers and intermediate brokers in the global commodity chain to governments, labor advocates and multilateral organizations (Labowitz and Baumann-Pauly, 2014). The devastation as it unfolded live on television, the horror of watching lives being lost and futures forfeited, ruptured mainstream discourses of female empowerment through a benevolent capitalism. Rana Plaza produced a crisis of image as well as of ethics, bringing to mind heartless capitalists indifferent to everything but the pursuit of profit. In this backdrop, a disparate set of actors scattered across the globe could not but come to a general consensus. This transnational, multibillion dollar industry's future hinged on the ability to "fix" working conditions, to protect labor, inside factories. Put differently, this called for a recalibration of the sourcing practices at the heart of the global supply chain. What this meant and how it was to be achieved was a different matter, subject to serious contestation.

Much has changed in the five years since that fateful morning of April 23, 2013. Amendments to the 2006 Labor Act to ease barriers to forming or joining unions, the formalization of a National Tripartite Plan of Action (NTPA), two international multi-stakeholder agreements – the Accord on Fire and Building Safety and the Alliance for Bangladesh Worker Safety – as well various ILO sponsored activities fell into place almost immediately afterward. The NTPA and others had been under discussion and spurred on by the fatal Tazreen fire the preceding year. Increased public advocacy and international pressure have led to more recent initiatives that go beyond building and fire safety – addressing questions of sexual harassment, violence in the workplace, insurance, financial inclusion and so on – in the intervening years (e.g. Fairwear, Sarathi). Bangladesh now has some of the world's top "green" garment factories, and the post-Rana Plaza fears of imminent decline have faded away. The Accord in particular has been pronounced a game changer, a model for transnational practices of oversight that could be replicated elsewhere. (In this respect Bangladesh has gone from the site of a "tragedy" to – once more – a place for experimentation, a global laboratory (see Hossain, 2017; Murphy, 2012).

Despite such transformations, certain aspects of working conditions and labor relations appear to be resolutely immune to change. Specifically, gains "have been severely limited in regard to wages, overtime hours, and work intensity *in part due to the sourcing practices* of the brands and retailers that sit at the top of global supply chains" (Anner, 2018, p. 1, emphasis added). Late payment of wages, workplace harassment, repression of trade unions and unionists remain standard (Human Rights Watch, 2015; Siddiqi, 2017).

It is the structural continuities, the invisible but persistent traces of the past as manifested in the recursive nature of mass demonstrations, work stoppages and strikes of 2006, 2010, 2013 and most recently 2016/2017 that constitute the core of this chapter. A reading of these worker uprisings reveals that specific forms of protest, *and* of labor repression, have remained remarkably constant since 2013.

The analysis proceeds on the premise that fundamental contradictions and constraints remain untouched by the legal and others reforms – much needed as they were – that occurred after 2013. My argument is nested in a broader analysis of the ways that dominant, neoliberal framings of the "problem" of labor in the garment sector privilege some issues while occluding or dismissing others. The Accord-Alliance solution and corresponding ILO initiatives to form factory-level unions illustrate the limited nature of existing interventions. The technocratic approach to "fixing" the problem elides the realm of the political, leaving untouched critical issues – such as persistent and systematic delays in payments – that fundamentally shape workers' experiences on the shop floor and beyond.

Rescripting labor "unrest"

Recurring but seemingly free standing moments of "uprisings" or "agitation" share a common structural trajectory. They begin with an initial provocation, usually an incident limited to a single factory (for instance, the death or overt mistreatment of an individual worker, as happened with Windy garments, or the retaliatory dismissal of a group of workers). The refusal or inability of management to adequately redress the injustice ensures the story will travel at great velocity through informal circuits, eventually producing outrage and garnering solidarity from coworkers in nearby factories. News of the individual injustice works to resurface lingering industry-wide grievances. The original incident is often lost as the broader mobilization takes place. Localized protests eventually spill out into the streets, blocking major thoroughfares and forcing the pubic to pay attention. The occupation of public space temporarily halts both industrial production and everyday urban mobility. Invariably marked by violence, such crises tend to be resolved through personal intermediation, along with the reframing and criminalizing of certain kinds of labor protest, specific legal moves and discursive framings. How do we understand the response of state functionaries and industry stakeholders during "waves of labor unrest?"

Keeping in mind Lila Abu-Lughod's proposition that the study of resistance is valuable as a diagnostic of power, I examine sites/modes of labor confrontation for what they can tell us about the workings of power.[1] I am interested in the ways that state,[2] capital and transnational actors/NGO priorities shape dominant narratives of labor protests and of labor repression. Through a reading of a 2010 case against Moshrefa Mishu as it traveled through the judicial system, juxtaposed to conversations with workers, lawyers and labor rights activists, I map shifting registers of acceptable and unacceptable forms of protest. Under what conditions do certain kinds of action carry moral force? What narrative structures parse out legitimate from illicit violence? What is the work of violence here? I situate these questions in relation to critical changes in the neoliberal global economy. What does it mean, for instance, that the Bangladeshi state and its development partners actively encourage "union formation" in export processing zones in order to attract foreign investment?

I am particularly interested in the uses of colonial-era provisions on sedition and dissent to discredit labor organizers and repress worker mobilizations. I draw on experience gleaned from long-term ethnographic study of the garment sector, conversations with primarily non-NGO union leaders and close textual analyses of a number of First Information Reports (FIRs). I suggest that a strategic invocation of sovereignty and the national interest, sutured to technocratic understandings of the problem, allows those who represent the state – ministers, law enforcement officials and government lawyers – as well as those with a direct stake in the industry, to forge a particular logic of exception. The effect is to produce a scenario in which routine (labor) laws need not apply. Here I draw on Georgio Agamben's concept of a state of exception to map the formation of this logic of exception. However, I follow Cotula's analysis of EPZs in Bangladesh in that "the exception is part of a wider set of interrelated problems rather than the overarching foundational problem" (Cotula, 2017, p. 442).

A note on neoliberal governance and its sentiments

Neoliberalism itself is a much-contested category. My concern here is not with debates around definition or the specifics of normative prescriptions that go under the sign of neoliberalism. Rather, my analysis is informed by what I call neoliberal sentiment – the discursive parameters and commonsense produced and promoted by neoliberal modes of governance. Here I approach governance as "a discourse to manage and promote the social stability fundamental for capital's accumulation," a process that relies critically "on the networked active participation and self-management of non-state actors such as NGOs and other civil society groups as well as business" (Massimo de Angelis, pp. 233–234).

Nasser Hussain remarks that global systems create new universal forms of normativity and legality (Hussain, 2003, p. 141). Among other things, neoliberal governance in the transnational realm relies on a language of democracy, equality and rights. By this logic, if the market is ultimately moral, then multinational corporations and their affiliates cannot be *seen* to be exploitative. In this context, the absolute horror of Rana Plaza as it unfolded in real time constituted a moment of acute crisis by exposing the underbelly of the global supply chain and potentially unleashing "market-unfriendly" sentiments. The sheer scale of the damage ensured that Bangladesh and its garment-producing infrastructure would be subject to global scrutiny. Further, the industrial disaster threatened to undermine the powerful narrative of the market as site of female empowerment for women in the South. In the circumstances, it is instructive that the collapse of Rana Plaza, a multipurpose multistoried building that housed several garment factories, was widely understood predominantly to be the outcome of (a lack of good) governance, corruption and negligence as well as the greed of an individual factory owner. It goes without saying that implementation and oversight are shockingly poor in Bangladeshi factories, and within the construction industry. Regardless, no one associated with the numerous other commercial ventures housed in Rana Plaza lost their lives. Sensing imminent danger, these establishments shut down operations. Clearly, more than shoddy buildings and inadequate inspections were at stake. This line of inquiry cannot be easily accommodated in a straightforward lack of governance narrative.

Neoliberal sentiment is gendered; echoing its imperial originals, this framing makes women and girls central to the process of development. Correspondingly, female empowerment – of the girl child, of the laboring woman and so on – is invariably an individual endeavor. We see this in the many NGO efforts to empower Bangladeshi garment workers through training on legal literacy, as well as on improving bargaining and leadership skills. While such training is undeniably valuable, the premise underlying the approach (of teaching people to be responsible for their own fates) relies on the assumption that "the problem" is individual rather than systemic. Among other things, collective efforts to mobilize for structural change in the long run can easily be discredited or dismissed as ineffective in this environment. Further, as we will see, the language of democracy and reform – paradoxically – demarcates acceptable forms of protest from those deemed illegitimate, dangerous and against the national interest. In effect, dominant, primarily Euro-American analytical frameworks, and narratives of solidarity, foreground certain features of global garment production as problematic while occluding or dismissing other kind of crises not so visible to global audiences.

A recent ILO-sponsored analysis of the Accord and of the NTPA concludes that after an initially positive start, the activities lost pace and intensity, a consequence in part of the underlying power structures of transnational apparel chains and the actual imbalance of power among the stakeholders (Khan and Wichterich, 2015). The asymmetry of power across the commodity chain has had invisible effects on workers. Mark Anner's research shows how international retailers have systematically pushed down prices, squeezing the profits of "local" capitalists who then attempt to compensate by speeding up the assembly line and reducing the number of workers (Anner, 2018). Anner suggests that violations of labor rights go up as a result. Further, lead firms are able to shift the risks associated with a volatile market to their suppliers who invariably shift the burden on to workers (Anner, 2015, p. 298). Other scholars have argued that the Accord/Alliance interventions have been primarily technocratic in nature, and depoliticizing in effect (Ashraf, 2017; Tanjeem, 2017).

Garment nation

Any analysis of labor organizing in Bangladesh must keep in mind the conditions of precarity under which the garment industry "took off," the nation's place within global political-economic structures and the predicaments of producing for an export economy that often leads to a "race to the bottom." When glossed as government deregulation of the business environment in order to attract or retain foreign investment, questions of who bears the cost of deregulation must be addressed. If retaining competitiveness calls for slashing wages and living standards for workers, as it invariably does, then the long-term prospects for worker well-being are not necessarily positive (see Chan and Ross, 2003).

Bangladesh's exclusive "comparative advantage" is its cheap(ened) and relatively unskilled female labor force. Paradoxically, what is an advantage for the national economy can actually be fatal for the union or individual worker demanding increased wages and improved working conditions. If low labor costs are central to being globally competitive then labor repression can be justified as a valid "cost" of maintaining the nation's competitive edge (Neveling, 2017). This line of argument becomes even stronger in a place like Bangladesh where the economy is inordinately dependent upon the apparel export industry. Last year, that is, in 2017–2018, the value of garment exports totaled US $30.61 billion. Measured differently, garment exports accounted for an astounding 83% of Bangladesh's total exports last year (www.bgmea.com.bd/home/pages/tradeinformation).[3]

Whatever the exact figures, it is evident given the scale that the social and economic multiplier effects are enormous. According to the BGMEA, more than 20 million were directly and indirectly assisted by the income generated from employment in the industry (Human Rights Watch, 2015). In 2015, another source claimed that the industry "indirectly supports as many as 40 million Bangladeshis," equivalent to about 25% of the population

(Bangladesh Social Compact). Banking, insurance, infrastructure and other related sectors, including hospitality, have also seen significant growth.[4]

The outsize economic power of the industry is reflected in the political realm. At one point in time, at least 30 factory owners or their relatives held seats in parliament. This translated into 10% of the total (Chalmers quote in ILRF). Beyond the formal political sphere, the autonomous, privately run BGMEA wields tremendous political power, much of it invisible. Significant policy decisions related to industry and by extension to workers' rights cannot by pass the BGMEA, which at times operates as a parastatal enterprise. Negotiations in 2018 around the minimum wage make this evident.[5]

The sector's success – it is now the second largest exporter of garments, after China – has allowed Bangladesh to shed definitively the image of an economic basket case. The spectacular rise of the industry lends itself to the telling of a near perfect success story – the singular engine of national economic growth and social progress. The nation's much anticipated (not yet fulfilled) entry into middle-income country status rests on sustained economic growth powered by the garment sector. The government's goal is to reach US $50 billion apparel exports by 2012, the country's 50th anniversary.

It should come as no surprise that the industry looms large in the national imagination. For much of the population, especially the globally aspiring middle classes, garment exports are a source of considerable pride.[6] This discursive relationship to the industry provides insights into prospects for mobilizing workers' rights movements. Public sympathy for workers, especially after the Rana Plaza collapse, remains high. Yet, when workers take to the streets, actual material support tends to be low. Further, as we will see later, there is a danger of nationalist discourses being invoked for labor to make "necessary sacrifices" for economic development and growth (see Neveling, 2017, p. 140).

Suffice it to say, there are other ways to tell the story of progress, not least because garment workers themselves have benefitted the least from economic growth (see ILRF, 2015, p. 12). In the past three decades, Bangladesh's poverty rate has been halved; life expectancy along with literacy rates and per capita food intake has increased appreciably. The extent to which such material advances are due to neoliberal industrialization as opposed to targeted public sector policy is open to debate. Further, excessive dependence on a single industry renders the country extraordinary vulnerable to global market volatility.[7] Rather than economic autonomy, Bangladesh has shifted from a state of aid-dependence to one of global trade dependence (Rehman Sobhan). Given these conditions, it is no surprise how easily labor resistance can be recast as sedition, as action that directly challenges nation sovereignty and interest.

Unions or NGOs? Accounting for labor

The inability of garment workers to refuse to enter the visibly dangerous premises of Rana Plaza laid bare the urgent need for collective bargaining mechanisms to secure the interests of labor. Accordingly, the hurriedly passed 2013 Amendment to the Bangladesh Labor Act modified requirements for factory-based union formation. Yet, as the spontaneous protests of 2013 and of 2016 make evident, the expanded space for union formation did not translate into greater rights for workers.

In an important comparative study, Mark Anner tracks modes of worker resistance in global supply chains in relation to the specificity of "local" labor control regimes (Anner, 2015). According to his typology, the labor control regime in Bangladesh is shaped by market conditions of high under- and unemployment, as well as the contingencies of the international market. Referring to the "waves of labor protests" in the country, Anner concludes that market despotism contributes to weak domestic bargaining power so that such protests are not able to bring about substantial transformation without international NGO and labor pressure. Under such circumstances, labor activists and allies pursue a transnational approach to organizing as a matter of pragmatism. Curiously, he does not mention state repression in his otherwise insightful analysis of the Bangladeshi case. Nevertheless, the study makes a critical intervention, linking domestic patterns of control with the international dynamics of supply chains. As Anner notes, the formation of national states has been "notoriously tied to patterns of labor control, with the state's use of its security forces to control labor unrest" (Anner, 2015, p. 294).

It is not incidental that unions have the potential to contain as well as promote labor militancy. Among other things, the situation calls for an interrogation of the broader political context that informs *processes* of union formation, including the extent of bureaucratic discretion in determining membership and agenda. Research indicates that only certain kinds of unions receive certification – despite possessing relevant paperwork, others are rejected (Siddiqi, 2015). It is equally critical to situate the new international desire for unions in shifting ideologies of neoliberal governance. The push by the United States and the European Union for some form of collective bargaining in EPZs signals a shift in the representational forms of transnational governance and registers of power.

The proliferation of factory-based trade unions under the aegis of the ILO is limited in power and scope, ill-equipped to confront the invisible structures that constrain workers' voices and actions. The trajectory of the hunger strike at Tuba enterprises in 2014 offers a sobering illustration.[8] Recall that for a few days summer of 2014, the labor movement in Bangladesh seemed poised for major insurgency. In late July, around 1,500 garment workers from five factories of the Tuba Group halted production. The striking workers were desperate. They had not been paid for three months; Eid was around the corner. The web of debt in which they were necessarily entangled – for rent, school fees, urgent medical care and of course daily provisioning – was closing in on them. So they occupied the shop floor, determined not to leave until they were paid. In an unusual move, a number of workers, as well as a prominent left-wing labor organizer, Moshrefa Mishu, went on hunger strike. A temporary platform of 15 trade unions – the Tuba Group Sramik Sangram Committee – came together to coordinate the action. Volunteers from Gonoshashasthyo Kendra, a prominent health rights organization, took turns to monitor the hunger strikers' condition. The atmosphere was disciplined and somber but not without hope. On one floor, increasingly weakened bodies with feeding tubes attached to them sprawled over hastily pushed together cutting tables. On another floor, hundreds of workers milled around, faces etched in anxiety, as they listened to members of the Sramik Sangram Committee speak at a makeshift podium. Relatives, university professors and other allies came through regularly.

Public sympathy was high – no surprise since the memory of Rana Plaza was still raw in people's minds. The contained, almost domesticated space of protest – inside the factory and out of the way – may have shaped public perceptions as well as media portrayal, which was uncharacteristically supportive. These were not "irrational" workers on the street disrupting traffic or damaging public property. Whatever the reason, the hunger strike momentarily displaced the dominant narrative of worker protest – of "outside" agitators or faceless and invariably male "rampaging" mobs stirring up trouble. Instead, a differently gendered and highly visual narrative emerged – that of mothers, sisters and daughters whose hard work sustained their families and by extension the national economy. This framing – of women toiling night and day for nation and family but denied what was rightfully owed – gave workers' demands for back pay and a holiday bonus unmistakable moral force.

Late payment is a common industry practice and the source of much grievance. Thus, the issue resonated deeply with workers from other factories who began to express open support for their colleagues at Tuba. After a few days, this highly publicized event seemed on the verge of mobilizing industry-wide collective action. After all, the hunger strike is an iconic and symbolically laden act of nonviolent resistance, recalling among other things, Gandhi's actions in the anti-colonial movement.

Increasingly alarmed about a replay of worker resistance in 2006 and 2010, the government pressured the BGMEA (the powerful factory owners lobby) and the Tuba Group to settle before Eid holiday. Perhaps sensing that events (and the narrative) were slipping out of control, the government moved to end the hunger strike on the 11th day. Nonviolence provoked violent state suppression. The operation was carried out with near military precision over the course of several hours. First, the authorities cut off the building's water supply. They then prevented anyone, including relatives and medical personnel, from entering the premises. Armed with an ample supply of tear gas and pepper spray, police stormed the multistory building. They fired rubber bullets and teargas shells on the hundreds of demonstrators who had by then gathered in the area. Clashes lasted for over an hour and resulted in serious injuries. Police detained the movement's two key leaders: Moshrefa

Mishu of the Garment Workers Unity Forum and Joly Talukder of Garment Workers' Trade Union Center. Reuters reported that "some workers who smashed vehicles and pelted police with stones to show solidarity with their colleagues on strike" were also detained. In a last ditch attempt, the Tuba Group Shramik Sangram Committee called a country-wide strike the following day. By then the momentum had been lost, even though the violence of the state was on full display. Goodwill toward the hunger strikers remained, in a dissipated and frayed form. Although there was condemnation of the police action, media attention focused primarily on a university professor who been badly injured. The majority of Tuba workers, many of them injured, despondently lined up at the offices of the BGMEA to collect two months' wages and no bonus. Work in other factories carried on as usual.

As it happened, four of the five TUBA Group factories had newly established government and BGMEA sanctioned unions. The now globally prominent labor leader and one time child worker Nazma Akhter had been in negotiations with the BGMEA on behalf of the unions. The hunger strike was the direct outcome of the failure of these talks, a failure that workers took to be Akhter's inability or unwillingness to secure a deal. Akhter's proximity to the BGMEA was already under scrutiny; for many workers and their allies, the TUBA incident simply confirmed what they long suspected. To progressive labor activists, Akhter embodied the shadowy figure of the dalal or collaborator. The trope of *dalal*/double agent is a recurring one in labor narratives of unionization (as the scholarship on colonial India, shows the dalal or broker was critical to the control of labor). The specificity of today's version draws on the extensive surveillance and policing characteristic of the Bangladesh garment industry. As a prominent labor rights activist said to me: "The only good outcome of the Tuba hunger strike is that Najma Akhter was finally uncovered for what she was, a dalal."

Unlike the Rana Plaza collapse and its aftermath, the hunger strike was barely covered in the international press, even though the garment industry was very much under global scrutiny. This was a remarkable absence, given the extent of international interest in the sector. Nor did the country's "development partners" seem especially concerned, thereby affording the government and the BGMEA some space for maneuver. State violence was enabled by this relative transnational invisibility.

National interest and logics of sedition

It is significant that the 1990 reinstatement of parliamentary democracy in Bangladesh coincided with the so-called end of history and the triumph of the market. The language of liberal democracy and human rights, and accompanying narratives of progress carry particular symbolic force in "civil society" circles as a result. This plays out in the backdrop of the nation's inordinate dependence upon the global trade regime, the disproportionate influence of "development partners" in policy matters and a densely NGOized landscape. At the same time, in the twenty-first-century grammar of democracy, "violence" as a form of protest is no longer tolerated. Suffice it to say, what constitutes violence is open; the prevailing discourse determines the repertoire of available and acceptable practices of resistance. Forms of protest that do not fit the donor sanctioned democracy and human rights narrative, that cannot be absorbed, are discarded as unusable or rendered illegitimate. The sanitized discourse of reform effectively renders invisible the many structural barriers to organizing. NGOized advocates of labor whose funding depends on donor protocol know this all too well. For instance, the Bangladesh Worker Solidarity Centre, which does valuable work and one of whose leaders was abducted and later found murdered, has clear instructions to avoid street action.

Further, what constitutes violence relies on the narrative's recognition of a proper object of grievance. It is legitimate to protest against collapsing buildings but not the nonpayment of wages, especially if one is occupying public space and disrupting traffic. As I was told numerous times during fieldwork, donors will provide training on fire and building safety to labor leaders, even fly them over to New York and Washington DC but will not raise the issue of wages or corporate culpability. It is at this juncture that the slide between righteous protestor and irrational vandal is secured. (In the obverse, this allows us to map the conditions through which *legal* violence becomes possible and even necessary. Naming an act violent justifies, for instance, the breaking up of a nonviolent strike so violently.) So what is this logic? I argue that in this case (post)colonial logics of sedition and security inform the Bangladeshi state's efforts to contain so-called labor unrest. Sedition is a somewhat elastic concept – unmoored from its original meaning advocating revolution or strategies to undermine the authority of the colonial state. Notably, the government reserves the right to prevent any demonstration or strike it deems "disruptive" to the community or harmful to the "national interest." Suffice it to say, what counts as the national interest or as disruption is open to the logics of power. As one commentator observes,

> Since the rise of Bangladesh's garment industry in the late 1970s, every decent-sized demonstration has been declared disruptive. Even the 2006 labour unrest – which, after decades of industrial growth, led to the formulation of the country's minimum wage – was identified by the government as an international conspiracy to destroy the country's garment industry.
>
> (Emran, 2013)

Thus, in the realm of labor politics, to be seditious is to be against the national interest. Labor agitation can and is often cast anti-national. The significance of the garment industry, not just in the economy but in the dominant social imaginary, in relation to the possible futures of the nation, secures this framing. Not surprisingly, security discourses are invariably sutured on to the narrative of the agitating workers as anti-national. Increasingly, there is a rhetorical collapse between the worker and the militant/terrorist. And quite conveniently, the figure of the anti-national – and that of the dalal – helps to occlude the BGMEA's disproportionately powerful role in national politics. Labor activists/organizers learn to live in the shadow of the Intelligence Services (DGFI) and the police: they learn to live with everyday surveillance. The threat of being implicated in manufactured court cases is real and immediate. "cholen ektu cha kheye ashi" (Come, let's have a cup of tea at our office) are ominous words no activist wants to hear. This is a command, not invitation. There is no guarantee one will return.

Living with the surveillance state

To illuminate some of these points, I turn to the 2010 arrest of Moshrefa Mishu, a left-wing political activist since her university days and now the head of Garment Workers Unity Forum. I reproduce below the full account of Mishu's arrest in the records of Bangladesh Legal Aid and Services Trust (BLAST) whose executive director represented the former in court. The sequence of events reads more like an Immigration and Customs Enforcement in the United States (ICE) raid to detain undocumented persons or intelligence services on the trail of a potential terrorist:

> Twelve persons from the Detective Branch, all but one of whom were in plain clothes, arrived at Mishu's residence around midnight and directly entered her bedroom. She was informed that she would be taken to the DB for questioning but not informed of the grounds of her arrest or any specific case with which she was suspected of being involved. There was no arrest warrant, which suggests she was picked on Section 54. She was not given chance to carry essential medication with her. She was forced into a microbus and driven around for an hour before being taken to the Dhaka Detective Branch office. (sounds like an ICE raid). Mishu was falsely implicated in three separate cases and shown arrested in connection with Khilkhet PS Case No. 13 (2) 2010. Harsh conditions in police custody exacerbated her asthma and chronic back pain so that early on, she required hospitalization. Her lawyers applications for bail were turned down twice until finally through an appeal to the high court division of the Supreme Court, she was granted bail on health grounds in March 2011.

The FIR waiting for Mishu did not name her but a subsequent petition to place her on a ten-day remand identified her as a rioter. The petition referred to her as Dhurto Ashami (a cunning prisoner), "known to provoke and instigate innocent/blameless workers in various factories across Bangladesh." The labor leader was accused not just of fomenting trouble among workers, but of creating country-wide instability, enabling the destruction of the nation's resources and *ruining the image of the country abroad.* (Here we see a recurring slide between private and national property.) Police argued in the petition that they needed ten days of intensive interrogation in order to "identify others involved in conspiracy as well as to identify the godfathers of destruction/sabotage so as to prevent instability the country."

Mishu as political subject disappears in this rendering of events. Constructed as national menace, she along with 16 named workers and 3,000–4,000 unnamed others were charged with violating colonial era legal provisions on rioting. The fate of the nation appears to be at stake in the "good worker" versus the "bad instigator," narrative. Several words and phrases recur in the FIR and subsequent petition for a ten-day remand in police custody, almost by rote:

> *"unruly workers," armed with "deadly weapons", (sticks, rods and bricks) set out to incite rioting (danga hangama), "disturbing law and order, creating chaos." destroying property or conspiring to destroy Bangladesh's industry.*

This reiteration invests an almost visceral meaning to the figure of the violent rioting instigator/worker (to be distinguished from the good, naïve worker). It also recalls the logic of security. It is the violence of the police that then becomes legitimate.

Concluding thoughts

In these circumstances, how do workers and independent labor advocates respond? Even as the professionalized NGO model of unionizing has taken hold, other forms of independent collectives around women workers have begun to emerge. The Garment Sramik Shonghoti (Garment Worker Solidarity, loosely affiliated with a left political party), a non-registered, member-funded organization, has been at the forefront of such initiatives. Over the years, the founder Taslima Akhter had often remarked to me of the difficulties of independent organizing "in these times," when workers had little money to spare for union activities, students and other potential volunteers saw little appeal in this line of work and generous funding through labor rights NGOs was widely available. Foreign-funded NGOs have the money to provide transportation, food and even legal aid.

The last time I met her, she spoke of fear, not finances. I had gone to her Hatirpool office just after the December 2016 Ashulia work stoppage and mass arrests. She was occupied fielding phone calls from workers who had been instructed to return to work but were unsure about presenting themselves at their factory gates in case they risked arrest. Several workers had already contacted her after being fired for participating in the demonstrations. A few had been arrested, one under the notorious Special Powers Act.[9] Unsure of how to respond, Taslima arranged for a meeting with lawyers at BLAST for advice. Taslima was concerned about the cost of hiring lawyers. Her experience of the recent past convinced her to find ways to assist workers in confronting the law. How do you handle verbal disputes with managers so that they don't escalate? What do you do when you're blacklisted? I was struck by the fact that these were the kind of trainings she sought, not on labor laws nor on the rights of workers.

To reiterate, the deployment of the rhetoric of protection, external conspiracy and national interest allows the state – and others associated with the garment industry – to create a space of exception in which routine labor laws need not apply. The discursive framing of the outspoken or resisting worker as foreign agent, anti-national conspirator or disloyal patriot – as a *dalal* of some kind – effectively enjoins the state and other forces to use extraordinary or extralegal means. Thus, it should come as no surprise that in 2016, a number of protesting workers were charged under the Special Powers Act of 1973, a draconian law reserved generally for political repression. It is worth recalling Saskia Sassen here, who long ago pointed out that the process of globalization does not involve a simple disappearance of the state form but rather calls on the national state and its powers to create *local* conditions hospitable to the flourishing of a *global* system (cited in Hussain, p. 143, italics in the original). Building on Sassen, legal theorist Nasser Hussain observes that within the new order one finds multiple instances of local crises and their "management" by familiar exercises of emergency powers (ibid.). Resort to laws of sedition and dissent appears to be the Bangladeshi state's preferred modes of managing labor crises. Workers who protest are treated as the exception; once they are recast as anti-nationalists, they can relegated to a space of exception – not in terms of the bare life described by Agamben but cast outside of the regulative space of labor legislation and its protections.

Notes

1
> We respect everyday resistance not just by arguing for the dignity or heroism of the resistors but by letting their practices teach us about the complex inter-workings of historically changing systems of power.
>
> (Abu-Lughod, 1990, p. 53)

2 I do not take the state to be a homogenous entity. While it is shot through with contradictions and competing interests, the "state effect" is to project the idea of unified national interest at stake. See Timothy Mitchell. Further, the Bangladeshi state cannot be understood without taking into account its relation to transnational capital (and the location of actors that mediate this relationship). I return to this point later in the chapter.
3 The BGMEA site notes that their data source is the Export Promotion Bureau, which is then compiled by organization.
4 Of those 19 foreigners killed in the Holey Bakery attacks, the majority were involved with the garment industry.
5 See, for instance, Faisal Mahmud (2018) "Protests over Bangladesh's minimum wage for garment workers." *Asia Times.* September 17. http://www.atimes.com/article/protests-over-bangladeshs-minimum-wage-for-garment-workers/

6 Such as when Bangladeshi firms contracted to make T-shirts for the World Cup in 2015.
7 In 1995, a US-led boycott over child labor led to the retrenchment of an esti-mated 200,000 workers. The phasing of the MFA and the 2008 recession were both sources of tremendous social and political anxiety.
8 This section draws on events analyzed in Siddiqi 2015.
9 Most were charged with violations of 11 separate sections of Bangladesh's Penal Code (derived from the 1860 colonial code and mostly unchanged). Key charges included various "Offences Against the Public Tranquility" such as Section 147 – punishment for rioting; Section 148 – rioting armed with a deadly weapon; and Section 149 – every member of unlawful assembly guilty of offense committed in prosecution of common object (a provision clearly meant for collective punishment).

References

Abu-Lughod, Lila (1990). "The Romance of Resistance: Tracing Transformations of Power Through Bedouin Women." *American Ethnologist*, 17(1): 41–55.

Anner, Mark (2015) "Labor Control Regimes and worker Resistance in Global Sup-ply Chains." *Labor History*, 56(3): 292–307.

Anner, Mark (2018) *Binding Power: The Sourcing Squeeze, Workers' Rights and Building Safety in Bangladesh since Rana Plaza*. Research Report. Center for Global Workers' Rights, Penn State University.

Ashraf, Hasan (2017) "Beyond Building Safety: An Ethnographic Account of Health and Well-Being on the Bangladesh Garment Shop Floor." In Prentice and de Neve (eds.) *Unmaking the Global Sweatshop: Health and Safety of the World's Garment Workers*. Philadelphia: University of Pennsylvania Press.

Chan, Anita and Ross, Robert J. S. (2003) "Racing to the Bottom: International Trade without a Social Clause." *Third World Quarterly*, 24(6): 1011–1028.

Cotula, Lorenzo (2017) "The State of Exception and the Law of the Global Econ-omy: A Conceptual and Empirico-Legal Inquiry." *Transnational Legal Theory*, 8(4): 424–454.

Hossain, Naomi (2017) *The Aid Lab: Understanding Bangladesh's Unexpected Suc-cess*. New York: Oxford University Press.

Human Rights Watch (2015) *Whoever Raises Their Head Suffers the Most: Workers' Rights in Bangladesh's Garment Factories*. https://www.hrw.org/report/2015/04/22/whoever-raises-their-head-suffers-most/workers-rights-bangladeshs-garment (last accessed May 5, 2019).

Human Rights Watch (2017) *Bangladesh: Stop Persecuting Unions, Garment Workers*. www.hrw.org/news/2017/02/15/bangladesh-stop-persecuting-unions-garment-workers (last accessed January 10, 2019).

Hussain, Nasser (2003) *The Jurisprudence of Emergency: Colonialism and the Rule of Law*. Ann Arbor: University of Michigan Press.

International Labor Rights Forum (ILRF) (2015) *Our Voices, Our Safety: Bangla-deshi Garment Workers Speak Out*. Washington DC: ILRF.

Khan, Mohammad Raisul Islam and Wichterich, Christa (2015) *Safety and Labor Conditions: The Accord and the National Tripartite Plan of Action for the Garment Industry of Bangladesh*. Geneva: ILO.

Labowitz, Sarah and Dorothy Baumann-Pauly (2014) *Business as Usual is not an Option: Supply Chains and Sourcing After Rana Plaza*. New York: NYU Stern Center for Business and Human Rights.

Locke, Richard (2013) *The Promise and Limits of Private Power: Promoting Labor Standards in a Global Economy*. Cambridge: Cambridge University Press.

Murphy, Michelle (2012) *Seizing the Means of Reproduction*. Durham: Duke University Press.

Neveling, Patrick (2017) "Capital over Labor: Health and Safety in Export Processing Zone Garment Production since 1947." In Rebecca Prentice and Geert de Neve (eds) *Unmaking the Global Sweatshop: Health and Safety of the World's Garment Workers* (pp. 123–146). Philadelphia: University of Pennsylvania Press.

Prentice, Rebecca and Neve, Geert de (2017) *Unmaking the Global Sweatshop: Health and Safety of the World's Garment Workers*. Philadelphia: University of Pennsylvania Press.

Siddiqi, Dina M. (2015) "Starving for Justice: Bangladeshi Garment Workers in a 'Post-Rana Plaza' World." *International Labor and Working Class History*, 87: 165–173.

——— (2017) "Before Rana Plaza: Toward a History of Labor Organizing in Bangladesh's Garment Industry." In V. Crinis and A. Vickers (eds.) *Labour in the Clothing Industry in the Asia Pacific*. New York: Routledge.

Tanjeem, Nafisa (2017) "Can Workers of the World Unite?" Unpublished PhD dissertation. Rutgers University.

Part III

Rethinking solutions in Bangladesh

7 Bangladesh's private sector
Beyond tragedies and challenges

Rubana Huq

Introduction

Prior to the collapse of Rana Plaza, Bangladesh and its ready-made garment (RMG) sector were a simple story of success. There were three historical turns that dominated its economic fate and lifted its status from a "bottomless basket" to one of the fast growing nations in the world. After the European Union (EU)'s generalized system of preferences, which amended the rules of origin requirements on the 18th of November 2010, the apparel sector became the biggest destination of export and turned Bangladesh into the second highest garment-exporting nation of the world overnight. The incredible and rapid rise of the industry is illustrated by the fact that exports rose from $30 million per year in the early 1980s to more than $30 billion per year today. This rise was only possible through the efforts of the growing workforce in the industry. However, workers' safety regulations had been overlooked for years in many factories. The Rana Plaza disaster provided a chance for Bangladesh to reevaluate safety practices and initiate a process for factory safety remediation interventions.

It is interesting to note that the export figure did not dip after the tragedy. Ready-made garment exports remained robust as garment factories engaged with remediation work and buyers sensed that reforms were underway. Furthermore, there were no other markets that could offer efficient production capacity at such low prices that could replace Bangladesh. Thus, Bangladesh pledged to tread into a new era of responsibility and reform. From the point of view of brands and retailers, it was convenient to believe in Bangladesh rather than engage in the difficult process of moving production over to new markets. The fact that most buyers did not shift orders to other manufacturing countries points to their desire to keep their relationships with Bangladeshi suppliers.

Interventions after Rana Plaza

As a response to the Rana Plaza tragedy, the North American and European buyers introduced a uniform code to monitor progress in the sector. Subsequently, the Accord and Alliance came into existence and developed codes on structural, fire, and electrical safety of the industrial units. The Accord, with European signatory brands, began to overview around 1,500 factories, while the Alliance, with 700 factories, represented the North American brands and retailers.

At the same time, the Government of Bangladesh took a decision to establish a National Action Plan (NAP), reformed the Labor Law, and increased the minimum wage. The National Tripartite Plan of Action (NTPA) on fire safety in the RMG sector was signed on March 24, 2013 in response to the Tazreen factory fire and the Joint Tripartite Statement was adopted on May 4 after the Rana Plaza tragedy on the 24th of April, 2013. It was decided that the NTPA would assess the structural integrity and fire safety of RMG factory buildings, strengthen labor inspections, offer training for workers and management to increase awareness of occupational safety and health, and oversee worker rights. The signatories to this plan were the International Labour Organization (ILO), the Bangladeshi government, and the Bangladesh Garment Manufacturers and Exporters Association (BGMEA). Over 1,200 factories would initially come under the NAP. It was also decided that factories excluded by the Accord and Alliance would be supervised under the plan.

Between 2016 and 2017, the journey of remediation and accountability continued and Bangladesh came under increased international scrutiny. The attention shifted from merely physical remediation to a more comprehensive discussion of workers' overall safety and rights. There was an increased demand for collective bargaining from trade unions. Various advocates began to require unions at the factory level or at least an elected workers' representative entity, in the form of a workers' participatory committee.

Amidst this situation, the ILO began to play an important role. With the annual International Labor Conference (ILC) held in Geneva in 2017, Bangladesh came into focus as the ILC mounted pressure, asking Bangladesh to explain the cases of labor abuse and expressing discontent on the labor laws prevalent in the export processing zones (EPZs), as well as a few clauses in the existing Bangladesh Labor Act 2013. The draft EPZ law was then recalled from the Parliament and was put up for amendments following a visit by the European trade delegation who had also assessed the progress of the sector. In 2018, Bangladesh was no longer singled out by the ILO and EU, as by then a Tripartite Coordination Council, consisting of trade unions and the industry and government, had been formed for the RMG sector and a Standard Operating Procedure for Trade Union formation was also formulated. The possible threat of withdrawal of the advantages of the "Everything But Arms" initiative by the EU guaranteeing duty-free privilege to Bangladesh has kept Bangladesh on its toes. However, significant progress has been made as the threshold to form unions has been lowered from 30 to 20, and EPZ laws are being amended to somewhat align it to the Bangladesh Labor Act 2018 (proposed).

The RCC was set up in May 2017 to supervise and monitor the remediation of factories under Bangladesh's National Initiative. As of September 2018, there were 3,843 factories in Dhaka and 723 in Chittagong that were members of the BGMEA. Among these, approximately 3,000 were operational. Out of the 809 National Initiative factories undergoing follow-up by the Department of Inspection for Factories and Establishments (DIFE), 107 were fully remediated. By March 2018, more than half of the factories had achieved at least 50% remediation, and 111 factories achieved at least 80% remediation.

The biggest discussion in 2018 was about the tenure of the Accord and Alliance. With the Accord coming to an end on November 30, 2018 and with the Alliance ending on December 31, 2018, brands were left wondering about the future of the RMG industry in Bangladesh with respect to compliance codes. The Alliance on its own took special initiatives to form a Special Monitoring Organization (SMO) which would include brands, the BGMEA, trade unions, and the ILO. The plan failed to move forward as the government did not want to be a part of an organization that would be formed with foreign initiative. As for the Accord, a special ruling from the High Court specified that it would cease after November 30, 2018, and could only be extended for six more months. In the meantime, the Accord, sensing its departure, initiated a new version of Accord and called it The Accord: Version 2. This version proposed to extend its jurisdiction into other sectors and into more areas of improvement, namely labor. This was deemed unacceptable by the manufacturers and the government. Hence, a transition Accord was framed to ensure a smooth transition to a new organization called the Remediation Coordination Council (RCC).

These factories are all working for brands and retailers who have either signed up with the Accord, Alliance, or have continued operating under NAP. However, the level of sustainability for the industry as a whole that has been achieved remains questionable. This prescriptive approach dictated by the international stakeholders cannot continue indefinitely. A homegrown solution that requires accountability and responsibility among the business owners is the only viable way forward.

The Accord and the Alliance came in with clear initial rules of engagement. First, a factory had to be registered with them through the brands and then the assessment would be done. The issues which were covered largely focused on the structural, fire, and electrical integrity. The critical areas under fire safety included the scope of workers' assembly, fire resistant exits, fire extinguishers, door width, the direction of the door swing, landings, handrails, staircase width, exit signs, housekeeping policy, emergency evacuation plans, fire pumps, occupancy load, boilers, and generators. On the structural issues, there were questions on columns, detailed engineering reports, load capacity, floor plans, as-built designs, etc. Electrical queries centered around a sound safety program, earthing system, emergency power switchboards, substation room, detection and protection devices, transformer, distribution boards, and safety signage.

Table 7.1 Status of factories by initiative

Initiatives taken by	Initial inspected factories	Inspected and active factories	Referred to review panel	Closed factories	Remediation progress	100% remediated factory	Suspended/closed/terminated factories
Accord	1,620	1,620	57	26	90%	142	420 (suspended-124 closed-296)
Alliance	829	672	35	9	90%	400	173
NAP (ILO)	1,549	771	40	5	—	107	566
Total	3,998	3,063	132	40	—	649	1,159

Source: Bangladesh Garment Manufacturers and Exporters Association (BGMEA).

After five years of inspection and monitoring on the above issues and remediation, the number of factories in the industry has been reduced due to the closures suggested by the Accord/Alliance/NAP. The following chart shows the status of RMG factory inspections through September 2018. The remaining smaller units have been consolidated and moved into larger factories in cases where the groups or organizations could afford to do so. Those who could not afford to remediate eventually had to shut down. In spite of the total number of operational factories decreasing, the business volume did not fall, and in many quarters it rose. Larger factories and those well resources gained more market share as a result (Table 7.1).

In many cases, factories have accomplished more than the minimum compliance requirements. Across the entire industry, there are now nearly 70 eco-friendly green buildings, which is the highest for any garment industry in the world. However, the prices buyers are willing to pay have not commensurately increased with this increased focus on sustainability on the part of the manufacturers.

Meanwhile, workers' wages have gone through numerous revisions. The minimum wage was increased from Bangladesh Taka (BDT) 1,662.50 in 2006 to BDT 3,000 in 2010, then to BDT 5,300 in 2013, and finally to BDT 8,000 in 2018. This final revision in 2018 amounted to a 51% increase.

Response by the Mohammadi Group

As an exporter, I was also asked to remediate and comply with the requirements of the brands which had signed up with the Accord and the Alliance. Out of eight factories, I handled the remediation and relocation of five factories. The primary approach taken was to shift a number of older factories into new buildings which had been under construction at the time and nearing completion; this task appeared simple at face value. There were two new buildings, and the job was to shift three factories to the new locations and remediate two other existing factories. The cases are briefly shared below so that readers can gain in-depth insights into the costs and the challenges of the entire process.

Case study 1: Factory 1 with compliance issues relocated to Factory A, a brand new unit

Factory 1, a small factory of 600 workers, shifted to a new building, Factory A, at a different location. Issues regarding the old factory included observations on unsealed penetrations and openings located in the exit stair enclosures, rooms used for combustible storage on the ground floor were not separated by fire-rated construction, areas used for combustible storage were not separated by fire-rated construction, and the fire detection and alarm system installation required detailed review to confirm compliance with National Fire Alarm and Signaling Code (National Fire Protection Association (NFPA) 72) and Accord standards. Electrical issues (original) included observations on quality of safety training program and electrical distribution board/panels being adjacent to water source.

The relocation was difficult for workers, since the new location was in a different area that required a significant commute or moving entire households. Moving to the new area also proved problematic since natural gas was not available for household use there. This resulted in a large number of workers resigning. Management arranged daily commuter transportation for workers traveling to the new location, which is still an ongoing operation. The unavailability of natural gas meant the factory had to be operated on diesel generators. The construction of Factory A, a LEED gold-certified building, was also complex and more expensive than initially planned. Compliance issues with fire safety and electrical design were identified by auditors, requiring additional modification of construction and new investment.

Case study 2: Factory 2, an older unit with compliance issues shifted to a new Factory B

Factory 2, with 2,000 workers, had been operating in a rented building; thus, renovations to meet compliance were not feasible. The 2,000 workers in the factory were moved to Factory B, a newly constructed building. This relocation proved less challenging than Factory 1, since the new location was closer to the old one. The workers were awarded compensatory relocation bonuses. However, construction and design issues were identified in Factory B as well. These included observations on exit stairs needing fire-rated constructions to protect the openings and penetrations, the fire alarm system being an unlisted system and antiquated, and not in accordance with NFPA 72. The engineers also noted that the building was equipped with single-station smoke alarms, and the required standpipe system was not installed in accordance with the Accord standard and NFPA 14 (Standard for the Installation of Standpipe and Hose Systems).

There were also new issues of the width of aisles being less than 0.9 m (36 in.) on the first floor and second floor, the dining space was not separated from the store room by fire-rated construction on the ground floor, and the aisles along means of egress were obstructing storage on most of the floors. The original electrical issues included the unavailability of an electrical single-line diagram (SLD) and drawing of the lightning protection system (LPS). New observations included the transformer silica gel being discolored, the transformer cable size being inadequate, generator exhaust system was kept exposed/not insulated, the cumulative breaker size was greater than cable capacity, etc.

Eventually, the significant and challenging construction issues were solved. The key achievement of this relocation process was successfully managing workers' needs while moving to meet compliance requirements.

Case study 3: 600 workers being transferred to Factory A

This relocation was carried out most recently. The affected workers gained information about the process from previously relocated workers from Factory 1, and this significantly strengthened their negotiating position. This led to the provision of transportation, as well as compensation packages that the workers accepted. While the smoother resolution of worker demands was a success, meeting compliance requirements for the new building still proved challenging.

Case study 4: 400 workers being kept on existing premises

This was a relatively easy case as the building was rated green in structure already and the management just had to take care of the basic fire and electrical issues at a reasonable cost.

Case study 5: 800 workers being kept on existing premises

This was also an easy case as the retrofitting issues and original issues for this factory were totally completed, which included storage rooms and areas being separated by fire-rated construction from the adjacent work areas along with the exit stairs being separated from work areas and other spaces on each floor by fire-rated construction. Fire hydrants were properly installed as well. However, the new findings included the LPS being inadequate for the factory, power cables was found covered by sand in the distribution panel while terminating, outdoor cable trays were not covered to protect from effects of weather, and the heat source (or exposed steam line) was found adjacent to electrical installations (cable channel/duct). All had been done so far with the hope that no other new issues would surface.

A summary of the incurred cost is provided in Table 7.2.

Table 7.2 Cost summary for woven factories requiring remediation

Factory name	Structural ($)	Fire ($)	Electrical ($)	Total cost ($)
Factory A	50,000	265,063	22,625	337,688
Factory B	212,500	149,424	25,875	387,799
Factory 4	10,000	19,651	16,000	45,651
Factory 5	250,000	81,259	26,750	358,009
	522,500	515,396	91,250	1,129,146

Source: Mohammadi Group.

Over a million dollars have been spent in remediating two existing factories and shifting three factories to two new locations. This costing does not include the workers' compensation packages or any other costs apart from the structural, fire, and electrical heads. The primary insight gained from these experiences is that workers and their needs must come first. When workers are informed and aware of their rights, it leads to better management of difficult relocation processes. Local management is capable of carrying out complex measures to achieve compliance despite significant challenges, which points toward an encouraging future where self-governance can become the standard.

Limitations to monitoring and compliance

While the remediation process has been successful in general, a host of limitations have also become apparent. One major issue with the process has to do with equity and justice toward businesses. While the larger businesses were able to organize the resources required to complete the required remediation and relocation, often, the smaller businesses fell short. Some consolidated into larger businesses, but many had to cease operations completely. By disproportionately affecting the smaller businesses, the process proved to be inequitable.

As a result of this entire process, sustainable practices in the industry have developed and grown. However, this growth has been largely prescriptive and pushed by third parties as a part of these agreements. The question remains whether the industry can continue on this path independently, especially with the pressure of continuing to deliver products at the lowest cost possible. Unless buyers demonstrate a commitment to sustainability and recognize the increased costs incurred, this trend toward more sustainable practices will not continue, even though businesses may agree with it in principle.

After 2013, customers agreed to increased prices; however, with subsequent pressures toward increased productivity and the additional costs needed to fulfill compliance requirements, the manufacturers have struggled to meet expectations. Increasing bank debts, combined with increased production demands from buyers, have impacted the general health of factories.

Manufacturers have faced increased pressure on three fronts: complete remediation measures, deliver higher production quantities, and accept lower prices. As the industry as a whole was operating at maximum capacity already, delivering higher quantities was not possible; but manufacturers acquiesced to more competitive prices. As a result, margins began to diminish. Some manufacturers used other enterprises to subsidize their RMG operation, while some others relied on new credit lines from banks. With increased wages going into effect in January 2019, the overall impact of these pressures on the industry remains to be seen.

In the initiation period of Accord and Alliance, there was an expectation among businesses that buyers would assist suppliers financially with remediation measures. In reality, they mostly offered assurance of business continuity and pointed out that they were the ones paying for the audits and the assessments. Buyers did not consider it to be their responsibility to help with the cost of remediating factories. International financial organizations had continued with the arrangement of funds at low interest rates (around 3%–4%); however, at the time of disbursement through the central and commercial banks, the rates rose to 8%–9%. Thus, manufacturers did not receive the financial support they had originally thought to be a part of the buyers' pledge, and this led to increased difficulty of continuing the required improvements.

Going forward, as new markets emerge, the position of the brands and retailers will shift. As new capacities are added, the pressure on prices in Bangladesh will also continue to grow. This phenomenon is not new. Even with increased capacities, manufacturers have continued receiving orders with lower margins and a lower FOB price. The latest tool has been offering vendors off peak price or a special capacity price, meaning that in the months where orders are less, manufacturers are offered lower unit prices and in months where additional capacities are taken by brands and retailers, the manufacturers are expected to offer the most competitive price.

Why self-monitoring is important: *Shonman*

Currently, with the Alliance leaving Bangladesh at the end of its term and with the Accord in a state of transition, the role of the RCC is going to be more important than ever before. The RCC is headed by the Ministry of Labor, which in collaboration with DIFE will oversee the local remediation effort.

Initially, the RCC planned to work with 1,293 operational factories. However, this number may depend on the new factories being added to the National Initiative or as factories leave the Accord and Alliance. The RCC will also contribute to building capacity of regulators and establish a coordinated approach to safety inspections. Ultimately, the RCC hopes to offer a "one-stop-shop" service issuing factory building, fire, electrical, and occupancy permits.

Prior to 2013, brands usually maintained ad hoc protocols and requirements with their suppliers. As a result, numerous bilateral agreements were formed between brands and their suppliers. Previously, most of the corrective action plans focused on social conditions and working hours. Auditors assessed the availability of facilities and services such as doctors, nurses, day care, and child labor prevention for workers. Pillar strength, availability of fire hydrants, and other structural safety issues were often not prioritized. After the Rana Plaza tragedy, auditors have been assigned to evaluate structural, electrical, and fire issues. The Accord and Alliance primarily trained a group of local engineers with valuable construction experience to perform audits. A uniform code of conduct based on basic premises of safety and labor issues, accounting for the local context, can transform the industry to be more proactive.

With the Accord set to end in November and the Alliance by December 31, 2018, the industry, instead of following prescribed modes being set by either brands or the government, needs to be prepared for self-monitoring. The best way forward would be a way to transition into a plan of self-monitoring initiated by the industry itself. For the sake of reference, I am calling this *Shonman*. Through this transformation, the industry must move toward sustainable self-monitoring and demonstrate that prescriptive approaches to these problems can be gradually replaced. A uniform code of conduct can also simplify supplier relationships for buyers by eliminating the need for ad hoc agreements while also consolidating the requirements and desired practices for manufacturers. This step to self-monitoring would also synchronize the goals of the brands and the manufacturers themselves.

Other initiatives that go beyond third-party monitoring

Only compliance imposed by brands cannot also be the be-all and end-all in our sector. A more humane approach to doing business is the only way to true compliance. With that goal in mind, I have taken steps to ensure better working conditions in the factories reflecting my leadership skills and strong commitment to the betterment of the workers.

My factories have a fair price shop, which ensures the workers' right to fair prices for their daily commodities. At the end of the day, the worker finds this shopping convenient. The management provides the salary of those running the shop, the basic setup, and the initial stock, and then there is no major extra cost for the factory to sustain this over time.

The Mohammadi Group also gives scholarships to garment workers, who wish to pursue higher education. The Asian University for Women (AUW) in Chittagong has introduced a special "Access" program for two years that allows the workers to get used to the environment. Considering the socio-cultural divide that exists, admission to such a university for these workers opens up doors of opportunities and helps them to dream of a life beyond their sewing machines. The workers also face an admission process to get inducted to the university. The Mohammadi Group workers participate in the Pathway Scholars program, where selected workers are offered the opportunity to obtain a bachelor's-level education from AUW. The employers provide five years of wages to the workers, and their tuition is paid through charitable donations. The encouragement of higher education among workers is one of the initiatives I am most proud of (www.thedailystar.net/op-ed/my-heroes-207757).

The Mohammadi Group also has schools for workers' children. The schools are called "Sharafer Patshala." These schools have students attending up to grade 5. We have preschool going children as well, who follow a visual method for learning. The teachers for the preschoolers are workers themselves, who take turns and dedicate half of their time to school and the rest to the factory. In addition, they get paid BDT 500.00 extra per month. Being teachers raises their self-esteem, and the children are also achieving extraordinary results. Eleven children scored a GPA of 5.00 out of 5.00 on their primary school examinations this year.

The central bank has a scheme of low-cost housing for workers at 2% interest rate. Fifty-five owners applied for this loan and only two were given a sanction against this. Loan disbursement has not started, but land has been purchased and developed, ready for immediate construction, located near the factory in Banglabazar in Gazipur. In the process, the design has been finalized as per recommendations from the workers.

The next area of focus is on retiring workers. Workers retiring from factories need to transition into a sustainable form of livelihood. It is up to them to decide if they want to return to their village homes or remain in Dhaka. A possible opportunity for them is to continue in the industry in a less labor-intensive capacity by forming small businesses such as sewing lines and finishing setups. We, as their previous employers, could help them by taking equity positions in these ventures and providing the initial support to set the business up. Safety standards may be maintained in accordance with ILO recommendations.

Conclusion

It has been more than five years since Rana Plaza collapse. It has been five years since factories have consolidated and moved to newer locations. It has been five years since manufacturers have struggled to sustain and grow their businesses. Five years is a long time for an industry to set its own standards.

If the industry is subjected to prescriptions from stakeholders from abroad, then the basic ability and the intention of the industry to reform itself will be in doubt. If the RCC is seen to be the rescuer, then brands may also end up questioning the efficacy and the intent of the initiative and whether it is free of bias. In both cases, reform and implementation may also end up being questioned. Thus, it is in everyone's interest that the industry come together and form its own platform, one that will be appropriate for the owners, workers, brands, unions, and the rest of the stakeholders. This way, trust will not be lost and well-meaning attempts will be belittled.

Shonman, in Bengali, means *respect*. The ready-made garment industry has learnt a huge lesson post-Rana Plaza which will haunt the nation as a collective tragedy. The only way out of this tragedy is through an initiative that promises transparency, readiness, and remediation steered by a higher degree of commitment and ethics from the industry players themselves. There is really no other alternative.

Acknowledgment

I would like to thank Kashfia Nehrin, graduate student in UC Berkeley's Masters of Development Practice program, for excellent research assistance.

Appendix 1: Structure of *Shonman*

Steering Committee – the Steering Committee of *Shonman* would be constituted to include the following representatives:

a. BGMEA	According to the proposed Steering Committee (SC),
b. DIFE/NAP	neither the BGMEA nor the brands will have a veto
c. Trade union	or majority vote. All decisions would be taken on a
representatives	consensual basis. The SC shall appoint an objective
d. Brand	review panel, consisting of manufacturers, brand, and
representatives	DIFE.
e. Ombudsman	The SC members will choose an Ombudsman for the
	purpose of instilling objectivity and transparency for
	the process in order to strongly address any corruption,
	negligence, or bias. In the case of dispute or vote tag,
	judgment of an independent Ombudsman will prevail,
	taking into consideration views of all parties.

A rough proposal could be set to look like the following:

RCC Case Management Board	Shall be dealing with monitoring factories under Alliance and Accord, NAP and new factories created after December 2017.
COO (Chief Operating Officer)	The SC shall appoint a suitably qualified COO to oversee the operations of "Shonman."
CTO (Chief Technical Officer)	The SC shall appoint a suitably qualified CTO to oversee the technical operations of "Shonman."

(Continued)

RCC Implementation Board	Will be responsible for RCC Technical Task forces, case handlers, QC teams including fire, electrical and safety engineers, and regulators including DIFE, FSCD, CDA, and CEI. The Board will also be responsible for monitoring engineering firms selected by ILO and CTO.
RCC Financial Management Board	Will liaise with BGMEA and BKMEA and ILO for funds. However, there may be additional need to ask for contribution/participation of wider stakeholders if deemed necessary by the SC.

Appendix 2: Approach

Scope	New factories registering after March 2019 will be included in "Shonman."
Assessment of factories	Will be done on an individual basis, and failure to relocate or remediation of that particular unit under scrutiny will not impact the other production units belonging to the same "group."
Registration	"Shonman" will be registered in Bangladesh under the relevant act.
Funding	1. For the initial period, June 2019–June 2021, signatory buyers will be requested to assist "Shonman" with third-party audit fees, so that independent verification of the existing factories can continue. Note to reader: this is because the vast majority of remediation and assessments will already have been completed and only some follow-up would be pending with the exception of NAP factories: CAP follow-up of the NAP factories will be supported through the RCC. 2. New Factories entering the pool of suppliers will have to pay for their inspections based upon the square footage of their facility. 3. From July 2021 onward, Shonman will become fully self-financing and external contributions would be discontinued.
Audits	Independent third-party auditors having prior audit and certification experience will be contracted to undertake all structural, fire, and electrical audits.
Miscellaneous	Laws of the land, with regard to compensation, closure, and penalty, will prevail.

Appendix 3: Possible articles of association for *Shonman*

The parties will be committed to the goal of a safe and sustainable Bangladeshi RMG industry, which will ensure safe workplace and fair practices.
Supervision, remediation, and training:

Role of signatories	The signatories shall appoint an SC
Role of SC	1. The SC shall have responsibility of overviewing cases, implementation, and financial management. 2. The SC shall also continue to perform managerial functions. Decisions will be made on the basis of a majority vote.

Dispute resolution	Any dispute between the parties to, and arising under, the terms of this agreement shall first be presented to and decided by the SC, which shall decide the dispute by majority vote of the SC within a maximum of 21 days of a petition being filed by one of the parties. Upon request of either party, the decision of the SC may be appealed to a final and binding arbitration process.
Arbitration	Any arbitration will be governed by the laws of Bangladesh and administered by the BIAC.
Fire and building safety	1. Teams led by the CTO with fire and building safety expertise and impeccable credentials, and who are independent of and not concurrently employed by companies, trade unions or factories, shall be appointed.
	2. Thorough credible safety inspections of the new factories and routine monitoring of the old ones shall be carried out by skilled personnel selected by and acting under the direction of Implementation Board. The safety inspectors will be available to provide input into legislative review and to support capacity building work with regard to inspections.
	3. Signatory companies wishing to have their inspection program considered integral to the program shall provide the Safety Inspector full access to the findings of their inspections and he or she will integrate these into reporting and remediation activities, as per the requirement of "Shonman."
	4. Written inspection reports of all factories inspected under the Implementation program shall be prepared by the Safety Inspector within two weeks of the date of inspection and shared upon completion with factory management, the SC members, CTO and COO.
	5. If the inspection identifies a severe and imminent danger to worker safety, the Safety Inspector will immediately inform IG-DIFE factory management the SC.
	6. Where corrective actions are identified by the Safety Inspector as necessary to bring a factory into compliance with building, fire, and electrical safety standards, the supplier will implement these corrective actions, according to a schedule that is mandatory and time-bound, with sufficient time allotted for all major renovations.
	7. The CTO appointed by the SC will establish an extensive fire and building safety training program. The training program will be delivered by selected skilled personnel by the training coordinator at the facilities for The Safety Committee and WPC of the respective factories. These training programs shall cover basic safety procedures and precautions, as well as enable workers to voice concerns and actively participate in activities to ensure their own safety. Signatory companies shall require their suppliers to provide access to their factories to training teams designated by the training coordinator.

(Continued)

Right of the workers	1. Signatory companies will require their supplier factories to respect the right of a worker to refuse work if he or she has reasonable justification to believe that the workplace is unsafe, without suffering discrimination or loss of pay, including the right to refuse to enter or to remain inside a building that he or she has reasonable justification to believe is unsafe for occupation. 2. A toll-free help line for workers will be set up to report safety issues, etc. at any factory. 3. The CTO shall establish a worker complaint process and mechanism that ensures that workers from factories supplying signatory companies can raise in a timely fashion concerns about health and safety risks, safely and confidentially, with the Safety Inspector.
Record Keeping	1. The SC shall have a regular updated aggregated list of all suppliers in Bangladesh used by the signatory companies, based on data which shall be provided to the SC and regularly updated by each of the signatory companies. However, volume data and information linking specific companies to specific factories will be kept confidential.
Report	1. Written inspection reports, which shall be developed by the Safety Inspector for all factories inspected under this program, shall be disclosed to relevant stakeholders. 2. Quarterly aggregate reports that summarize both aggregated industry compliance data and a detailed review of findings, remedial recommendations, and progress on remediation to date for all factories at which inspections have been completed shall be shared with all relevant stakeholders.

Appendix 4: Supplier and brand obligations

Roles and responsibilities of the signatories	1. Each signatory company shall require that its suppliers in Bangladesh participate fully in the inspection, remediation, health and safety, and, where applicable, training activities, as described in the Agreement. If a supplier consistently fails to do so within a specified period of time, the signatory will promptly implement a notice and warning process leading to termination of the business relationship if these efforts do not succeed. 2. Signatory companies to this agreement are committed to maintaining long-term sourcing relationships with Bangladesh, as is demonstrated by their commitment to this three-year program. Signatory companies shall continue business at order volumes comparable to or greater than those that existed in the year preceding the inception of this agreement with factories at least through the first two years of the term of this agreement.
Transparency of the funding	The SC shall ensure that there are credible, robust, and transparent procedures for the accounting and oversight of all contributed funds.

8 Post-Rana Plaza responses

Changing role of the Bangladeshi government

Shahidur Rahman

Introduction

On December 14, 2010, dozens of workers jumped to their deaths and more than 100 were injured when a fire swept through a Bangladeshi garment factory. On another occasion, a nine-storey factory building owned by Spectrum garments collapsed on April 11, 2005, resulting in death of 64 employees and injuring 84; hundreds of workers were left jobless as a consequence. These two events are not exceptions: about 686 garment workers died and hundreds injured between 2000 and 2009 (Rahman 2014). Although these incidents have been widely reported in national and international press, no major steps have been taken to prevent the recurrence of such events. The workers of the readymade garment (RMG) industry, mostly young women who migrated from the rural areas of Bangladesh to escape abject poverty and social exclusion, remained vulnerable to accidents like these and to uncertainty of their job. The demands of the workers to protect them from such uncertainties and adversity through reforming legislation and strengthening capacity building have rarely addressed by the key stakeholders. No effective action had been taken by the government until the building collapse of the Rana Plaza on April 24, 2013, where 1,136 workers were killed, and many more suffered grave injuries. The deadliest tragedy sent shockwaves around the world and pushed the government to come up with some constructive and effective ways to ensure labor safety at workplace, beginning a new regime extending from mid-2013 to the present.

Against this backdrop, this chapter responds to two questions: (a) what kind of changes have been initiated by the government after that disaster? (b) Has the government taken adequate steps to prevent another industrial accident? The objective of this study is to critically evaluate the responses of the government on two areas – labor legislations and capacity building of the government. The research questions have been examined by assessing the government's actions on: amendments to the Bangladesh Labor Act 2006 and capacity building of DIFE (Department of Inspection for Factories and Establishment), a key government department responsible for the safety of factory building. The study argues that the government has made some important changes immediately after the tragedy by introducing amendments to Bangladesh Labour Law 2006 and by strengthening the capacity of institution responsible to inspect factories. In spite of these positive changes, there has been a continuity of labor-related problems evident in five institutional features: union's role, minimum wages, compensation for accident, participation committee, and DIFE's inspection process.

Kingdon's (2003) theory of focusing event and Anner's (2015) despotic market form have shaped the theoretical framework of this chapter. The first explains why the government has taken the initiative to change its role towards industrial policy and the latter explains the continuation of previous culture. To examine this argument, two methods which have been used in this study are documentary research and Key Person Interviews. Six garment owners, one union leader, one NGO staff involved in labor rights, and two from government labor-related department participated in face–to-face interview with the author. They were selected considering their history of working in this industry for a long time and diverse experiences. Interviews of around 1.5-hour duration were conducted in Bangla, usually by two researchers and occasionally by trained research assistants. The interview schedule contains open-ended questions, which were translated into English and examined for consistency by at least one other researcher fluent in both Bangla and English.

This chapter is organised as follows. After introducing the theoretical framework, the responses of the government to this accident have been discussed shedding light on two areas: labor law and capacity building. The succeeding section critically analyses the role of the government, followed by the concluding remarks.

Theoretical framework

The proposal of insertion of a social clause in trade agreements in the 1990s and early 2000s has pressurised the exporting countries to comply with the minimum international labor standards (Berik 2017). The social clause did not work out because of the opposition of advocacy of neo-liberal policy, suppliers, most southern trade unions and civil society. Lead buyers have exercised influence over the suppliers through the requirement that they follow a code of conduct specifying international labor standards and agree to regular auditing by the lead firm and/or a third party. Yet evidence suggests that buyers' code of conduct produces limited results (Locke 2013; Locke and Romis 2006 Vogel 2008). This can be attributed to several reasons: codes of conduct are designed to limit legal liability (Rodríguez-Garavito 2005), audits may be conducted by an agent of the buyer exhibiting an inherent conflict of interest (O'Rourke 1997), and auditors sometimes lack skills required to conduct a thorough audit (Pruett et al. 2005). The absence of effective compliance at workplaces has continued because of the limitations of these institutional approaches and in public policy, workers' safety has not been considered as a key agenda.

Agenda setting in public policy is concerned with finding the problems deemed more important to the public, and determining the causes and solutions to that problem (Hilgartner & Bosk 1988). The agenda-setting process is therefore a system of exploring problems and implicitly assigning priorities to these problems (Birkland 2013). Two phenomena shape this process: changes in indicators of underlying problems and focusing events (Kingdon 2003). Kingdon (2003) portrays focusing event as the emergence of a powerful symbol involving sudden crises and shocks affecting policymakers on a personal level that promote policy change. Owing to the fact that Kingdon's definition was too broad to be fit in empirical research, Birkland came up with another approach. Birkland (1997: 22) defines a focusing event as one that is

> sudden, relatively rare, can be reasonably defined as harmful or revealing the possibility of potentially greater future harms, inflicts harms or suggests potential harms that are or could be concentrated on a definable geographical area or community of interest, and that is known to policy makers and the public virtually simultaneously.

By raising awareness about a specific problem or an issue leading to harm, a focusing event opens an opportunity for the policymakers to deal with the problem in an efficient way. However, it is often debatable if a major event can be deemed a focusing event; while some might attach adequate importance thereto, others might not. Even if an event gets the attention, contestation over goals or means may prevent a workable policy option (Farley et al. 2007). Following a focusing event, political institutions play a key role in both providing opportunities and creating constraints for policy change (Hacker 1998). Birkland (2006) argues that an event-driven policy change may be rare because organisations are oftentimes unwilling to adapt to changing situations. Furthermore, it is a triage process where pressing matters compete for elite and public attention (Jones 2001). However, in most focusing events, there is a pressure from key stakeholders powerful enough to identify the current condition as policy failure and demand for policy change where an attentive public exists (Baumgartner & Bryan 1993; Birkland 2006). It increases attention towards a public issue or problem leading to harm, referred by Slovic as "dread risk." Key policymakers play a role as proactive problem-solvers by focusing on changes in national policy. In particular, Birkland argues that focusing events have profound influence on legislative change as they, coupled with actions taken by the government, influence the salience of a focusing event for firms (Schuessler et al. 2018). Firms in a country with weak norms around CSR face strong pressure from the national-level government policies (Fransen & Burgoon 2012).

However, the changes brought by the focusing event would face challenges and some degree of non-standard labor relation would continue.

The reason of such continuation would be explained by using Anner's thoughts on despotic market labor control. Anner (2015) mainly offers three models of labor control comprising the state, market, and employer as separate regimes. The author argues that in the case of state labor control such as in China, labor is controlled by an arrangement of legal and extralegal mechanisms while employer labor-control regimes use highly oppressive employer actions against workers as can be seen in Colombia. In market labor control regimes, "unfavourable labour market conditions discipline labour; strong worker-organising is curtailed because workers are afraid that active participation in a union may result in job loss and prolonged unemployment or underemployment" (Anner 2015). Low-income countries with very weak labor rights exemplify despotic versions of market labor-control regimes. In such a case, the intensity of labor control depends on the flexibility of labor market. Since there are very limited alternative job opportunities available, workers embrace the unsafe working conditions, faced with poverty and finding underemployment a nonviable option. The employer takes advantage of the situation. However, these three models are not mutually exclusive, and countries do typically exhibit a combination of various types of labor control.

Government responses post-Rana Plaza

Ineffectiveness on the government's part can be traced to the presence of very outdated and convoluted legislations concerning labor standards. Before the major revamp on the labor laws during 2006, there were as many as 50 separate, and often inconsistent, legislations passed in various times (BEF 2009). From these 50 different legislations, 15 were passed during the colonial rule, 23 during the Pakistan period, and only 12 after the independence of Bangladesh. A large majority of the laws were in fact framed in the British context during the colonial era, and thus were unable to meet with the demands of a new country struck with very different challenges. To ensure a solid framework for labor laws by making revisions to prior laws and consolidating them into a single comprehensive code, a 38-member National Law Commission was set up in 1992. The commission was led by a former judge of Supreme Court of Bangladesh, its members, and eight labour leaders representing various unions and organisations (BEF 2009). Laws of neighbouring countries were considered as a framework during this process and opinions of stakeholders as well as public were also included into this new legislative process. In 1994, the Commission submitted to the government as a unified and comprehensive labor code by repealing and consolidating 25 existing legislations. Four years later, the Tripartite Labour Law Reform Committee (LLRC) was formed and comprised representatives from the government, workers as well as employers. This committee reviewed the draft labour code and recommended changes wherever necessary. In 2006, the Labour Act was finally passed by the parliament in effect from October 11, 2006. While the Labour Act 2006 was an ambitious project, the Rana Plaza tragedy proves the ineffectiveness of the act.

Reforming labor laws

After the building collapse at Rana Plaza, the Bangladesh Labour Act 2006 was amended on July 15, 2013, focusing on the obligations of rights to freedom of association and most importantly occupational health and safety. Hence, training and provisions of safety equipment, mandatory fire drills, reports of accidents to authority, finance to treat sick employees, compensation for worker death, labor inspection programmes, etc., were stressed in the amendments. Further, labor inspectorates were developed with several organisations in order to boost working conditions and worker safety. Realising the obligation and potentials, the Government of Bangladesh developed the National Occupational Safety and Health Policy 2013. While minor amendments were made after the Labour Act 2006, international scrutiny as well as suspension of trade privileges by the USA was a catalyst in the Bangladesh government's officially adopting 87 amendments to the original Labour Act of 2006 after Rana Plaza disaster. These changes are significant because they have a better insight on what workplace safety measures are necessary and on the desired measures to eradicate the issues. The most significant ones raised were concerned with the need of amendments directly related to workplace safety, trade unions, and collective bargaining.

The amended Act calls for better regulation of stairs and gangways, which are to be monitored under CCTV and to be open during business hours. A clause has also been added to Section 78 of the original Act, which requires employers to provide personal safety equipment and offer trainings for the use of such equipment. In factories with 50 or more employees, fire drills are mandatory every six months, as opposed to as it had been once a year. Section 80 urges factory inspectors to report serious accidents to authorities such as the government, police stations, fire service, etc. (Rubya 2015). Section 89 includes a new mandate for the establishment of health centres for factories with 5,000 or more employees (ILO 2013), and if an employee develops occupational sickness, employers must finance employee's treatment until he or she has fully recovered if said employee had worked for two years. Prior to this, compensation for work-related deaths was given after three years of service. Additionally, the maximum amount of compensation awarded in the case of workplace deaths to the dependants of the deceased would be 100,000 taka which must be deposited in the labor court by the employer. If a worker suffers permanent disablement because of a workplace injury, the compensation would be 125,000 taka. This would be assessed for the period of their disablement for one year or less (BLAST 2014).

The new amendments have also addressed collective bargaining by allowing for workers to call on external experts to advise them on collective bargaining. In the public industrial sector, workers will be allowed to elect 10% of their enterprise officers from outside the workplace. This however does not apply to the private sector (ILO 2013). The right to strike has also been revised by the Bangladeshi government, now requiring two-thirds vote by a union's leadership, previously requiring three-fourths (Rubya 2015). As for the trade union, notable changes made to union formation include eliminating the condition that required the Director of Labour to submit the names of union officers to employers. The workers no longer need approval from factory owners in order to create unions. Furthermore, under the amended laws, five unions could be formed within the same factory, an increase from the previous stipulation of two. Workers are also able to appoint external experts to assist in their collective bargaining. Section 205 of the BLA 2006 requires employers hiring more than 50 workers in any establishments to set up a "participation committee."

Because of the new amendments, there has been a sharp rise in trade unions after the Rana Plaza collapse due to international pressures. According to the Labour Ministry, a total of 326 trade unions have been registered with the Directorate of Labour since 2013, putting the total number of trade unions at 464. In comparison, there were 138 trade unions in 2012, and the number rose sharply with registrations every year, with 185 trade unions forming in 2014 alone. Syeda Sultan Uddin Ahmed from Bangladesh Institute of Labour Studies noted that the number of trade unions "increased due to international pressure including human rights organisations, global trade unions, consumer groups as well as retailers" (ILO 2015).

Capacity building

The activities of factory building safety and fire prevention largely took place within the context of the National Tripartite Plan of Action (NTPA) on Fire Safety for the RMG sector in Bangladesh. This was in fact developed in the aftermath of the devastating fire at Tazreen Fashions by the Government of Bangladesh in collaboration with ILO. The plan was devised with a view to taking comprehensive actions to prevent further loss of life from fire-related accidents. It identifies activities on three levels: legislation and policy, administrative, and practical activities. Formally adopted on March 24, 2013, the Rana Plaza collapse led to an urgent need to reassess the Plan of Action so that it also addressed structural issues. This revised document, now entitled the NTPA on Fire Safety and Structural Integrity for the RMG sector in Bangladesh, was subsequently adopted on July 25, 2013. As per NTPA, the DIFE is inspecting factories not covered by Accord and Alliance which is known as National Initiative (NI). The NI, with the programme support of the ILO and Bangladesh University of Engineering and Technology (BUET), has set a target to inspect 1,827 factories and until August 24, 2017 completed assessment of 1,549 factories. A Remediation Coordination Cell (RCC) has been formed to manage the remediation work of the factories inspected by the NI. The RCC is supported by ILO with funding from three countries, namely Canada, the United Kingdom, and the Netherlands. This unit is staffed by seconded members of regulatory bodies including the Department of Inspections for Factories and Establishments, Fire Service and Civil Defence, RAJUK (*Rajdhani Unnayan Kartipakkha*, government department of capital city development), Chief Electrical Inspector, Public Works Department, and Chittagong Development Authority. The changing structure of DIFE is appreciated by respondents as one entrepreneur mentioned in fieldwork saying: "The DIFE is becoming a stronger authority than before. I think DIFE can play a vital role to inspect factories since they have already recruited graduated engineers."

The collapse of Rana Plaza also brought about the weak capacity of the authorities involved in factories to ensure safety and acceptable working conditions. The government did not have the capacity to deal with factory building safety and occupational and health safety of the workers. It was in this context that the labor inspectorate needed a complete overhaul to be effective. The Government of Bangladesh has made several major commitments to revamp DIFE. The number of inspector has been increased from 183 pre-Rana Plaza to 575 post-Rana Plaza, and the budget was increased from US$0.97 million before 2013 to US$4.1 million in 2015–2016 (Shipar 2017). Different national and international organisations along with the development partners have extended their support to build up the capacity of the government. As part of its activities, the ILO is conducting a series of training courses for newly recruited labor inspectors on the national labor law, fire and building safety, and inspection techniques. A labor inspection programme was initiated on August 16, 2015 to enrich the skills of inspectors needed to boost working conditions and worker safety. The course was developed by DIFE and BIAM (Bangladesh Institute of Administration and Development), with the support of ILO. The programme seeks to instil labor policies, programmes, OSH (Occupational Safety and Health), and Bangladesh labor laws in its participants. Meanwhile, for the reform process, the Ministry of Labour, Government of Bangladesh and ILO are collaborating for wider implications of the inspectorate. The road map includes effective information management systems, basic equipment, and transport for inspectors, accountability units as well as a public database for inspection to promote transparency. Previously there was no comprehensive and uniform inspection checklist in use. After the Rana Plaza collapse in 2013, a new checklist was developed by the DIFE with the support of ILO's RMG programme funded by Canada, the Netherlands, and the United Kingdom (ILO 2017). The US Department of Labor funded a project on "Promoting Fundamental Principles and Rights at Work" for capacity building of trade union representatives and employers' organisations and promoting effective labor-management relations (Shipar 2017) (Figure 8.1).

In this chapter, from a theoretical context, the above-mentioned initiatives installed in after the Rana Plaza can be seen as the positive impact of

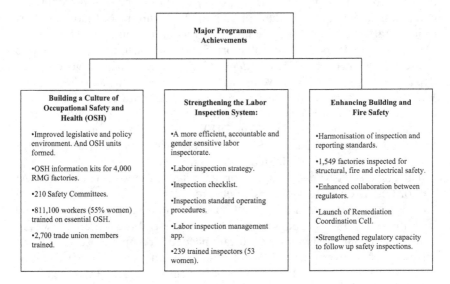

Figure 8.1 Government programs since Rana Plaza disaster.
Source: BGMEA, 2017.

a "focusing event" to explain the shifting role of the government to ensure compliance with labor standards. Given its scale, the Rana Plaza provided unforeseen leverage for workers and their allies to ensure building safety in garment supply chains (Berliner et al. 2015). Three mutually reinforcing preconditions of a focusing event are acknowledgement of a problem that needs resolution, offering a policy as a solution to the problem, and political pressure compelling policymakers to act (Kingdon 2003). In the Rana Plaza case, the government acknowledged lack of factory building safety in Bangladesh, which led them to reform the existing legislations and other policies to ensure workers safety. Most importantly, there was a political pressure from the global unions, NGOs, consumers, buyers, and other national and international organisations. The USA withdrew GSP facility and it created a panic amongst the Government of Bangladesh and the garment owners. The government did not have any choice but to accept the decision of the transnational partners to install a mechanism to inspect the factories in a transparent way. As a focusing event, the Rana Plaza tragedy was considered as dread risk that has placed immense pressure on regulators to fix the problems involved in the event. Government institutions came forward with intervention plans to change policies from constitutional to regulatory in legislature.

Critical evaluation

The Rana Plaza tragedy has placed the government to a position of obligation, at least vocally or upfront, to raise their concern for labor standards. Since then, workers' safety has gained more importance; although in reality, some aspects remain unchanged. It is argued in the introduction section of this chapter that there has been a continuity of labor-related problems and it is examined in this section by presenting a critical evaluation of union's position after the Rana Plaza, minimum wages, amendment on compensation for accident, participation committee, and DIFE's inspection process.

There was pressure from various organisations on an international level as well to address on the establishment of trade unions, and as a result, there are a lot of trade unions in place. However, it is still questionable as to how much these unions can work for the workers' rights and related matters. Despite an initial rise in the number of registered unions, union density continued at around 3% and remained divided along political lines (Moazzem 2017; Zajak 2017) and collective bargaining was rare (The Financial Express 2017). For instance, as per the amendment proposed in 2013, union leaders will only be allowed to select their leaders from their own establishments. This enables employers to fire union leaders under the pretence of work-related issues, and not related to the union. According to Human Rights Watch, this is a common issue globally, but has been common practice in Bangladesh (Human Rights Watch 2013). Furthermore, there are a number of organisations playing a double role of garment workers' organisations and non-registered trade unions because the amendments do not make union registrations easier. The government offices still have power over registration and continue to accept or reject these applications at their will (Human Rights Watch 2016). According to a labor activist,

> If you do a research on those who have formed trade unions so far, you'll see that most of them are those with maintain a good link with either owner groups or political affiliations with the ruling party. The real proponents of labour rights have faced unnecessary bureaucratic problems from the Director of Labour to register union.

However, while the numbers are significant, the disparity between the number of factories and the total number of unions is still to be noted. While there are 464 and increasing trade unions, there are more than 3,500–4,000 factories in Bangladesh, exhibiting stark lack of representation. At the same time, unions are still seen in a negative light from the owners, who view them as disruptive forces in the industry. The President of Bangladesh Garment Workers' Employee League mentions how unions cannot be made effective due to workers' leaders being harassed for being involved in a union, which makes fewer unions effective in factories. On a similar vein, Babul Akhter, president of Bangladesh Garment and Industrial Workers Federation, said that "in a true sense, there are only 33 readymade garments factories in which unions can meet their demands through collective bargaining" (ILO 2015).

The new law has kept the previous provision of 30% membership in a company for forming trade unions, which negates the idea of free trade unionism

(The Daily Star 2016). Labor leaders urged the Bangladeshi legislators to accept a 10% threshold for union formation and from one factory instead of entire company (Rubya 2015). After the pressure of the ILO, EU and US, the government has recently approved a draft of Bangladesh Labor (Amendment) Act, 2018 and under the proposed law workers' participation required to form trade unions at factories will be reduced to 20% from the existing 30% (The Daily Star 2018a). The right to strike is still a cumbersome process because it requires two-thirds of union's members to vote for the strike (Human Rights Watch 2013). Again, the government has the right to end a strike if it causes adverse effects to the community and is detrimental to the national interest. Such provision encourages the garment owners to showcase how labor protest can disrupt the economic growth from the main export-earning industry of the country and take advantage of this situation. In addition, another weakness of the Labour Act amendment (2013) is the failure to modify the penalties of factory owners and other individuals associated with accidents and disasters. The failure to notify authorities of accidents is a fine of only 1,000 taka, while the loss of life or failure to report it is an imprison up to six months or a fine of up to 3,000 taka (Labour Act 2006) which is seen as grossly inadequate given the serious nature of the crimes. Less effort has been channelled to produce an effective compensation. Because of the pressure from labors all around the world and international consumers, buyers have sometimes come forward with financial assistance to workers who suffer any accidents in order to protect their image. Lack of support from legislation on compensation is shared by a union leader (Table 8.1):

> The only thing that would have been helpful after Rana plaza is to fix a compensation, around 10–15 lakh with the advice of economists and others. This was presented in high court but nothing changed. Compensation remained 1,00,000–1,25,000 Taka.

At the same time, the Building Construction Act, which prevents the construction of hazardous structures, penalises anyone who does so. While

Table 8.1 Changes of workers' wages

Grade	2006 (taka)	2010 (taka)	Increase over 2006 (%)	2013 (taka)	Increase over 2010 (%)	2018 (taka)	Increase over 2013 (%)
Grade 1	5,140	9,300	80.93	13,000	39.87	18,257	40.44
Grade 2	3,840	7,200	87.50	10,900	51.38	15,416	41.43
Grade 3	2,449	4,120	68.23	6,805	65.16	9,875	44.67
Grade 4	2,250	3,763	67.24	6,420	70.60	9,347	45.59
Grade 5	2,046	3,455	68.87	6,042	74.87	8,875	46.89
Grade 6	1,851	3,210	73.42	5,678	76.88	8,420	48.29
Grade 7	1,662	3,000	80.45	5,300	76.66	8,000	50.49

Source: Fair Wear Foundation (2015), The Daily Star (2019).

this also applies to the garments industry, there are no direct labor laws within the Act or its amendments, which discuss alternative grounds for punishment (Rubya 2015). Frustration appears from labor leader saying

> Nothing changed in the amendment about the labour law. There are many cases against the Rana Plaza owners - accident case, murder case, building law case. Some owners got bail. But even in four years, Sohel Rana didn't get a sentence. This gives a message to others that nothing will happen to them as well.

In order to fix minimum wages, the Minimum Wages Board was formed in Bangladesh under the Minimum Wages Ordinance in 1961. The responsibility of the Board is to set minimum wages for different sectors. The minimum wage was fixed at Tk 3,000 in 2010, Tk 1,662.50 in 2006, Tk 940 in 1994, and Tk 627 in 1985 (The Daily Star 2018b).

It means that the minimum wage increased by Tk. 2,373 from 1985 to 2010 in 25 years.. Although the minimum wage has increased, in dollar terms, from USD$13 to USD$43 per month, thousands of workers took to the streets on July 2010 burning cars and blocking traffic to protest against this decision on wage hike which fell far short of their demands. Following the Rana Plaza incident, the minimum wage once again increased to Tk.5300, amounting to a 76.66% increase of that of 2010. The workers were still unhappy as they found it very difficult to make ends meet with this salary. According to Living Wage Benchmark Report (2015), the estimated living wage ranges from 13,630 taka (Dhaka satellite town) to 16,460 taka (Dhaka city). It shows a 9,000-taka gap between minimum wage and living wage, and because of such disparity, labor movement erupted in 2016 in Ashulia. However, the way the government handled this labor unrest exemplified the problem of execution of legislation and the continuity of unjustified labor control. In 2016, labor unrest erupted with demands for wage increases leading to the dismissal of 1,600 garment workers and arrests of 34 trade unionists (Anner 2018). The movement primarily started in a factory when land owners had increased the house/room rents of the workers. Other problems included no increase of basic facility and laying off workers in a particular factory. It pushed them to raise their voices to revise the minimum wage. As per the labor law, the government is supposed to ensure a wage rate analysis and check the status of the market to revise the wage structure every five years but it could be done earlier in case of special cases such as done in 2010 and later in 2013. In response to continuous labor unrest, the government finally declared a new pay structure in 2018 and the minimum wage is set at Tk. 8,000 (The Daily Star 2018b). Although the minimum wage has been increased by 51% from the previous wage declared in 2013, it has been criticized by global unions and activists. Clean Clothes Campaign (2018) argued: "The announced minimum wage of 8,000 taka is problematic in a number of ways. Not only is the total amount far below any credible living wage estimate, it is hardly even an increase (from the current minimum wage of 5,300 taka) given inflation in the country over the past five years, and given the increases that should have already been implemented based on legal requirements".

The Bangladesh Labour Act (2006) has also favoured the garment entrepreneurs by opening up a space to opt for Participatory Committee (PC) consisting of elected workers. Legally, it may be possible for a PC and trade union to work simultaneously; however, in reality they are not seen as operating together. In most cases, the factories have a PC in place, as PC members act as insiders for the owner party, making it easier for the factory owners to operate under this system. Generally, a PC is to be formed only when a trade union is not possible for particular issues. The transparency of the election process of the PC is also highly questionable. According to a labor activist (2018): "Though established in the labour law as an alternative, it is most definitely not as effective as a trade union and it really allows owners to use this as loophole to get away without a trade union." Again, a positive approach of the Labour Act (2006) and consequent amendments is the inclusion of safety committee in each factory. However, questions could be raised about the effectiveness of this committee since workers would be undermined by the management. Some safety measures such as fire exits are still vague, and not much has been added in terms of detail of the standard of fire doors. The Labour Act of 2006 mentioned worker PCs in factories employing more than 50 workers. This workers' platform has been strengthened after Rana Plaza by a 2013 amendment required worker representatives in PCs to be elected by secret ballot (Manzur et al. 2017). The survey conducted by the researcher of this paper finds that 78% of senior management reported the presence of a PC in their factory and 70% of these PCs included elected workers' representatives. Obviously this initiative has engaged workers of each factory to discuss their issues directly with the management without any interference from the outsiders. However, the presence of PC has challenged trade unions since very few factories have unions. However, all garment owners who participated in interview with the author claimed to be "very satisfied" with the management-PC relationship. To the management, it seems the overwhelming presence of PC in factory has overshadowed the justification of having a union at workplace. The common issue raised by PC in their factories was non-economical such as annual leave; economic concern such as living wage was not a common agenda in the committee. It appears that unions are more effective than non-union representation in dealing with economic issues such as wages and lay-offs since they are not controlled by management (Kaufman & Kleiner 1993).

Following the Rana Plaza incident in 2013, the EU took action through a "sustainability compact" jointly with Bangladesh, the ILO, and the USA. The compact aimed at improving labor, health, and safety conditions for workers, as well as responsible behaviour by businesses within the industry. The EU expects the Government of Bangladesh to comply with 17 points.

The compact came right after the USA announced it would be removing its trade preferences from Bangladesh, and it was since feared that the EU would soon follow suit. As a large portion of EU's garment imports comes from Bangladesh, there has been a degree in leniency in policies related to trade. Not only did the GSP privileges remain intact, but in a meeting on 20 October, 2014 in Brussels, representatives from the EU also indicated that the EU will continue to provide GSP facilities for Bangladesh even after it progresses to a middle-income country (Bdnews24 2014). Like sustainability compact, the US Trade Representative (USTR), responsible for recommending and developing the US trade policies, also came with another set of labor right issues (USTR 2016). Although significant progress has been made by the government, the EU and the USTR believe that more efforts need to be invested in the following issues: (a) regulations implementing the amendments of Bangladesh Labour Act, (b) government delays in completing inspections and hiring additional inspectors, (c) slow response to unfair labor practices, and (d) labor reforms for EPZ (The Daily Star 2017).

In context of inspection and remediation, factory remediation under the Accord and the Alliance made significant progress compared with NI. The garment owners who took part in interviews with the author believe that the remediation progress of the factories under NI was highly disappointing. Upon completion of the inspections, remediation works are underway in the factories, and 77% of the findings in Accord factories, 79% of the findings in Alliance-affiliated factories, and 20% NI have already been fixed (BGMEA 2017). The DIFE could also be criticised for not having a sufficient number of qualified engineers to inspect the factories. For instance, one of the respondents said: "I don't have any space to challenge what the NI is doing. The inspectors lack technical coordination and lack of expertise in dealing with building safety." The DIFE appoints a third-party engineering firm to inspect the factory and to suggest how to fix the structural, fire, and electrical problems. However, there has been no follow-up information about remediation work after the inspection. On the contrary, the inspection teams of the Accord and Alliance have been visiting the factories, thoroughly examining the fire, electrical, and structural condition of the building, providing corrective action plans to the management with time frame and also maintaining follow-up of the process. Such a rigorous action plan is missing in the NI. Again, the Bangladeshi suppliers within NI are not under any pressure from the buyers since DIFE is working with the leading buyer countries such as Canada, the Netherlands, and the UK, not with the specific buyers, unlike the other two transnational institutions. The absence of a compelling pressure from buyers has created an opportunity for the factories to ignore the remediation. Furthermore, whereas the Accord and the Alliance have sent their own engineers to do the inspection, the NI has appointed external organisations to do the inspection and DIFE staffs supervise the works of those organisations. According to a senior staff of DIFE, there was no inspector from National Initiative who went to inspect... What we have done is that we have appointed 26 structural firms to do inspections. We haven't appointed people like Accord has. So I will not be able to do inspection on par with Accord.

A better understanding of process could be achieved if the DIFE would send their own inspections who have the credible qualification to do the job.

From the theoretical point of view, Anner's (2015) despotic version of market labor-control regime explains the continuity of some labor-related problems discussed above. Outside of the garment sector, it is very difficult to secure employment as the job market for women is very limited in Bangladesh and as a result they adjust with the wages that is below the living wage. The only "solution" is for these employees to continue with their jobs accepting the existing labor act and sharing their problems with PC whose role is questionable for management control. Garment workers are vulnerable because of the ineffective role of union. Although the number of union has increased significantly the culture of intimidation of union member has continued. An immense change has been produced by the EU's "Sustainability Compact," yet labor unrest has not been handled in efficient way. The issue of compensation for workers affected by industrial accident is not compatible with the current global standard. Workers' vulnerability is not only limited to working conditions; they are concerned of factory building safety since the inspection process governed by the DIFE is not promising.

Conclusion

This chapter draws attention to the role of the government after the building collapse of Rana Plaza. The study finds that the government has played a comparatively proactive role to ensure safety of workers compared to its previous efforts. The changes have brought 87 amendments to the Labour Act 2006, which have addressed the weaknesses of labor law and tried to minimise the gap between policy and practice. The changes include the presence of a significant number of trade unions, formation of participation and safety committee at workplaces, use of safety equipment, access to external resource to advise on collective bargaining, and so on. A noticeable change is also evident in capacity building by reviving the government administration and monitoring system to prevent another Rana Plaza. The number of inspectors has been increased; the structural, fire, and electrical conditions of the factories are being checked; an RCC has been formed; and a number of training have been offered to different stakeholders on different areas in collaboration with the ILO and other partners. While important progress has been made within the last five years, this chapter also finds some labor issues continue to be ignored. Although there are more trade unions than there were before 2013, questions could still be raised about their effectiveness which is evident in the way the government handled labor unrest in Ashulia in 2016. There is no way to deny that participation and safety committee are far from evading the control of the owners. Workers are still not satisfied with the amount of compensation and legal punishment set for the management in the case of violation of labor law.

However, what is positive is that until the Rana Plaza tragedy, social compliance was the main concern for stakeholders. The structural, fire, and electrical safety of the factory building did not garner much attention. The majority of the factory owners were not concerned about the building safety mechanisms at all. Now, social and physical compliance are the key indicators of sustainability in the global apparel industry, at least for doing business with lead buyers. The government has acknowledged the problem and has been working together with other stakeholders, although it is hard to say whether a culture of safety has been installed into the entire industry regardless of the size of factories. There is however a possibility that the distance between workers and owners will reduce and social dialogue will function as an initial step towards finding a common ground on different issues. The momentum that started five years ago should continue and the government needs to play an exemplary role by addressing the drawbacks of the entire process in a systematic way, and utilise the resources available from different stakeholders to prevent another incident similar to the one at Rana Plaza. There is no way to deny that the capacity of the government needs to be strengthened so that dependence on transnational or private governance approach would be reduced and a self-reliant independent body would lead effectively. To make it happen, the cooperation of and collaboration with different stakeholders is essential which has already initiated and should be continued.

Acknowledgement

I would like to thank the Volkswagen Foundation in cooperation with the Riksbankens Jubileumsfond and the Wellcome Trust for funding the project on which this chapter is based.

References

Anner, M. (2015) Labor control regimes and worker resistance in global supply chains. *Labor History* 56(3): 292–307.

Anner, M. (2018) Binding Power: The Sourcing Squeeze, Workers' Rights, and Building Safety in Bangladesh since Rana Plaza. Penn State University, *CGWR Research Report*.

Bangladesh Employers' Federation (BEF) (2009) A handbook on the Bangladesh Labor Act 2006. Online, available at: www.ilo.org/dyn/travail/docs/352/A%20 Handbook%20on%20the%20Bangladesh%20Labour%20Act%202006.pdf (accessed 15 May 2017).

Bangladesh Legal Aid Services and Trust (2014) Note on compensation for workplace deaths and injuries in Bangladesh. Retrieved from www.blast.org.bd/ content/news/note-workplace-deaths-and-injuries.pdf.

Baumgartner, F. R. and Bryan, D. J. (1993) *Agendas and Instability in American Politics*. Chicago: University of Chicago Press.

Bdnews24 (2014) Bangladesh to continue getting GSP trade privileges from EU. Retrieved from https://bdnews24.com/business/2014/10/24/bangladesh-to-continue-getting-gsp-trade-privileges-from-eu (accessed 24 October 2014).

Berliner, D., Greenleaf, A. R., Lake, M., Levi, M. and Noveck, J. (2015) *Labor Standards in International Supply Chains: Aligning Rights and Incentives*. London: Edward Elgar.

BGMEA (2017) The Apparel story. BGMEA newsletter, May–August, 2017.

Berik, G. (2017) Revisiting the feminist debates on international labor standards in the aftermath of Rana Plaza. *Studies in Comparative International Development*, 52(2), 193–216.

Birkland, T. A. (1997) *After Disaster: Agenda Setting, Public Policy and Focusing Events*. Washington, D.C.: Georgetown University Press.

Birkland, T. A. (2006) *Lessons of Disaster*. Washington, D.C.: Georgetown University Press.

Birkland, T. A. (2013) Focusing Events in the Agenda Setting Process. Clean Clothes Campaign (CCC). (2006). "Spectrum: One year after the collapse". Retrieved from https://cleanclothes.org/resources/newsletters/ccc-newsletter-22.pdf/view (accessed 20 May 2006).

Clean Clothes Campaign (2018) Outrageous new minimum wage announced in Bangladesh. September 21, 2018. Retrieved from https://cleanclothes.org/news/2018/09/21/outrageous-new-minimum-wage-announced-in-bangladesh.

Fair Wear Foundation (2015) Bangladesh country study 2015. Retrieved from www.fairwear.org/wp-content/uploads/2016/06/BangladeshCountryStudy2016.pdf (accessed 11 January 2017).

Farley, J., Baker, D., Batker, D., Koliba, C., Matteson, R., Mills, R. and Pittman, J. (2007) Opening the policy window for ecological economics: Katrina as a focusing event. *Ecological Economics*, 63(2): 344–354.

Fransen, L. and Burgoon, B. (2012) A market for worker rights: Explaining business support for international private labor regulation. *Review of International Political Economy*, 19(2): 236–266.

Hacker, J. S. (1998) The historical logic of national health insurance: Structure and sequence in the development of British, Canadian, and U.S. medical policy. *Studies in American Political Development*, 12(01): 57–130.

Hilgartner, J. and Charles, B. (1988) The rise and fall of social problems: A public arenas model. *American Journal of Sociology*, 94(1): 53–78.

Human Rights Watch (2013) Bangladesh: Amended labor law falls short. Retrieved from www.hrw.org/news/2013/07/15/bangladesh-amended-labor-law-falls-short (accessed 21 March 2017).

Human Rights watch (2016) Bangladesh: Garment workers' union rights bleak. Retrieved from www.hrw.org/news/2016/04/21/bangladesh-garment-workers-union-rights-bleak (accessed 21 March 2017).

International Labor Organization (2013) ILO statement on reform of Bangladesh labor law. Retrieved from www.ilo.org/global/about-the-ilo/newsroom/statements-and-speeches/WCMS_218067/lang--en/index.htm (accessed 20 March 2017).

International Labor Organization (2015) Better work. Retrieved from www.ilo.org/washington/areas/better-work/lang--en/index.htm (accessed 21 March 2017).

International Labor Organization (2017) Inspection checklist a new step in labor inspection reform. Retrieved from www.ilo.org/dhaka/Whatwedo/Projects/

safer-garment-industry-in-bangladesh/WCMS_543296/lang--en/index.htm (accessed 2 February 2018).

Jones, B. D. (2001) *Politics and the Architecture of Choice: Bounded Rationality and Governance.* Chicago: University of Chicago Press.

Kaufman, B. E. and Kleiner, M. M. (1993) *Employee Representation: Alternatives and Future Directions.* Madison: Industrial Relations Research Association.

Kingdon, J. W. (2003) *Agendas, Alternatives, and Public Policies* (2nd edition). New York: Longman.

Living Wage Benchmark Report (2015). Retrieved from www.isealalliance.org/sites/default/files/resource/201712/Dhaka_Living_Wage_Benchmark_Infographic.pdf.

Locke, R. M. (2013) *The Promise and Limits of Private Power: Promoting Labor Standards in a Global Economy.* Cambridge: Cambridge University Press.

Locke, R. M. and Romis, M. (2006) Beyond Corporate Codes of Conduct: Work Organization and Labor Standards in Two Mexican Garment Factories (MIT Sloan Working Paper 4617-06). Retrieved from Social Science Research Network http://papers.ssrn.com/abstract=925273.

Manzur, S., Brown, D., Knudsen, J. S. and Remick, E. (2017) After Rana Plaza: From building safety to social dialogue. Working paper.

Moazzem, K. G. (2017) Strengthening social dialogue mechanism under weak enabling environment: Case of RMG sector. Presentation 23 April, 2017, Dhaka.

O'Rourke, D. (1997) Smoke from a hired gun: A critique of Nike's labor and environmental auditing in Vietnam as performed *by Ernst & Young.* Transnational Resource and Action Center.

Pruett, D., Merk, J., Zeldenrust, I. and de Haan, E. (2005). Looking for a Quick Fix: How Weak Social Auditing is Keeping Workers in Sweatshops [Monograph]. Retrieved October 25, 2015, from www.cleanclothes.org/.

Rahman, S. (2014) *Broken Promises of Globalization. The Case of the Bangladesh Garment Industry.* New York: Lexington Books.

Rodríguez-Garavito, C. A. (2005) Global governance and labor rights: Codes of conduct and anti-sweatshop struggles in global apparel factories in Mexico and Guatemala. *Politics & Society,* 33(2): 203–333. doi:10.1177/0032329205275191.

Rubya, T. (2015) The ready-made garment industry: An analysis of Bangladesh's labor law provisions after the savar tragedy. *Brooklyn Journal of International Law,* 40(2): 7. Retrieved from http://brooklynworks.brooklaw.edu/cgi/viewcontent.cgi?article=1042&context=bjil.

Schuessler, E., Frenkel, S. J. and Wright, C. F. (2018) Governance of labor standards in Australian and German garment supply chains: The impact of Rana Plaza. *Industrial & Labor Relations Review,* 72(3): 552–579.

Shipar, M. (2017) Steps taken by Ministry of Labor and Employment and other related stakeholders after Rana Plaza collapse at Savar. Online, available at: https://cpd.org.bd/wp-content/uploads/2016/04/Presentation-of-Mr-Mikail-Shipar-Secretary-Ministry-of-Labour-and-Employment.pdf (accessed 12 January 2018).

The Daily Star (2016) *Trade Union in EPZs Gets Nod.* 16th February, 2016 issue. Retrieved from www.thedailystar.net/frontpage/trade-union-epzs-gets-nod-511831.

The Daily Star (2017) *EU Finds Fantastic Progress under Sustainability Compact.* Online, available at: www.thedailystar.net/business/eu-finds-fantastic-progress-under-sustainability-compact-1402675 (accessed 9 May 2017).

The Daily Star (2018a) Govt eases trade union rules. September 4, 2018. Retrieved from www.thedailystar.net/news/city/bangladesh-labour-act-amendment-2018-cabinet-approved-banning-child-labour-1628449.

The Daily Star (2018b) Tk. 8000 a month. September 14, 2018. Retrieved from www.thedailystar.net/business/news/bangladesh-rmg-garment-workers-minimum-salary-8000-taka-announced-1633342.

The Daily Star (2019) Workers' wages rise in 6 grades. Retrieved from www.thedailystar.net/business/bangladesh-garment-workers-salary-structure-be-revised-1686979.

The Financial Express (2017) *Collective Bargaining Largely Absent in BD*. Retrieved from http://today.thefinancialexpress.com.bd/print/collective-bargaining-largely-absent-in-bd-1513190403 (accessed 14 December 2017).

United States Trade Representative (2016) *Standing Up for Workers: Promoting Labour Rights through Trade*. Online, available at: https://ustr.gov/sites/default/files/USTR%20DOL%20Trade%20-%20Labour%20Report%20-%20Final.pdf (accessed 5 January 2017).

Vogel, D. (2008) Private global business regulation. *The Annual Review of Political Science*, 11: 261–282.

Zajak, S. (2017) International allies, institutional layering and power in the making of labour in Bangladesh. *Development and Change*, 48(5), 1007–1030. doi:10.1111/dech.12327.

9 Behaviour of the buyers and suppliers in the post-Rana Plaza period

A decent work perspective

Khondaker Golam Moazzem

Introduction and objectives

The post-Rana Plaza period (2013 onwards) has been specially marked for various national and global initiatives particularly the 'Sustainability Compact' and the 'National Plan of Action' with a view to fix the decent work agenda in the apparel value chain of Bangladesh. The key activities related to decent work which had been carried out include amendment of labor laws, activities on workplace safety, security and workers' health, strengthening public agencies responsible for workers' safety and rights, transparency in reporting on workers and their organization-related information, responsible business conduct among the buyers, etc. Implementation of such multidimensional initiatives required cooperation and collaboration of major players of the value chain including suppliers, buyers, local public monitoring and implementing agencies, workers, consumers, international organizations and development partners. Among all the players, the buyers and the suppliers (tier 1 and tier 2 enterprises) are supposed to be the two most important players in implementing those decent work-related activities as part of their commitment to develop the sustainable value chain.

The 'decent work' is defined by the ILO as

> opportunities for work that are productive and deliver a fair income, security in the workplace and social protection for families, better prospects for personal development and social integration, freedom for people to express their concerns, organize and participate in the decisions that affect their lives and equality of opportunity and treatment for all women and men.

In other words, four elements are covered under decent work agenda. These are employability, decent wage, workplace safety and workers' rights. Enforcement of these elements in the production segment of the value chain is guided by supplying country-specific rules and regulations. This then is considered to be the responsibility of the suppliers. However, buyers' codes of conduct is their major business guideline to assess suppliers' level of compliance on decent work-related issues including social issues. Therefore, the buyers also play a key role in the enforcement of the decent work agenda in the value chain.

It is important to note that the post-Rana Plaza initiatives have concentrated on few issues of decent work agenda such as workplace safety and workers' rights. The present study takes an effort to examine what have been done from the particular angle of the aforesaid four elements of decent work agenda.

The industrial accident of Rana Plaza in 2013 (and the fire in the Tazreen Fashions garment in 2012) reflected sheer negligence of the key stakeholders in ensuring workers' safety and security. In this backdrop, market players were pushed to show increasing commitment on social compliance in their business practices (USFIA, 2017) with a view to mainstreaming the decent work agenda in the value chain. The key question is how the buyers and suppliers have taken part in implementing different activities related to decent work agenda in the post-Rana Plaza period and how distinctive those activities were compared to those of the pre-Rana Plaza period. Based on the findings of these questions, the chapter tries to identify the gaps in the activities in implementing the decent work agenda and the role of other stakeholders in the implementation process.

This chapter comprises five sections. After the introduction, the second section discusses about different types of suppliers and buyers and the nature of contractual relationships between the two and different types of engagement in implementing decent work agenda. The third section analyses different roles that brands and buyers have played from the lens of decent work agenda during the post-Rana Plaza period; this has been compared with their activities during the pre-Rana Plaza period. Based on this analysis, the fourth section identifies the key lessons learned in the process of engagement of the buyers and suppliers and the gaps in achieving the agenda. Finally, the fifth section puts forward a set of suggestions for implementing the decent work agenda in the RMG sector.

The buyers and suppliers in Bangladesh's apparel value chain: an overview

The two major market players that are popularly mentioned as 'buyers' and 'suppliers' in the apparel value chain are not of homogenous entities. Different enterprises operate at different tiers in the apparel value chain – brands and retailers operate at tier 1 level, different types of suppliers operate at tier 2 level and sub-contractee enterprises operate at tier 3 level. The suppliers of the apparels sector of Bangladesh are usually categorized as tier 2 and tier 3 enterprises. According to the CPD-RMG Survey 2018,[1] the sector is overwhelmingly dominated by small- and medium-sized enterprises/suppliers (Figure 9.1). Small-sized enterprises with less than 500 workers comprise 48% of total enterprises followed by medium-sized enterprises with having workers in between 500 and 2,500 (43%) and large-sized enterprises with

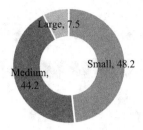

Figure 9.1 Distribution of RMG enterprises (%).
Source: Moazzem, 2018.

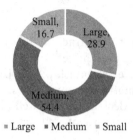

▪ Large   ▪ Medium   ▪ Small

Figure 9.2 Distribution of employment in RMG enterprises (%).
Source: Moazzem, 2018.

employment above 2,500 workers (only 7% enterprises). However, the share of employment is higher in medium-sized enterprises followed by large- and small-sized enterprises respectively (Figure 9.2). The differences in terms of share of enterprises, employment and export orders at the suppliers' end influence the nature of contractual arrangement to be established with the buyers.

On the other hand, buyers comprise brands, retailers, international buyers and buying houses. According to the CPD-RMG Survey 2018, local and international buying houses and buyers dominate the RMG market as one-third of the suppliers are still exclusively working with buying houses/buyers (34.4%) followed by 47.8% suppliers are working either with brands/retailers or with the buyers/buying houses. About 17% of total suppliers have exclusive contractual relation with brands/retailers (Figure 9.3). However, the average number and number of orders offered by the brands/retailers to the suppliers are significantly higher than those of the buyers/buying houses.

The type of buyers working in the apparel value chain and the nature of their contracts with the suppliers are determined by suppliers' production capacity, quality of work and capacity to maintain buyers' code of conduct (CoC). Suppliers' production capacity depends on their size of workforce, use of technologies, management capacities, level of efficiency, etc. In

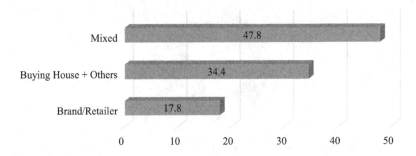

Figure 9.3 Contractual relationship between suppliers and buyers (%).
Source: CPD-RMG Survey, 2018.

this backdrop, the exclusive contractual relationship with brands tends to happen with large-scale enterprises, while mixed nature of contractual arrangements and exclusive relationship with buying houses tend to happen with medium- and small-scale enterprises. Overall, the role of buyers and suppliers in ensuring decent work-related activities needs to take into account their diverse types, nature of contractual relations, level of enforcement of buyers' CoC, etc.

Role of the buyers and suppliers on decent work issues during pre- and post-Rana Plaza period

Workplace safety-related problems during the pre-Rana Plaza period

The level of workplace safety maintained in the factories during the pre-Rana Plaza period had been monitored by the buyers apart from those by the public monitoring agencies (DIFE, Directorate of Labour (DoL), Fire Service and Civil Defense (FSCD) and other agencies). Based on the CoC, buyers/brands were supposed to review the compliance standard of RMG enterprises. There were three different types of compliance monitoring mechanisms: (a) first-party monitoring done by the buyers, (b) third-party monitoring done by the appointed agencies of the buyers and (c) monitoring done by supplying countries' public monitoring agencies. Often, the buyers relied either on first-party or on third-party monitoring to assess the operational compliance of suppliers such as ergonomic balance within the factory, required facilities for workers, wage- and nonwage-related compliances. The physical structural compliance related to workplace safety and security such as fire-, electrical- and building-related issues had not been part of buyers' own assessment mechanism for which they depended on the assessment done by the local public monitoring agencies.

No official data are available about the nature and level of role played by the buyers and suppliers in ensuring workplace safety and security in RMG enterprises. An indirect approach to assess their nature and level of role is to analyse the quality of workplace safety maintained in RMG enterprises during the pre-Rana Plaza period as related data are available. The enterprise-level data of the status of compliance on fire, electrical and structural integrity of the building are available on the websites of the Accord and the Alliance – two brands/retailers/buyers led monitoring initiatives, who assessed over 2,200 enterprises since they formed after the Rana Plaza tragedy. The present study used data of 1,583 factories inspected by the Accord till March 2017, which reflect the condition of workplace safety of the assessed factories during the pre-Rana Plaza period.

The frequency of three sets of problems (fire, electrical and structural) identified in the selected factories widely varies in terms of factories' location, factory size and their year of establishment. The average number of problems per factory related to fire, electrical and structural integrity that were observed in 1,583 factories were 41, 27 and 9 respectively.[2] In other words, electrical problems were most frequently observed in factories followed by fire- and building-related problems. Such factory-related non-compliances were ignored by concerned local authorities while they assessed the physical compliances.

The frequency of electrical, fire and structural integrity problems was the highest in medium-sized enterprises: 67.1% of all electrical problems, 65.9% of fire-related problems and 66.5% of structural problems were identified in medium-sized enterprises (Figure 9.4).[3] Though the frequency of problems is low in large factories, the average number of electrical, fire and structural problems per factory is high for this category. In other words, the gaps in the number of problems are not so high between large-, medium- and small-scale enterprises. Besides, the level of electrical, fire and structural problems is found to be linked with factories' length of operation. These problems

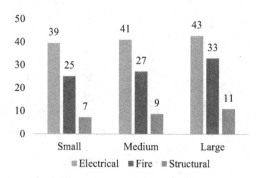

Figure 9.4 Size-wise problems per factory.
Source: CPD-RMG Survey, 2018.

were high in factories which established earlier and are still being used without major renovation. The highest problems have been identified in factories which were established between 1991 and 2012 (Figure 9.5). Over 80% of electrical, fire and structural problems have been observed in the factories which have been established between 1991 and 2012.[4] The higher number of structural problems in factories established before 1990 portrays that the older buildings have more problems due to wear and tear of time.[5]

Overall, older factories without necessary repair and maintenance found to be with weak compliance standards; such factories found among large-sized enterprises as well. Hence the popular perception of large enterprises are 'better complaint' in terms of maintaining safety standards may not necessarily be fully true. In other words, brands and retailers that usually worked with large factories did not pay adequate attention to the problems on physical compliance-related issues. At the same time, the problems identified in small- and medium-sized enterprises are not so small reflecting that there were serious oversight problems in small, medium and sub-contractee factories where buyers, buying houses and partly brands/retailers placed their orders. This suggests their needs to have equal attention to be paid to small- and medium-sized enterprises which usually have more contractual arrangements with buying houses and buyers but less with brands/buyers/retailers.

Analysis of the Accord data also identified the nature of problems in case of fire, electrical and building structures. According to Moazzem et al. (2018b) most of the electrical problems are related to 'electrical prevention' – about 85.9% problems are under that category while the rest (14.1%) are 'behavioural' problems. The frequency of problems of fire issues is found to be higher under the category of 'means of egress' (about 57.2%) which is followed by the category of 'fire prevention' (about 23.0%), 'fire protection/control' (15.7%) and 'behavioural' (about 4.1%). Almost 70.6% of structural integrity problems are under the category of 'physical' while the others are under 'behavioural' category. Overall, a large share of problems under each

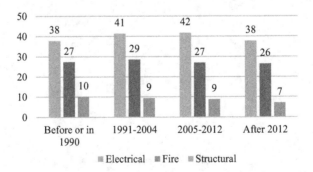

Figure 9.5 Year-wise problems according to establishment year.
Source: CPD-RMG Survey, 2018.

category are related to technical and behavioural problems – remediation of these problems requires both investment for building technical capacities and investment for raising awareness among the users of the factories. In other words, the sustainability in the workplace safety would depend not only on fixing the technical problems but also on regular monitoring and follow-up with appropriate means and instruments. The roles of suppliers and buyers are very important in addressing these gaps through appropriate means and instruments.

Workplace safety-related issues during the post-Rana Plaza period

The role of the buyers to monitor the workplace safety has evolved particularly with the changing demand during the post-Rana Plaza period. The formation of the Accord led by the European brands/retailers and the Alliance led by the North American retailers with a view to monitor the workplace safety are a major departure from the traditional monitoring mechanism of the buyers. The mandate of the Accord and the Alliance were monitoring and inspecting the factories which worked with member companies of these two initiatives; identifying the fire, electrical and building structure problems, developing the corrective action plans (CAPs) with the supplying factories and following up the progress of the CAPs; taking punitive measures in the case of lack of progress of CAPs; and providing technical support and, if necessary, financial support for undertaking necessary remediation. In other words, the physical structural compliance-related problems for which they earlier relied on the assessment of the local authorities have now been done by the brands/retailers as like first-party monitoring. Out of 3,596 enterprises operated in the export-oriented RMG sector, a total of 2,286 (1,572 Accord inspected factories, 714 Alliance inspected factories) enterprises have been monitored under the two initiatives. In other words, about 64% enterprises have been covered under these two initiatives while another 36% enterprises were out of these two initiatives. These remaining enterprises are mostly small, sub-contractee enterprises with contractual relation with local and international buying houses and buyers. It is important to note that these enterprises have been monitored under a separate public sector-led initiative called the 'National Initiatives' (NIs).

The role of the buyers and suppliers in post-Rana Plaza period can be examined in two ways: first, to review the level of remediation of fire, electrical and building structure problems under the three initiatives and second, to examine whether an institutional arrangement has been fixed based on the experience of these initiatives for ensuring sustainable monitoring practices. The progress of remediation of different structural problems reflects how the buyers and suppliers played their role in ensuring workplace safety during post-Rana Plaza period. It is important to note that the present study considered the progress status of remediation of different problems that were identified by the Accord during its first and second reviews which took

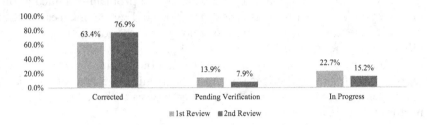

Figure 9.6 Progress status of electrical problems in first and second reviews.
Source: CPD-RMG Survey, 2018.

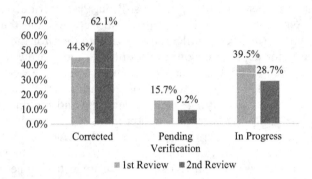

Figure 9.7 Progress status of fire problems in first and second reviews.
Source: CPD-RMG Survey, 2018.

place in February 2017 and August 2017. The state of progress of remediation of electrical, fire and structural problems has been stated as 'corrected', 'pending verification' and 'in progress' in the status reports of Accord-led inspected factories.

In the case of electrical problems, about 63.4% have been 'corrected' during the first review; about 76.9% of the remaining problems have been 'corrected' during the second review (Figure 9.6).[6] In the case of fire-related problems (37,413 problems), 44.8% have been detected as 'corrected' during the first review and 62.1% of the remaining problems have been identified as 'corrected' during the second review (Figure 9.7). In other words, more problems have been corrected over time by the enterprises. In the case of structural problems, the level of progress was rather slow as has been identified in both the first and second reviews. During the first review, only 21.9% problems have been 'corrected' (Figure 9.8), while in the second review about 35.4% of rest of the problems have been 'corrected'.

Major progresses are observed in the case of fire and electrical issues, while progress in structural issues was lagging behind. Constraints of

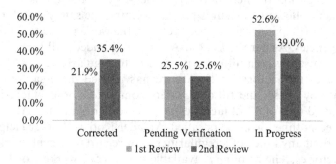

Figure 9.8 Progress status of structural problems in first and second reviews.
Source: CPD-RMG Survey, 2018.

financial resources, lack of incentives for undertaking necessary investment to make the factory complaint due to limited business prospect and plan for relocating factories were the possible reasons regarding the slow progress in remediation-related activities in the factories. While the medium sized-factories have found with more problems, the percentage of problems 'corrected' is high in the case of large factories. In the case of small-scale enterprises the progress of remediation (from 'in progress' to 'corrected' is 46.6%) is rather slow. Most of the small factories suffered due to their limited investment capacity and partly due to lack of interest to invest for remediation due to limited business prospect at the existing location of the factory.

The differences in the pace of implementation of different safety concerns are partly related to different level of investment capacities of the enterprises. This mainly happens in the case of small-scale factories. The responsibility on slow progress of remediation owing to lack of capital for making necessary investment would be imposed partly to the buyers as per the understandings of the Accord/Alliance. Under these initiatives, the brands/buyers are supposed to play a proactive role for making necessary arrangement for funding for the suppliers if required. Although a number of small-scale funding initiatives had been undertaken such as International Finance Corporation (IFC) created fund, Japan International Cooperation Agency (JICA) fund and Agence Francise de Development (AFD) fund, due to procedural complexities most of those funds remained unutilized. There was no special fund for remediation-related activities at the national level; individual factories took loan from banks at market rate of interest. Since the activities are not considered 'commercially' viable, many small enterprises did not get positive response from banks for their request for funding. As a result, many small factories closed down. In other words, the buyers and the suppliers under the initiatives of Accord and Alliance maintained a limit in their activities to improve the workplace safety.

In continuation of their initiatives, the Accord and the Alliance have undertaken follow-up measures for maintaining the safety standards with the direct participation of the management, the workers and the officials of public agencies. As per the Labour Act 2013 (amended), all RMG factories have set up safety committees with a view to regularly review the safety condition of the factories. The Accord has trained these safety committees phase by phase, and till date, safety committees of 353 factories have been trained (out of 1,572 factories). On the other hand, the Alliance has introduced hotline for workers called 'Amader Kotha- Worker Helpline' to inform about any kinds of irregularities with regard to decent employment in the factories. The helpline is available to 1,491,582 workers of 1,004 factories. Since introduced in 2014, a total of 14,545 substantive issues have been reported in the Alliance factories. Those are the attempts to further strengthen the local ownership of the private sector-led monitoring initiatives in the RMG sector.

The institutional obligation for improving workplace safety under the agreement of Sustainability Compact drives the suppliers of the Accord- and Alliance-led initiatives to undertake necessary measures. Besides, they are in fear of losing contracts of their brands/buyers unless be compliant as per the CAPs which pushed them to make necessary investment for remediation. Thus, from the suppliers' point of view they are largely driven by the number of 'push factors'. On the other hand, the buyers' initiatives were driven by both push and pull factors. The pressure from the right-based organizations and consumer groups immediately after the Rana Plaza tragedy pushed the buyers to fix the problems by undertaking measures beyond traditional means. At the same time, such engagement of the buyers in improving workplace safety in a supplying country is quite unique in the context of value chain governance of the apparels sector. The huge investment made by the buyers for improving the compliance standard in a supplying country is rather a pull factor. Given the differences in the perspectives of the buyers and the suppliers in engaging in remediation-related activities, the process of institutionalization of the workplace safety may face difficulties in the future.

'National initiatives' on workplace safety for other factories

As mentioned, there are about 41% enterprises which have no contractual relations with the members of Accord and Alliance. These enterprises have been monitored under the 'NIs' which is managed by the public monitoring agency, DIFE. Given the limited human resources and lack of technical expertise, the monitoring and inspection of these enterprises had been done by several private agencies in technical cooperation of the ILO. Because of lack of preparedness of the DIFE, the follow-up review of the progress of CAPs had been discontinued for long time. In 2018, the government has formed the 'Remediation Coordination Cell (RCC)' with a view to follow up the CAP-related activities of the NI member factories. Unlike the Accord and the Alliance, there were no buyers/buying houses involved in monitoring the implementation of the safety-related activities in these factories. Hence, a huge difference is observed between the private sector-led initiatives and the public sector-led initiatives of monitoring the workplace safety in terms of technical capacity of the monitoring team, logistics and human resources, capacity to implement the decisions including capacity to undertake punitive measures, etc. (Rahman and Moazzem, 2017; Moazzem and Khandker, 2018).

NI-led enterprises are relatively small in size and largely worked with buyers/buying houses or did subcontracting of local large enterprises as tier 2 or tier 3 enterprises. According to the RCC, out of 1,549 NI enterprises only 809 factories were found to be in operation. Of these, 107 factories have completed their full remediation works related to fire, electrical and structural safety issues as per the CAP which was only 13.2% of total factories. Till March 2018, 422 factories remediated more than 50% and 111 factories have remediated more than 80% of compliance-related problems identified in the CAPs. Of the total problems identified, 27% are fire related, 31% are electrical related and 29% are structural safety-related problems which have been remediated till date.

Compared to the initiatives undertaken by the Accord/the Alliance, the NI was found with number of weaknesses including slow progress in monitoring- and implementation-related works, maintaining substandard in inspection process, constraints of human resources, slow progress in monitoring and reviewing process, weak in taking decision against non-complaint factories and unwanted influence of associations such as BGMEA and BKMEA in the decision-making process. In fact, the NI is merely an extension of the public sector-led traditional monitoring initiatives and could not upgrade itself to maintain standards as maintained by those of the Accord and the Alliance. Overall, the elements of institutionalization in the NI-led activities are much weaker.

A comprehensive harmonized monitoring initiative covering all factories is of critical importance in order to implement a sustainable monitoring system. The activities of the Alliance ended in December 2018; on the other hand, the activities of the first phase of the Accord were ended in May 2018 but a part of the safety-related activities remained unfinished. In the meantime, the Accord has restructured in the name 'Transitional Accord' and has recently sought the permission for extension of its activities for another three years. However, there were strong reservations from the government as well as from the BGMEA to allow its activities for full three years. The Accord is now facing a case in the High Court with regard to the extension of the timeline. Overall, the good organizational learning for maintaining workplace safety fell in trouble to get institutionalized without the cooperation of local stakeholders.

Employability-related issues during the pre- and post-Rana Plaza periods

Workers' employability is one of the important areas of concern in the apparel value chain. During the pre-Rana Plaza period, the employability-related issues were addressed through traditional means of 'in-house' training without any special initiatives from both the buyers and the suppliers. In order to ensure regular supply of workers, the suppliers' associations such as BGMEA and BKMEA in collaboration with the government operated a number training centres for providing basic training to entry-level workers. Besides, there are private commercial training centres in different industrial clusters for providing basic training to the workers. There were no arrangements for specialized training for the workers either at public or private sectors. The role of the buyers in strengthening the employability of workers was rather absent.

During the post-Rana Plaza period, workers' employability issue did not get any special attention from both the buyers and the suppliers. However, workers' employment background has improved over time in the case of their average age, average academic attainment, average length of services, etc. However, the sector has yet to standardize the minimum qualifications of workers for entering into the RMG job market. For example, factories did not maintain minimum academic qualification for workers seeking RMG-related jobs; consequently, workers with no formal education (though small in percentage) are still found as production workers (Figure 9.9). While the length of service in garment factories has increased, production workers with work experience of more than 15 years are rarely found. Factories are still non-compliant in terms of providing documents which workers are entitled to – for example, majority of factories still do not provide job experience certificates to workers. Lack of standardization of jobs still remains a major concern in all categories of factories. The problems may be less acute in large-scale enterprises and with enterprises having contractual arrangement with brands.

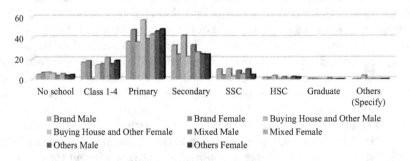

Figure 9.9 Distribution of workers according to their academic qualification.
Source: CPD-RMG Survey, 2018.

In the case of skill development, workers received more training in factories which have contractual arrangements with brands/buyers followed by those with contractual arrangements with buying houses and those having mixed contractual arrangements (Table 9.1). Factories working with brands are usually found to be large-scale enterprises and these enterprises tried to maintain the compliance standards on workers' training. However, these changes in various employability indicators have little relation with various activities undertaken by the buyers and the suppliers during the post-Rana Plaza period. Unlike the combined initiatives of buyers and suppliers for workplace safety under the agreement of the Sustainability Compact, there is no initiative of the two in improving the employability situation in the RMG sector. More importantly, since there are no special activities on employability undertaken under the national and international agreements, there is no institutional pressure to the buyers and the suppliers to make the factories compliant on employability.

Against the wind, the post-Rana Plaza period has experienced sharp changes in the composition, growth and skill of workers, particularly those of female workers. According to the CPD-RMG Study 2018, the composition of female and male workers has been gradually changing (53:47 from 64:46 in 2015) mainly because of rapid rise of male workers vis-à-vis those of female workers. Female workers are perhaps been replaced by male workers because of their limited knowledge about multiple advanced machineries compared to that of male workers (Moazzem et al., 2018). Moreover, technological upgrading in Bangladesh's garment sector is likely to have slowed down the growth of employment in the garment sector (Moazzem and Khandker, 2018). Besides, job market is likely to get pressured as there is a tendency to replace workers by machines when workers' wages have been adjusted. Such replacement of workers usually has adverse impact on employment and most likely on female employment. In the absence of special drive under institutional arrangement/agreement, there are no major initiatives observed in either side of the value chains to address employment-related concerns. Hence, a special effort is necessary from the buyers' and

Table 9.1 Workers' received training from their currently employed factories and factories contractual relation with buyers

Nature of response	Brand		Buying house and other		Mixed		Others	
	Male	Female	Male	Female	Male	Female	Male	Female
Yes	89.6	89.9	83.9	81.1	79.3	85.0	80.3	82.8
No	10.4	10.1	16.1	18.9	20.7	15.0	19.7	17.2
Total	100	100	100	100	100	100	100	100

Source: CPD-RMG Survey, 2018.

the suppliers' side in order to protect employment in the apparels sector by assuring normal growth of employment particularly those of female workers.

Workers' decent wage-related issues during the pre- and post-Rana Plaza periods

Decent wage is a major component of workers' decent work agenda where key players of the RMG value chain such as suppliers and buyers have a direct role to play. Historically, workers in the RMG sector were paid low owing to avoiding timely revision of their wages particularly in the 1980s and 1990s. The pre-Rana Plaza period has experienced adjustment of wages with long time gaps (i.e. 1983, 1995 and 2006) and then adjustment happened in less time gap (2010). Because of long time gap, the revision of the wages could not even address the minimum livelihood requirement of workers. Hence, Bangladesh remained the lowest minimum wage providers among the competing garment-producing countries. A major constraint in this process was institutional weakness. The Minimum Wage Board for RMG workers – the tripartite negotiating platform for revision of minimum wages – was found to be weak in terms of its composition with weak representation of workers, lack of evidence-based discussion and debates, and overwhelming dominance of entrepreneurs in the decision-making process. There was almost no initiative from the buyers' side to better adjust workers' wages other than reiterating their commitment to comply with national rules for minimum wages.

The post-Rana Plaza period is marked by adjustment of wages number of times. Since the Rana Plaza tragedy, the minimum wage of RMG workers has been revised twice – December 2013 and December 2018. In December 2013, the minimum wages of the RMG workers were revised with changes in the composition and in the amount. The structure of minimum wage included a new allowance called 'transport allowance'. An annual increment was introduced which was 5% of the basic wages for workers who worked at least one year in a factory. The wages of grade I to VII workers had been increased by 39.8%–76.7%. For example, minimum wage of grade VII workers had been increased from US$39 to US$69. However, workers' demand for minimum wages was much higher (US$107) – an analysis on living wage for RMG workers carried out by the CPD (Moazzem et al., 2013). Hence, the revised wages for workers were way-below the decent wage required for the workers. Unlike the past, the brands had welcomed the revision of minimum wage in post-Rana Plaza period and announced to raise the CM charges for the suppliers with a view to accommodate the additional costs for increase in wages. During the period of second revision of minimum wages in 2018, workers' wages have increased but at a slower rate compared to that in 2013. The wage for a grade VII worker has increased by 50.9% (considering no annual increment). Compared to the past, the adjustment of wages in 2018 could not satisfy the demand for skilled workers (grades III, IV and V). Consequently, workers had to go for procession with the demand for proper adjustment of the wages in different grades. Unlike in 2013, the response from the buyers was not so specific in 2018.[7] Moreover, buyers' price of production orders to the suppliers has experienced consistent fall over the years which have been affecting suppliers' profit margin and have been weakening their capacity to adjust additional costs (Moazzem and Arfanuzzaman, 2018).[8] The suppliers have approached to the government seeking fiscal incentives in view of the adjustment of the minimum wages; in response, the government has provided three different types of fiscal incentives which include reduction of corporate tax rates from 15% to 12%, significant reduction of source tax (from 1% to 0.25%) and giving waiver from 4.5% VAT on using different domestic logistic and transport services. Thus, new minimum wages will be implemented mainly by taking less profit by the suppliers and partly by getting additional fiscal incentives from the government. The role of the buyers in this process is still not clear.

A major criticism from the workers' side is that after announcement of wages, factory management immediately raises the daily production targets for the workers as part of accommodating part of additional costs in the name of enhancing workers' productivity. Without addressing the other major cost components of the factories, targeting workers alone would imply 'over production' through pressing for 'overwork'. Such incidences of 'overwork' in the factories happened in the knowledge of the brands/buyers. Moreover, there is limited effort from the sides of buyers/brands to ensure living wage/decent wage for workers, although some brands took some efforts sporadically in different countries. There were some initiatives from the global brands and retailers and large suppliers to address workers' livelihood concerns by providing medicare facilities, fair shop facilities and subsidized schooling facilities for the children. However, those facilities have limited impact considering the demand of all garment workers of Bangladesh.

Overall, the issue of decent wages got more attention during the post-Rana Plaza period compared to that in the pre-Rana Plaza period. But the role of brands/buyers and suppliers cannot be considered adequate to ensure decent wages. Various efforts made by brands/buyers to address the wage-related concerns which were observed in 2013 were not continued afterwards. It appears that an institutional approach is necessary under international agreement and NI with a view to ensure workers' decent wage for their decent living.

Workers' rights-related issues during the pre- and post-Rana Plaza periods

Workers' right is an unaddressed issue of the decent work agenda in the RMG value chain of Bangladesh. The Pre-Rana Plaza period was criticized for a lack of organized voice of workers. There were negligible number of trade unions operated at the factory level (in less than 100 factory-level organizations were registered). But most of those were non-functional due to lack of scope for discussion and debate on workers' rights and entitlements including wages and overtime allowances and their timely payments and weekly and casual leaves and festival bonuses and other facilities/entitlements. Due to faulty and cumbersome procedures trade unions could not be registered; rather workers attempted to form trade unions often victimized. On the other hand, the workers' participation committees (WPCs) were almost non-functional because of lack of cooperation from the employers' side. Besides the committees had been formed in the selection process where management selected the workers' representatives who often did not represent the workers. Lack of voice and non-functional workers' organizations had been considered as some of the major weaknesses of establishing workers' rights.

The improvement of workers' rights was a major focus of the Sustainability Compact under which various regulatory and institutional reform measures had been identified for implementation. Given the nature of engagement, brands/buyers have a role to play along with those of suppliers in order to improve workers' rights in the workplace. Despite various initiatives, the post-Rana Plaza period did not bring major changes in the day-to-day operations of workers' rights. A number of measures have been undertaken with a view to better industrial relations and to establish effective workers' organizations in the workplace. The amendment of labor law titled 'Labour Act 2013 (amended)' made necessary changes in order to make it easy to establish trade unions at the workplace; besides, it introduced election system for workers' representatives in the WPCs. CPD-RMG survey 2018 shows that 71% of factories have introduced election-based WPCs in their factories (Table 9.1) and these committees regularly met and discussed issues of their interest. However, poor implementation of different decisions taken by these committees is still a major concern. A weak state of WPCs partly indicates that the brands/buyers are less involved in making these organizations effective/functional.

Trade union-related activities did not increase during the post-Rana Plaza period. Although there was a hype immediately after the amendment of labor law in 2013 to form new trade unions, that hype did not continue for long. According to the CPD-RMG Survey 2018, only 2%–3% enterprises have trade unions which are mostly available in factories where brands operate (Table 9.2). No trade union-related activities observed in factories where buying houses and mixed form of contractual arrangements with the suppliers prevail. Moreover, workers face different kinds of harassment from different quarters where limited level of cooperation is approached to workers from the buyers/brands. In other words, the role of buyers/brands in facilitating establishment of workers' organizations and their effective functioning remains at poor state. However, global trade union groups have shown increasing interest on trade union-related activities in Bangladesh. The consumer groups and right-based organizations have shown their concerns about workers' rights though that have limited visible impact.

ble 9.2 Existence of workers' organizations in sample enterprises

	Enterprises working under different contractual arrangements with										
	Brand		Buying house and other		Mixed		Others		Total		
	Male	Female	Male	Female	Male	Female	Male	Female	Male	Female	Total
of factories have WPC	85.0	81.2	58.1	78.4	78.7	82.9	75.2	67.8	81.1	79.4	80.0
of workers took at least some kinds of services from the WPC	13.0	10.2	22.2	13.8	17.8	16.9	19.4	15.4	15.1	12.3	13.3
of factories have trade union	2.3	3.5	0.0	0.0	0.0	0.0	2.2	4.2	1.8	2.8	2.5

rce: CPD-RMG Survey, 2018.

There is an attempt from the Accord to play a role in workers' rights issues by broadening their scope of work under the transition Accord. However, such changes in the Accord's scope of work were not appreciated by the suppliers and the government. Unlike the workplace safety, the problems related to workers' organizations especially those of trade unions are more complex and politically sensitive. Hence, the suppliers and government were less enthusiastic about Accord's work on trade union-related issues in the second phase. Moreover, an international organization such as ILO has been actively working with workers' organizations in improving industrial relations through social dialogue. Taking those into account, brands/buyers need to work closely with ILO and local stakeholders with regard to establishing better functioning WPCs and the trade unions in the RMG sector.

Overall, although various activities on workers' rights have been undertaken under the NI and international agreements during the post-Rana Plaza period, those activities have yet to develop any organizational learning under which institutionalization process of workers' rights and workers' organizations could be set in.

Stance of the buyers and suppliers towards ensuring decent work

Overtly focused on workplace safety issues but low or no focus on non-safety issues

The Post-Rana Plaza initiatives on the decent work under the Sustainability Compact and the NIs could not maintain balance in designing the programme focusing on four different components of the decent wage. The activities were overtly focused on workplace safety and security, but less or no activities on other three components such as employability, decent wage and workers' rights. Given the urgency in addressing the safety concerns immediately after the tragic industrial accidents in 2012 and 2013, putting priority on workplace safety issues is logical. However, there should have been a systemic approach to address other three issues phase by phase through the programme where less/no attention has been shown by the key stakeholders.

Ensuring workers' rights in the RMG value chain is the second most targeted activity under the international agreements and NIs. In this connection, necessary regulatory reforms have been undertaken by amending the Labour Act, introducing the labor rules, improving the processes for applying for the trade union and reducing the minimum share of workers for applying trade unions particularly due to the pressure of the ILO. With the amendment of the law, workers' representatives in the WPCs have been elected. Despite those changes, a number of new trade unions in the RMG factories did not rise; the existing trade unions were found to be either moderately or non-functional. The WPC activities did not ensure their effectiveness. The engagement of the buyers was not appreciated in full due to lack of clarity of their work as well as conflict with the activities of other organizations (such as ILO).

The decent wage issue has been widely discussed and debated but the initiatives undertaken were mostly confined to regularizing the adjustment of wages. The commitment to ensure decent living by providing 'living wage' had been raised by lead brands and buyers immediately after the collapse of the Rana Plaza; however, the commitment has gradually faded away without having comprehensive efforts afterwards. Most importantly, the absence of addressing the issue under the international agreement has gradually reduced the commitment from the buyers' side as the pressure from the key stakeholders including consumers and international workers' organizations eased. This urges the requirement of an institutional commitment in addressing the decent wages for workers in the global value chain.

The issue of employability was neither included in the agreements nor received any priority in the activities of the buyers and suppliers. The changes in structure and composition of the workforce observed in the post-Rana Plaza period in the case of average age of workers, their length of services, female-male ratio of workforce, etc., happened with the changes in product composition, requirement of skills in the production processes, usages of advanced technologies, etc. In contrast, a number of those initiatives have adverse impact on female employment, and also on preparation of female workers for advanced technologies. Without a targeted institutional effort, the commitment from the buyers and suppliers in addressing the employability concern would be difficult to ensure.

A comprehensive decent work agenda needs to address all four components which are difficult to achieve under the existing agreements/arrangement. Given the importance of institutional commitment in ensuring different targets, similar types of international agreement/NI would be required to address all components of the decent work agenda.

Absence of same level of participation by all categories of buyers and suppliers

The role played by brands/buyers and suppliers during the post-Rana Plaza period is a step forward towards improving decent work in the apparel value chain. The institution-driven decent work-related initiatives under the international agreements (the Sustainability Compact)/the arrangement (USTR action plan) pushed different stakeholders to comply with different regulatory, operational and management-related commitments. The engagements of brands/buyers and suppliers in this process are largely driven by two opposite set of factors – push factor and pull factor. In the case of buyers, the engagements were a blend of pull and push factors, particularly in the case of workplace safety and workers' rights issues; while in the case of suppliers the engagements were mostly driven by push factors. Besides all categories of buyers/brands and suppliers did not take part at similar level in those activities, i.e. workplace safety and security. Moreover, engagement of the buyers and suppliers in employability issues was not only absent but those were rather directed in opposite directions. A large segment of market players such as local and international buying houses, small-scale suppliers and subcontracting enterprises were by and large absent in the process of implementing various initiatives. The consumers were less aware and less engaged in ensuring decent work agenda in the value chain. Overall, the post-Rana Plaza initiatives have ensured participation of a large section of buyers and suppliers in the selected set of decent work activities but could not ensure participation of all stakeholders in full. Without active engagement of all stakeholders, the outcome of the initiatives would be less robust with limited possibility for sustainability.

Limited role of other market players in ensuring decent work agenda

An implementation of the decent work agenda by relying only on the market-based mechanism through the participation of the buyers and the suppliers would be difficult. A large part of the decent work agenda is related to social compliances where institutional approach is found to be more effective. Hence the market-based mechanism and institutional mechanism need to be blended efficiently. As part of implementing the institutional mechanism, appropriate rules, regulations, organizations, standard operating procedures (SOP) and awareness of the stakeholders would be important. These activities are to be developed, implemented and monitored by the government, international organizations (such as ILO), development partners and local and international workers' organizations, consumer groups, right-based organizations, etc.

In the post-Rana Plaza period, the government, the development partners, international organizations and local and international workers' organizations have participated at different levels under the commitment of the international agreements and NIs. However, the participation of the consumers was rather limited in those activities. Hence, comprehensive decent work agenda blended with market-based and institution-based means and instruments needs to be developed with the participation of major stakeholders with a view to ensure sustainable development of the value chain.

Learning on international standards for improving workplace safety

The organizational learning on workplace safety and security is a unique experience of the apparels sector of Bangladesh. As part of the process, a comprehensive guideline on workplace safety and security has been developed based on the relevant national rules and regulations as well as on relevant international regulations in case the national rules are not sufficient, such guideline has been vetted through a national-level consultative process; SOP for monitoring, follow-up and implementation have been developed; international experts on workplace safety have been recruited for management and operation; global steering committee as well as local level advisory committees have been formed; status of the problems and review of the progress of the CAPs have been reported in the website as part of transparency initiative; strict follow-up and punitive measures have been maintained on non-compliance issues; dispute settlement mechanism was established; the process recognized the factories for complete remediation through certification, etc. Following such a rigorous process helped implementing the CAPs efficiently. The public monitoring agencies such as DIFE and DoL are inexperienced in dealing with such extensive monitoring, reporting and transparency standards. Bangladesh's public monitoring agencies could restructure their operational modalities and upgrade their skills and capacities based on this global level example of monitoring of the Accord and the Alliance.

Limited progress towards institutionalization of the decent work agenda

The sustainability of the existing decent work-related activities would be difficult to ensure unless the individual/collective/organizational learnings could be converted into institutionalization process. According to Moazzem and Khandker (2016) the huge knowledge and experience gathered in the process of restructuring, remediation and value chain governance are treasure of 'organizational learning'. Such 'organizational learning' could be used by the stakeholders as a 'test case' for implementing the decent work agenda in the apparels sector. The main issue of concern is how effectively the existing initiatives will run in the absence of outside influence such as pressure under international agreements and NIs. Hence there is a need for 'systemic power' to institutionalize the whole process. To move to the ultimate goal of institutionalization, the government, buyers, workers, entrepreneurs and development partners all need to play proactive role in this process.

Suggestions for implementing decent work agenda in the apparel value chain: way forward

The post-Rana Plaza initiatives are a step forward in implementing the decent work agenda in the apparels sector value chain of Bangladesh. The international agreement of the Sustainability Compact, USTR Plan of Action and the NI had identified a set of activities which the stakeholders have committed to implement. However, the activities pursued have primarily focused on workplace safety issues and, partly, on workers' rights issues. However, these did not put focus on the other two components of the decent work agenda. Moreover, participation of buyers and suppliers was largely confined to brands, retailers, international buyers and large- and medium-scale suppliers. On the other hand, participation of the local and international buying houses and small-scale enterprises and sub-contractee enterprises was either low or absent. Moreover, the nature of their engagement was either proactive or reactive in nature depending on the level of influence of various push/pull factors. There is a significant organizational learning which has been gathered through this process. However, the scope for institutionalization of the decent work agenda, however partial this may be, is still uncertain because of the absence of a high level of commitment from all stakeholders including the buyers, suppliers, government, international organization, workers' organizations, consumer groups and rights-based organizations.

Since the decent work agenda is not driven by a market-based mechanism only, because of the inherent components of social compliances, an appropriate blend with institutional mechanism needs to be ensured. In this context, following activities need to be taken into account. *First*, a comprehensive decent work agenda needs to be developed putting focus on the four identified components. Implementation of the agenda should have the commitment of all key stakeholders under an international agreement and along with a national plan of action. *Second*, it is important to ensure participation of all stakeholders in the process of implementation of the decent work agenda; there is no scope for a section of the stakeholders not participating in this process. *Third*, participation and contribution of consumers and rights-based organizations will be required through raising of awareness on different related issues. *Fourth*, there should be a proactive attitude among all stakeholders towards implementing different activities of decent work despite the fact that some of the factors may cause adverse impact for a number of stakeholders. Without high level of commitment on the part of the stakeholders, the pace of implementation and the consequent generation of results would be rather slow. *Fifth*, sustainability of various initiatives will depend on how effectively the organizational learning of the decent work-related activities could be institutionalized.

Notes

1 The Centre for Policy Dialogue has undertaken a study titled 'New Dynamics of Bangladesh's RMG Enterprises: Perspectives on Restructuring, Upgradation and Compliance Assurance'. In short the study is called 'CPD-RMG Study 2018'. As part of the study, a nationally representative sample survey on 226 enterprises and 2,123 workers of those enterprises has been carried out on six key areas such as management, technology, products, cost and production, workers and remediation works.
2 The total number of fire, electrical and structural integrity problems identified in two reviews of Accord were 63,948, 43,231 and 13,695 respectively.
3 Since the number of factories is small in large-scale enterprises, the frequency of electrical, fire and structural problems is also low there.
4 The number of problems identified in factories established after 2012 is found to be low perhaps due to shorter length of use of these buildings. The average number of electrical and fire problems per factory is high in the factories whose establishment year is between 1991 and 2012 while the average number of structural problems per factory is high in the factories whose establishment year is before 1990 (Figure 9.7).
5 Due to technological advances and greater awareness about safety standards by factory management, few electrical, fire and structural problems have been detected in factories which have been established in recent years (e.g. factories established after 2012).
6 Only a small number of problems are found to be in the status of either 'pending verification' or 'in progress'.
7 An anecdotal information on buyers' response indicates that about 70% of buyers/brands would not accommodate the additional wage cost.
8 A detailed analysis on distribution of margin in the apparels value chain in Bangladesh has been discussed in Moazzem and Basak (2015).

References

Moazzem, K.G. and Basak, K.K. 2015. 'Margin and Its Relation with Firm Level Compliance: Illustration on Bangladesh Apparel Value Chain', Centre for Policy Dialogue, Dhaka.

Moazzem, K. G. and Khandker, A. 2016. *Post-Rana Plaza Developments in Bangladesh: Towards Building a Responsible Supply Chain in the Apparel Sector.* Centre for Policy Dialogue (CPD) and Pathak Shamabesh, Dhaka.

Moazzem, K.G. and A. Khandker, 2018. 'Ongoing Upgrading in RMG Enterprises: Preliminary Results from a Survey', Paper presented in a dialogue on 'Ongoing Upgradation in RMG Enterprises: Results from a Survey' held on 3 March, 2018.

Moazzem, K.G., A. Khandker, M.R. Ahmad and S. Ali (2018a). *Strengthening the Social Dialogue Mechanism within Weak Enabling Environment: The Case of Bangladesh's RMG Industry*, CPD Monograph 9, Centre for Policy Dialogue (CPD), Dhaka.

Moazzem, K.G. et al. (2018b). *New Dynamics of Bangladesh's Apparels Enterprises: Perspectives on Restructuring, Upgradation and Compliance Assurance*, Centre for Policy Dialogue (CPD), Dhaka.

Moazzem, K.G. and Md. Arfanuzzaman (2018). *Livelihood Challenges of RMG Workers: Exploring Scopes within the Structure of Minimum Wages and Beyond*, CPD Working Paper Series 122, Centre for Policy Dialogue (CPD), Dhaka.

Moazzem, K.G., S. Raz, D. Miller, C. Schlangen and I.v.d. Sluijs, 2013. *Estimating a Living Minimum Wage for the Ready Made Garment Sector in Bangladesh.* September. Available at: www.irinavandersluijs.nl/site/assets/files/1067/living_wage_report_bangladesh.pdf.

Rahman, M. and Moazzem, K. G. (2017). "The Legacy of Rana Plaza: Improving Labour and Social Standards in Bangladesh's Apparel Industry." In Hira, A. and Benson-Rea, M. (eds.) *Governing Corporate Social Responsibility in the Apparel Industry after Rana Plaza*. New York: Palgrave Macmillan.

United State Fashion Industry Association (USFIA), 2017. *Sourcing Trends & Outlook for 2017.* March 28. Washington. Available at: www.usfashionindustry.com/pdf_files/USFIA-Sourcing-Trends-Outlook-2017.pdf.

Part IV

Rethinking solutions

From an international perspective

10 Can place-based network contracting foster decent work in informal segments of global garment chains? Lessons from Mewat, India[1]

Meenu Tewari

Introduction

Over the past decade, a series of horrific workplace disasters in garment factories in Bangladesh, Peru, Honduras and other supplier countries, where much of the globe's output of low-cost clothing is produced, has served to shine a bright light on the dangerous and exploitative working conditions that continue to prevail in unmonitored segments of global garment chains. As firms search for ever lower prices in the face of intensified global competition and consolidation in a post-quota world, and as hyper-speed turnaround times have become the norm in this era of fast fashion, more and more of the globe's apparel output is produced by workers laboring for cascading tiers of no-name subcontractors. These opaque labor chains cannot be reached by the systems of private governance and elaborate third-party enforcement audits that companies have put in place over the last 30 years to combat poor working conditions, often with dire consequences (Locke 2013, Lund-Thompson and Nadvi 2010, Barrientos and Smith 2007, Barrientos 2008, Barrientos et al. 2011, Posthuma and Nathan 2010, O'Rourke 2002, Locke et al. 2007, Tewari 2010).

A global flashpoint arrived in 2013 when, on the heels of a horrific fatal fire at Bangladesh's Tazreen fashions, more than 1,100 workers perished in a catastrophic building collapse in Bangladesh's Rana Plaza, injuring many more (Manik and Yardley 2012 and 2013, Burke 2014, O'Connor 2014). The global outcry over the disaster was immediate and fierce. In the wake of the contestation and uproar that followed, a new experimental arrangement came into being: the Accord for Fire and Building Safety in Bangladesh. The Accord, for the first time, brought together at least 180 leading global apparel brands into a five-year binding agreement with two transnational labor union federations, seven Bangladeshi labor unions and multilateral organizations like the International Labour Organization (ILO) to inspect and ensure structural safety of all the factories where their orders would be executed over the next five years (Accord, 2013, Scheper 2017). They also agreed to maintain sourcing volumes from Bangladesh. A second nonbinding agreement between 28

US-based garment brands, the Alliance for Bangladesh Worker Safety, also informally committed to focusing on similar inspections and ensuring the structural safety of the factories they sourced from. This year both agreements are set to expire or be reviewed.

Are Bangladeshi workers safer today as a result of the Accord and Alliance? Are the gains deep enough to be sustained even after these global tripartite mechanisms are phased out? As the chapters in this volume, and others in the wider literature, begin to critically assess the effects of the Accord and Alliance on labor safety, I argue in this chapter that the structural challenges faced by low-wage workers in low value-added segments of global industries are deep. Alongside top-down, multilateral arrangements like the Accord, we also need to think of more proximate, home-grown and locally embedded initiatives that can simultaneously build vigilance and accountability from the bottom-up. This "sandwich" strategy of scrutiny (Fox 2014), where mobilization, engagement and oversight from the bottom meet reformist mechanisms from above, can serve to deepen workers' own agency while building local institutions (and institutional capacity) that will remain in place even after more global or national initiatives have passed.

In this chapter I report on lessons drawn from a new experiment in relational contracting that was introduced in Mewat, India, in 2008 by Gap Inc. The experiment seeks to ensure better paying, safer and more transparent working conditions for workers at the bottom of global garment chains – home-based workers who generally labor in anonymity behind tiers of no-name subcontractors. The novelty of the experiment lies in three key features: (i) it is a *place-based* work arrangement that is anchored in the community where workers live. Moving beyond worker hostels and the factory floor, the arrangement is centered around a community workplace that straddles the places where workers live and where they work. It is a labor-market-wide initiative and includes all workers in a community, not only those currently employed by a garment exporter.

(ii) Rather than top-down or bottom-up forms of governance, Mewat's supply arrangement has a *networked form of intermediation* that includes workers (and their civic advocates), global brands and the garment exporters they place orders with, and the state. Each partner has a distinct role, and collectively provides training, a community-based work platform outside the home and factory, a crèche and logistics support that links the workers with the export market. The arrangement is loosely overseen by public sector bureaucrats who hail not from the ministry of labor nor from the ministry of small and medium enterprises, but from social welfare ministries (women and child development, and rural development in the case of Mewat). These street-level social bureaucrats have worked in these communities for years to build civic arrangements around education and savings societies, and hence are familiar to local residents. (iii) The economic ties of the new supply arrangement are thus *built on the backs of long years of prior social work* and institution building in these communities supported by the state. Transparency and accountability around working conditions and payment mechanisms also rests on the presence of these prior civic and social arrangements that have been in place and are being continuously expanded. Workers and their civic partners negotiate rates with exporters, and based on hours worked, workers receive payments directly in their bank accounts opened as part of their involvement in local savings societies.

The rest of the chapter explains how the networked economic ties of the Mewat model work, how they are embedded within place-based, social community institutions, and what lessons this might offer other regions, including Bangladesh.

As described in Tewari (2017), this research is based on 24 interviews conducted in Mewat and in the National Capital Region (NCR) in 2011 and 2013 through a purposive, snowball sampling method. The author conducted interviews with Indian government official in the Ministry of Women and Child Development (MoWCD) and the Ministry of Rural Development (MoRD), the former director of global partnerships and social responsibility for Gap, the global brand that had coordinate the arrangement, a local buying house, two exporters, members of the civic organization Society for the Promotion of Youth and Masses (SPYM), which anchored the initiative locally, and a number of the workers involved in garment embroidery in Mewat's Hathin region, and one of two villages involved in the project. These open-ended qualitative interviews and focus groups were supplemented by internal reports on the program prepared by Gap, SPYM, the government and published accounts of other embroidery clusters available in the literature (Mezzadari 2011, Unni and Scaria 2009).

The model and its origins

The Mewat model originated in 2008 in the wake of Gap Inc.'s efforts to deal with the discovery of trafficked child labor in some of its North Indian factories a year earlier and the public shaming that followed (BBC 2007). "This problem [of trafficking] was bigger than what a single brand could handle alone," said Gap's then director of global partnerships and social responsibility. The company therefore turned to the Government's Ministry of Women and Child Development, and a consortium of other brands, the ILO and UN Agencies to brainstorm how brands could ensure that not just specific firms, but entire regions they sourced from could be free of some of the worst problems of trafficking, child labor and poor working conditions.

Under the leadership of an officer of the Ministry of Women and Child Development, and in consultation with other actors, Gap picked Mewat, a rural region in Haryana state with indigenous hand embroidery skills, and just an hour away from near garment export hub of the National Capital

Region, as the site for the new experiment that aimed to create a fair and transparent arrangement to cut out traditional middlemen from home-based subcontracting systems and assure fair wages and safe working conditions.

The Ministry official recommended Mewat not only because the region's largely Meo-Muslim community had a long tradition of embroidery skills that had never been seriously developed despite the proximity to major garment centers. The Ministry had been working in the region for over 15 years, partnering with local civic and community organizations to help create self-self groups among the local residents, especially women, help them open bank accounts, organize group savings societies and initiate income generation activities. After years of work trust had been forged between the reclusive community and the state, and the Ministry saw this as an opportunity to build on this work by layering over the social networks they had built over the years, new economic networks that would bring training and formal links with export markets to the region. The Ministry had been working with the SPYM,[2] an NGO in Mewat, whom Gap allied with to serve as the local anchor around which the new initiative was built. Two communities within Mewat – Hathin and Nagina – where the NGO had been most active were chosen as pilot sites.

The partners

The partners that came together to implement the Mewat model each had a distinct role to play. The Ministry officials were the "binding agents" of the team. They brought the different partners together and served as overall promoters of the initiative. Gap Inc. was the main coordinator of the program and designer of its supply arrangements. Gap's India office joined hands with a Delhi-based buying house (IM) to implement the project. Together they brought in two exporters from their supply networks, one for each of the two pilot communities that had been chosen – Hathin and Nagina. Each exporter was responsible for training workers in their respective community, upgrading their skills as needed, placing orders and developing a sourcing system in each community.

SPYM, the local NGO that had worked in Mewat for years, would anchor the initiative by renting a community workspaces in the heart of the two pilot towns and coordinating the workers and their time there. This space would be the "public" or "community" worksite for the project where local women would be trained and where they would come to work based on the hours they wanted to put in. SPYM would also provide some space for a crèche in the same building and staff the work centers with two supervisors to coordinate orders, supervision and payments. Gap provided two $5,000 grants to cover initial rent and set up costs, but eventually the work centers would be self-sufficient. They would cover their costs by retaining 20% of each order value as administrative overhead. If orders were consistent, this was expected to be sufficient to pay for the program.

Traits of the Mewat model

A network approach to intermediation

Five goals shaped the project's organizational design: (i) cutting out middlemen, (ii) curtailing competition between buyers to prevent undercutting of prices, (iii) providing a safe, easy-to-monitor working environment, free of child labor and human trafficking, (iv) training workers to meet the needs of the exporter and (v) ensuring workers were paid fair, timely and transparent wages. Let us examine how each goal or principle was achieved.

Cutting out the middlemen

To cut out middlemen and link the workers to the market, the network picked two regions in Mewat, as we noted, and brought in two Delhi-based exporters from their own supply networks: Gap brought OCL into Hathin, and IM-linked exporter RD to Nagina. The spatial division of labor was in part based on the kinds of products each exporter specialized in and the nature of skills each community had. OCL was mainly looking for hand embroidered beadwork on women's clothing, while RD was looking for more specialized large frame embroidery work in addition to handwork, a skill that workers in Nagina had.

The decision to bring in only one exporter into each community was motivated by a desire to prevent competition between buyers.

> From our experience with other prior models we realised that if you get two exporters without any MOU's [Memorandum of Understanding] into the same community, they try competing with each other...there is a whole price chaos which starts and then workers get divided because they don't want to do your order because in this particular season they will get 10 rupees extra on a particular garment. During the lean season they drive wages down. So we decided that we were going to do this differently.
>
> (GDGP interview 2011)

In effect, however, this arrangement created a monopsonistic situation where each exporter as the sole buyer of workers' output in each region had some market power in determining the size of orders it would place there with the ability to potentially influence rates.

The exporters were responsible for training workers in each region and upgrading their skills to the levels required for the products they intended to source from them. Besides training, the exporters had to also provide for work-time flexibility. Many of the women in this culturally conservative region had not worked outside their homes before and for them to even participate, balancing household responsibilities with any extra-household work was critical. To accommodate this uncertainty about actual labor supply per day, the exporters' strategy was to train widely. Anyone willing or interested in working at the center was provided training.

Before the first formal orders were placed in December 2008, the two exporters sent production supervisors to the communities to carry out detailed assessments of existing skill levels. The supervisors conducted time studies on simple orders, then targeted training to bring workers up to the basic skill levels they needed. The company's supervisors spent two to three hours every day for about a month training workers in various aspects of the kind of embroidery they would expect to source from the region. In Nagina, the project team worked with the exporter to train workers in the more complex large frame embroidery techniques. Gap subsidized this more sophisticated training, and even paid to bring two people "from Bareilly [an established center for frame embroidery in a neighboring state] to come and train these workers" (GDGP interview 2011).

The point of this relatively intense interaction with the workers was also to understand their work habits and gauge their constraints and the social structure of the community and its expectations about garment work. For example, the supervisors found that even minimal training went a long way given the workers' existing skills. This was evident in the unusually low rejection rates even in the earliest orders that were placed during the testing phase – a pattern that has continued since. But it also made it clear to them that some of the most skilled workers may not be able to put in as much time as they could like given family demands. By the time formal orders were placed in late 2008; therefore, about 800 women had been trained across the two sites and the exporters knew what to expect and what size of order they could place in each site (MK Interview 2011, AK Interview 2013).[3]

This focused training, according to the Gap DGP, helped improve performance from the very start and provided a rich pool of workers to draw from. "With one month's training they were producing for Gap and Monsoon and Next... which has never happened in any other community [we have worked with in India]" (GDGP Interview 2011). Subsequently, the exporters used downtime in orders to add more training hours and deepen the skills as needed. "Indeed the idea was to use seasonality to the program's advantage and provide training upgrades to the women in the slack season" (GDGP Interview 2011).

From the partners' perspective, the motivation behind this arrangement in which the buyer/exporter trained widely and prepared the workers in the communities they sourced from was that the factory's investment of its own time, money and effort to train and the workers would serve as an incentive to build longer-term ties between the workers and exporters. Not only would this help develop the community by providing steady work that enhanced local livelihoods but it could also help create a deeper handwork supply base in the region. The monopsonistic arrangement also allowed each firm to internalize the positive externality of the training it had invested in, overcoming a problem that generally leads to the potential under-provision of portable training by private companies (Brunello and De Paola 2004). In return for training the workers and developing local skills, each investing exporter got the benefit of sole access to an assured pool of handworkers in close proximity to their factories without the threat of rate increases or being outbid by other interested factories or having their workers poached (IM Interview 2011).

Providing a safe place to work with fair and transparent wage setting

To provide a safe place to work that would be child-labor free and provide decent working conditions, the program decided to bring women outside from their homes to the "community" based work center run by SPYM. In Hathin, the site that I visited in 2011, the project's worksite was in a community center in the center of town. SPYM had a large hall that served as the workspace, a small office and a crèche upstairs. "None of the women have to walk more than 10 minutes from their homes to reach these community centers" (SPYM Interview 2011). Locating the work centers in familiar community buildings, SPYM's long years of work with the government in the region and its embeddedness in the community gave the project legitimacy in the eyes of the local community that Gap, IM or the exporters working individually would have had a hard time achieving on their own as outsiders.

SPYM hired a local team of two men and one woman (a skilled worker from the community) to run and manage the work centers on a day-to-day basis; they were paid a salary by SPYM (initially from the grant that Gap gave them, and subsequently from 20% of the value of the orders that it retained for overhead). Initially SPYM negotiated rates with the exporters, but very soon the women workers took over this role. Gap and its partner (IM) did not interfere in rate negotiations except to ensure that minimum wages were paid.

Besides managing day-to-day operations, SPYM invested in the project in a second way. Despite the fact that the work was based on piece rates, and factories often can delay payments, the program partners and SPYM made a commitment to make regular monthly payments to the embroidery workers who worked through the center. The payments were made directly to workers' bank accounts. Having or opening a bank account was a tacit condition for working at the center; most already had them. SPYM paid the workers on the seventh day of each month for the hours they had worked during the previous month. Each worker maintained a passbook where she noted her hours worked, as did SPYM. SPYM later recouped its advance (or monthly) payments when the exporters paid for their orders. This "pre-payment" by SPYM was supported in part by the grant from Gap, and in part by SPYM's own funds. The primary intent of this interesting innovation was to maintain a regular income cycle for the workers and shield them from fluctuations in buyer payments that are often routine, while maintaining support from their families for their continued work at the center.

The active presence of the Ministry initially also brought the local elite along. The elite were comforted by the fact that "outsiders" were not taking over local work practices – the government was present. The local administration and elected councilors also did not oppose the project because of the Ministry's role. The leaders of the dominant local Muslim community as well as the minority Hindu community closely monitored the interaction of outsiders with the women of their community. The Ministry's direct presence in the project, and its longstanding work in the area, along with SPYM, went a long way toward getting the local elite to tacitly support the project. The Ministry for its own part was itself sensitive to local concerns and used its internal and informal channels to keep the leaders informed of the project's activities and aims.

The state provided legitimacy and accountability in the eyes of the community, but did not put any money into the project directly beyond in-kind facilitation of the partnership and the prior support it had given to SPYM for the development of SHGs across all 400 villages and towns of Mewat district. By contrast the brands, exporters and the NGO did put their own money into the project directly or indirectly. Gap gave a total of $10,000 to SPYM over a two-year period to help set up the project, the exporters invested time to train workers for a month before placing orders and SPYM used its own space and time.

Workers and their interests

Garment work is notoriously seasonal. It is also demanding. Orders have to be fulfilled within tight turnaround times, and coordinating across a flexible group of workers can be stressful. How did Mewat's women workers understand their new identities as participants in global export chains? How did their work-time constraints fit into the cycles of demand by exporters and their tight turnaround times? Who negotiated the contracts? Was there any competition over how much work each worker would get?

In the early days of the program, three aspects of the project's design helped consolidate a collective identity around work in each community. The shared workplace; the month-long training where women met and worked together and were tested together, coached together; and the sense of pride over their history of skill and the shared costs of defect and rejection rates on all workers had the unintended consequence of building a collective brand image around women's work in each community. The presence of company supervisors who supervised their work and trained them also brought a new proximity between each worker and the structure of export cycles. Earlier, working out of their own homes, women conferred and met only the middleman who looked for the lowest rates and had little time or incentive to explain to them the demands of quality, consistency and turnaround times. Interacting with the company staff helped the workers' understand their own role in the factory's work and export cycle and eventually the worth of their own work to the factory, and how to bargain intelligently.

For example, the hours that each worker put in dependent on her personal constraints and hence were flexible. But gradually a shared responsibility and collective identity developed among the workers and mechanisms emerged to troubleshoot difficult orders or ensure timely delivery. The work centers opened at 8:30 a.m. and remained open until 7 p.m. (or even longer when necessary). While no one worked continuously, throughout the first year when flow of orders was regular at least 60–100 women came to the center regularly. During peak loads, as many as 150 women worked at the center (Focus group, Hathin 2011). Despite the uneven working hours that each worker could individually contribute, they began to understand how much time and work hours each order would require and a tacit leadership structure emerged where the workers negotiated constraints to meet tight deadlines, "because it was about the image [reputation] of our community" (Focus group, Hathin 2011).

To reinforce this sense of community responsibility, Gap and IM brought in student interns and professors from the Pearl Academy of Fashion in New Delhi to analyze the group's work processes and engage them on the process of garment production, exports and good work practices. This involved local innovations and awareness around storage, "clean working" – wearing gloves to keep the items clean, scheduling strategies and ways to reduce defects. All sides testified to this learning dynamic and growth in confidence by pointing out that rejection rates were consistently very low (IM interview 2011, GDGP interview 2011).

As they learned more about how their work was valued by others, and as they observed fluctuations in fashion and in rates, they came to understand that in some seasons embroidery was in high fashion, and that their work was more important to the exporter's orders than at other times. They thus developed their own capacities to bargain with the exporters during those times. They noticed that while exporters reduced their rates during slack times, they did not raise them above the minimum during times when "embroidery was in season." If their work is worth more at that time, it was fair that they should be paid more. So while, initially SPYM negotiated rates, by the end of the first year the women themselves took over the process of negotiating rates, deciding which orders to take and which to decline (Focus group, Hathin 2011).

The sense of collective agency that the workers developed over their craft, then, was an important by-product of networked supply arrangement.

Outcomes and challenges

Initial success

The early success of the Mewat project was striking. By early 2009, a year after it was launched, about 800 women workers had been trained in basic embroidery skills across the two worksites. At any given time the number of workers at the Hathin work center ranged from 60 to a maximum of 150. The first 18 or 19 months were good times for the project. Workers in Hathin produced roughly 200,000 pieces between 2009 and mid-2010 or 10,000–12,000 a month on average (IM interview 2013), with individual workers earning between Rs. 1,000–5,000 per month depending upon the time they put in. "[I]f you look at the data, more than Rs. [2 million] has come into this community in a very short period of time [in the first 6–8 months of the program] because there are no middlemen involved" (GDGP interview 2011). Throughout the first year of its operation there was an excitement and a buzz around the project. IM, Gap, OCL and RD made presentations about their Mewat initiative to retailers and funders. The word spread and several curious exporters and retailers made field visits to see how the model actually worked (IM Interview 2011).

By 2010 the BBC had aired a short documentary on Mewat's success. Interviews with local workers illustrated how the project had changed their lives. The women who had worked at the center expressed deep satisfaction at earning their own income, working outside the home, building community ties and being able to invest in the betterment of their families' the everyday lives. They reported having invested in their children's education (shifting them to better schools, sending them to school), improved nutrition and helping retire family debt (Focus Groups 2013, SPYM studies 2013). Though the earnings each earned depended on the time they had been able to put in, everyone we spoke to wanted the work to continue – and hoped orders would continue to come in. Government officials and Gap representatives also pointed out the confidence and leadership that had emerged among the center's women in just a few seasons of operation. "About two seasons into this...the women started negotiating for better prices..." One of the exporters (OCL) remarked on the touch negotiations his team had with the center's women: "They have refused to do our work at cheaper prices" (Interview 2011). In our focus groups the workers reiterated this sentiment. "We are very well aware of MNREGA[4] rates in our region. If that is the [default] rate here, why should we work for anything less?" (Focus Group, Hathin, 2011).

But times change as do market trends. The Mewat experiment was launched in 2008 at a time when few saw the great recession coming. By 2010 end, the effects of the recessions had reached Mewat. Both Hathin's and Nagina's exporters lost large orders and cut back on their sourcing.

A related exporter tried to place an order for embroidered quilts rather than clothing, but fluctuations deepened and by 2011 work was barely trickling into Mewat. There had been turnover at Gap as well, and the India team saw great churn. Just when the work was dwindling, the organizational structure of the partnership shifted as well. Yet, it is in times of crisis that real lessons about adaptation and weaknesses emerge. By late 2011–early 2012 both the exporters OCL and RD had returned, but the orders were modest. Despite these challenges, the program has persisted. When I returned in 2013 the project had begun to adapt to its circumstances and was transforming itself from having a sole focus on export markets to diversifying into the domestic market as well.

Stepping back from the immediacy of the recession, however, it became clear that at least three factors related to the experiment's success also explained the challenges it faced later during times of stress. The recession only brought these weak links to light sooner. The first factor relates to the limitations of linking each community to a single exporter. When the recession shrank export demand, the project's commitment to a single exporter prevented the community from turning to others to bring in new orders. As the work fell away, some of the workforce started to stay away or move to other work, thus denting collective morale. Limiting each community's market access through a single exporter, the very feature of the project that Gap and IM initially lauded as one of project's innovations turned into a limitation and bottleneck at the time of a downturn later on.

Second, there was uncertainty over who would bear the institutional costs of program continuity during times of growth and during lean times. As noted, Gap had seen turnover of its personnel as director who had been the driving force of the innovation left Gap in 2010 and a series of short-term consultants with weaker knowledge about the program and fewer stakes in it took over. Post-recession, the exporters were also reluctant to send their supervisors to or their logistics team to cart raw inputs into the work centers from Delhi, and ship completed work out, leaving it up to SPYM to find ways to transport work in and out of the work centers when the chips were down. In conventional subcontracting arrangements this is exactly the role the subcontractor plays. "They pick the orders up from the firms doorstep and deliver the finished work back" (IM Interview 2011). SPYM did not have the fiscal capacity to do that.

A model where the innovative feature related to financial self-sufficiency rested on the consistent flow of orders and a certain quantum of continuous work (that could generate the 20% overhead to cover administrative costs) not surprisingly left SPYM, the civic partner, struggling to find the funds to tide over the center during difficult times. Unlike membership-based organizations like the Self-Employed Women's Association (SEWA, India) there were no dues to collect and SPYM as an NGO did not have separate fund to dig into. Gap's internal churn made any one time grant impossible and the state did not put in any money. As Sabel noted in a different context (1982: 36–37), the division of labor that the partners designed initially was acceptable to all partners at the start because of its relevance to their respective roles and strengths. But it did not translate into any map of how longer-term responsibility between the partners would be assigned. When crisis hit, the most powerful actors withdrew.

When the project began to recover in 2012–2013 and orders from OCL and RD began to return, the private partners acknowledged the contribution of SPYM as an institutional anchor, and its efforts at somehow having keeping the centers operational by paying the workers for work done on small orders. Even later, as orders from the original exporters began to return after the recession, SPYM had begun to explore linkages with domestic buyers to create redundancy and insurance during future export crises. SPYM's role has been critical. "SPYM's community work-center is still there, the workers are still there, the women still come when there is work, so the project endures" (IM interview 2013). Nevertheless, diffusing good labor standards broadly in a community on sustained basis requires institutional continuity. Could a small grant from the state – as a form of employment insurance – have helped the civic actor tide the downturn better? Should the public sector be a coanchor for projects such as these? Could the designers institutionalize protocols for handling economic disasters and downturns?

Finally, in some ways the very success of the program unleashed pressures that potentially undermined that success at least to some extent. As the project attracted public attention, it also brought closer political scrutiny from the community's conservative political and religious leaders resulting in some pushback. This pushback was a deeply gendered process and coalesced around two events. One was around debates about replication and scaling up. The strong initial success of the program had inspired the Ministry to look for ways to extend the project from the two pilots to all 400 towns/villages of Mewat. The government had funds for scaling up and the process could start by providing training to workers and women in all wards. Instead of sending supervisors to train workers in each ward, they had considered busing women from each ward to a joint government-industry run training center an hour away. The center was managed by the Apparel Export Promotion Council. While the government had funds to bus interested workers for 30 days of training, community elders put their foot down: "Their women would never go out of the district for work" (MK Interview, 2011). The effort to scale up the project thus not only backfired but local leaders became suspicious of even the local center's activities and sought to hold some women back. Collectively this slowed down the momentum of growth.

A second event that tipped the scale even further against the project came when the BBC aired the documentary it had made on Mewat's success on Channel 4 in May 2010. It showcased the women's rising confidence as income earners in their own right, displayed their camaraderie at the community workplace, and the satisfaction they felt at stepping outside the home for work that they enjoyed and leadership lessons they had learned. All of this, publicly displayed on their television sets, raised a red flag in the eyes of community elders and led to a serious backlash against the project. Some project staff, some of the exporters and even Gap's director reported receiving anonymous death threats, warning them to stay away and back off (GDGP Interview, 2011). A worried local administration counseled the Ministry to go slow and lie low for a while as the controversy blew over. This stepping back was soon compounded by the effect of the recession in late 2010, denting even more the program's early momentum (MK Interview 2011, GDGP Interview 2011). Ironically, then, the partial unraveling of the program in 2010 was as much a consequence of its own very public success, as it was of any external pressure such as of the recession that came down upon it.

These double-edged effects of program design thus illustrate the challenges of institutionally anchoring supports for informal workers in the lowest tiers of global contracting, and doing so in ways that allow programs to adapt and change as the circumstances they face, change. The program endures, albeit with some altered faces. OCL was preparing to ramp up orders as it was expecting embellishment to once again be in fashion in 2014. While all parties believe the program will continue, the structure of the model is changing and evolving.

Conclusions

What lessons does the Mewat experiment offer to countries like Bangladesh about building programs of accountability in urban and rural communities from the bottom-up? The program and its progression so far offer at least four lessons about how and under what conditions can labor protections can be extended to those at the bottom of global value chains. First, it shows that it is possible to build relational contracting networks even in the most informal segments of global production networks. These networked models, as in the Mewat case, are place-based, anchored in labor markets, and not just sectorally, but also territorially. For Bangladesh, where currently the greatest density of garment work is concentrated in one or two key cities, this might mean looking to hinterlands and rural areas where large numbers of workers live, many with a history of garmenting or embroidery skills that can be better tapped through the development of locally anchored community-based initiatives as in Mewat. Over the past three decades sectoral strategies or workforce development and training have been ascendant. It may be time to bring territory and spatiality back into work and workplace development initiatives.

Second, the Mewat model shows how responsive and accountable economic networks can be built upon, layered over and anchored within social sector institutions (Bartley 2011). In the Mewat case export supply networks were built on a web of institutions of personal finance developed over many years of work on women's financial inclusion and their participation in group savings societies. This earlier work by civic organizations and the public sector helped build a well of trust that the actors (public, civic, private) could repeatedly return to as conflicts and challenges demanded modifications and adjustments in operating practices (see Tewari et al. 2018). Bangladesh has a long history of vibrant civic institutions and nonprofit community organizations in rural and urban settings that could usefully double up as anchors of more accountable economic networks could be built.

Third, and related to the second, the Mewat case points at the importance of paying attention to the work of social bureaucracies in achieving economic ends. The Ministry of Women and Child Development in the Indian case had worked for years on social projects. That work, and the trust that it had helped nurture, was invaluable later when global brands like Gap arrived to build supply networks in these regions.

Finally, experiments like Mewat are important exemplars of the need to look beyond continuity of form, to continuity of the spirit of a program as it evolves. The particular partnerships or institutional arrangements that lead to initial success may look quite different from the structures needed for it to persist and evolve as it grows later on. It is significant that the recession nor the stepping away of Gap's director in 2010 did not doom the Mewat experiment. It adapted, and continues to exist in a new way and with a different market focus (hybrid markets, both domestic and export) and with both the old and new collaborators. Managing these changes over time is what is meant by building out a system of local governance through which the project sustains. This requires not only understanding what each partner in the relational network is good at, but fostering a coevolution of mechanisms to manage the partnership as it changes.

In this regard, finally, to reach workers at the bottom of global chains, it is clear that the state will need to get involved. The Mewat case sheds light on how intermediation by the state – and even its material involvement early on during the 15 years of organizing the communities socially – was of critical importance to providing a platform of legitimacy on which other private and collective actors could come together and collaborate. Scaling up is not the only way for the state to engage with workplace experimentation. Diffusing good labor standards requires institutional continuity. The state can be the actor that can bring continuity by holding open the space for new organizational partnerships to emerge even as private supply chains and markets shift. This is especially important in countries and contexts where 90% of the total employment is in the informal sector, outside the reach of both labor laws as well as the monitoring protocols and codes of conduct of buyers and private companies. The state's role is going to be critical if these spatialized experiments that are extending good labor practices down to the bottom tiers global value chains and into communities and places where workers live are to continue and succeed.

Notes

1 This chapter draws on research that was carried out under the auspices of the Capturing the Gains Project based at the University of Manchester and Duke University. An earlier version of the chapter was published in the *Indian Journal of Labour Economics*, 2017, "Relational contracting at the bottom of global garment chains: Lessons from Mewat." Vol. 60, No. 2, pp. 137–154, and the current version is adapted with permission from the *Indian Journal of Labour Economics*, Springer.
2 SPYM is not an indigenous organization in Mewat. It is headquartered in nearby Delhi and works nationwide with youth and women and children. But it has worked in Mewat for over two decades and has a presence there.
3 For context, the 800 women trained constituted about 15% of all women in the two communities. The total population of Hathin according to the 2011 census was 1,018: of which 543 were males and 475 females of all ages. Nagina is a larger town with 11,417 people, 5,928 men and 5,489 women of all ages.
4 The Mahatma Gandhi Rural Employment Guarantee Act (MGNREGA) was a works project introduced in rural areas and under hinterlands it piloted in 2006 and introduced in all districts of India in 2008. It established work programs (mostly infrastructure projects) guaranteeing 100 days of work in rural areas and rates were set according to piece rates based on a scale established by the Central government that is revised every financial year.

References

Accord. 2013. Accord on fire and building safety in Bangladesh. First Accessed May 15, 2015. https://bangladeshaccord.org/.

AK Interview. 2013. Face to face interview conducted by the author with a sourcing manager at the buying house, IM, Delhi.

Barrientos, Stephanie. 2008. Contract Labour: The 'Achilles heel' of corporate codes in commercial value chains. *Development and Change* 39(6): 977–990. doi:10.1111/j.1467-7660.2008.00524.x.

Barrientos, S., Gereffi, G., and Rossi, A. 2011. Economic and social upgrading in global production networks: a new paradigm for a changing world. *International Labor Review* 150(3–4): 319–340. doi:1111/j.1564-913X.2011.00119.x.

Barrientos, Stephanie and Sally Smith. 2007. Do workers benefit from ethical trade? Assessing codes of labor practice in global production systems. *Third World Quarterly* 28(4): 713–729. Special Issue: Beyond Corporate Social Responsibility? Business, Poverty and Social Justice. doi:10.1080/01436590701336580

Bartley, Tim. 2011. Transnational governance as the layering of rules: Intersection of public and private standards. *Theoretical Inquiries in Law* 12(2): 517–542.

BBC. 2007. Gap pulls 'child labor' clothing. Accessed April 16, 2015. http://news.bbc.co.uk/2/hi/south_asia/7066019.stm.

Brunello, Giorgio and de Paola, Maria. 2004. Market Failures and the Under Provision of Training. CESIfo Working Paper No. 1286., Munich.

Burke, Jason. 2014. Rana Plaza: One year on from the Bangladesh factory disaster. *The Guardian*. 19 April, 2014.

Focus Groups. 2013. Follow-up focus groups conducted in Hathin and Nagina villages in 2013.

Fox, Jonathan. 2014. Social accountability: What does the evidence really say? *World Development*, 72. doi:10.1016/j.worlddev.2015.03.011.

GDGP Interview. 2011. Face to face interview conducted by the author with Gap's former officer of Global Partnerships and Social Responsibility, New Delhi, March 2011.

Hathin. 2011. Focus groups conducted by the author in Hathin village in March 2011.

IM Interview. 2011. Face to face interview by the author with senior manager at IM Buying House, March 2011.

Locke, Richard. 2013. *The Promise and Limits of Private Power*. Cambridge, MIT Press.

Locke, Richard, Quin F., and Brause, A. 2007. Does monitoring improve labor standards? Lessons from Nike. *Industrial and Labor Relations Review*, 61(1): 3–31.

Lund-Thompson, Peter and Khalid Nadvi. 2010. Global value chains, local collective action and corporate social responsibility: A review of empirical evidence. *Business Strategy and the Environment*, 19(1): 1–19.

Manik, Julfikar Ali and Jim Yardley. 2012. Bangladesh finds gross negligence in factory fire. *New York Times*, 17 December, 2012.

Manik, Julfikar Ali and Jim Yardley. 2013. Building Collapse in Bangladesh leaves scores dead. *New York Times*, 24 April, 2013.

Mezzadari, Alessandra. 2011. Indian Garment Clusters and CSR Norms: Incompatible Agendas at the Bottom of the Garment Value Chain. Mimeo. SOAS.

MK Interview 2011. Face to face interview conducted by the author with the civil services officer at the Department of Women and Child Development, Government of India, New Delhi.

O'Connor, Clare. 2014. These retailers involved in Bangladesh factory disaster have yet to compensate victims. *Forbes*. 26 April, 2014.

O'Rourke, Dana. 2002. "Monitoring the monitors: A critique of corporate third party labor monitoring." In R. Jenkins, R. Pearson, and G. Seyfang (Eds.) *Corporate Social Responsibility and Labor Rights: Codes of Conduct in the Global Economy* (pp. 196–208). London: Earthscan.

Posthuma, Anne and Dev Nathan. 2010. Labour in Global Production Networks in India. New Delhi: Oxford University Press.

Sabel, Charles. 1982. The structure of the labor market, Chapter 2 in *Work and Politics, the Division of labor in industry* (pp. 31–77). New York: Cambridge University Press.

Scheper, Christian. 2017. Labour networks under supply chain capitalism: The politics of the Bangladesh Accord. *Development and Change*, 48(5): 1069–1088. doi:10.1111/dech.12328.

SPYM Interview. 2011. Face to face interviews carried out by the author with the leadership and staff of SPYM, Delhi and Hathin, March 2011.

SPYM studies. 2013. Internal assessments prepared by SPYM interns on the functioning of the Mewat program. Accessed by the author during visits to SPYM's Delhi offices.

Tewari, Meenu. 2010. Footloose capital, intermediation and the search for the 'highroad' in low wage industries. In *Labour in Global Production Networks in India* (pp. 146–165). New Delhi: Oxford University Press.

Tewair, Meenu. 2017. Relational contracting at the bottom of global garment chains: Lessons from Mewat. *Indian Journal of Labour Economics*, 60(2): 137–154.

Tewari, Meenu, Kelmenson, Sophie, Guinn, Andrew, Cuming, Gabriel, and Colloredo-Mansfeld, Rudolf. 2018. Mission driven intermediaries as anchors of the middle ground in the American food system: Evidence from Warrenton, NC. *Culture, Agriculture, Food and Environment*. doi:10.1111/cuag.12175.

Unni, Jeemol and Scaria, S. 2009. "Governance, Structure and Labor Market Outcomes in Garment Embellishment Chains." Working Paper 194, Gujarat Institute for Development Research.

11 Emerging solutions to the global labor transparency problem

Kohl Gill and Ayush Khanna

Introduction

In the aftermath of the Rana Plaza tragedy, much has been made of the disaster's technology context. While workers' own mobile phones were ubiquitous—indeed, they delivered some of the very first images of the disaster for global broadcast—the potential for this technology to contribute to supply chain transparency and accountability went largely untapped. The authors of this chapter, both technology toolmakers by training, were asked to contribute to this volume, specifically on the landscape of and forecast for such technical solutions to supply chain transparency.

LaborVoices was founded by the authors to address two problems simultaneously: the lack of transparency in global supply chains, and the absence of voice for workers around the world. LaborVoices partners with local organizations to reach manufacturing and agricultural workers directly and collect real-time anonymous information about their work conditions via mobile phone surveys. Once aggregated, these data provide global brands and their supply chains what has been missing: an early warning system based on direct feedback from workers. Just as important, the lines of communication established with workers and the information collected about factories in cities and countries across the globe give workers for the first time the power of information to make informed choices about where and how they work—information they can easily share with one another. LaborVoices reaches workers and gives them less detectable ways to organize, rebalancing the power scale in their direction with potentially major economic, social, and political implications.

Since inception in 2010, LaborVoices has employed its crowdsourced worker feedback model in 11 countries including Bangladesh, and has reached hundreds of thousands of workers in over a dozen languages. LaborVoices works with brands, government, and aid organizations, and also works closely with factory owners and labor organizations. So far, we have successfully gathered actionable worker feedback in the apparel, agriculture, and electronics industries.

In this chapter, we discuss solutions to supply chain transparency. This is by no means a new problem, so we begin with a recap of existing solutions, looking into their strengths and weaknesses. Using these, we create a framework for what the ideal solution might look like: not just for delivering worker impact, but also for driving benefits across supply chain stakeholders. This includes global brands, suppliers, consumers, and governments. Then, we introduce some existing solutions, and dive into case studies to understand exactly how they are delivering results. Specifically, we look at the underlying approaches and technology that enable these solutions. We end by examining the barriers these solutions must address to become successful at scale.

An overview of existing approaches to supply chain transparency

Supply chain stakeholders had implemented a variety of approaches to supply chain transparency prior to Rana Plaza, and even more in the immediate aftermath. These ranged from traditional social audits, to hotlines, helplines, and multi-stakeholder initiatives. Each of these approaches attempt to inform brands, and, in some cases, employers, trade unions, civil society, and government, to improve decision-making. These transparency tools have promised to show the actual policies, practices, and performance records of individual suppliers. The idea was that, armed with this information, government and brands would better protect and respect labor rights by applying regulatory and market pressure on suppliers, respectively.

The dominant technology to generate brand-facing transparency has been—and continues to be—social audits.[1] These audits are in-person inspections, usually conducted by a third-party auditing firm. The process dates back to the 1990s, with the top three firms[2] having a combined revenue of approximately $15 billion. The social audit regime grew out of the quality-control movement, and therefore carries damaging tacit assumptions—such as the assumption that working conditions change slowly, and can therefore be measured effectively by periodic inspections. Consequently, factory management has developed a variety of methods of gaming social audits, ranging from coaching workers on what to say to a visiting auditor, to cleaning up noncompliances immediately before an audit, to simple bribery of auditors, sometimes trading sexual exploitation of female workers for a "clean" audit.[3] Indeed, two of the factories within the Rana Plaza building were audited against the BSCI (Business Social Compliance Initiative) standard before the collapse, failing to highlight the structural issues.[4] Similarly, prior to the 2012 Tazreen factory fire, an auditor gave the facility an "orange" rating, failing to prevent the tragedy.[5]

To complement the periodic transparency provided by social audits, brands also instituted hotlines to gather urgent issues directly from workers. Some examples include the Fair Wear Foundation's helpline system, and consultancies like Clear Voice. These hotlines typically allow workers to call into a local or toll-free phone number, using their mobile phones or a landline, to connect directly with a live operator. These systems are sometimes as simple as an auditor handing out their business card to workers, inviting an occasional call to verify information gained in an audit. In other cases they are fairly complex, spanning multiple countries, with phone-banks of operators. The live-operator aspect of hotlines throttles the number of workers who can call, and raises the cost of increased responsiveness—they simply don't scale well. Because of this non-scalability, hotlines are often expensive, and therefore restrictive; only workers from particular factories are allowed to call particular hotlines. Because of these constraints, the user experience of hotlines, from a worker's perspective, is similarly constrained. These factors resulted in severe under-use of hotlines in general, and low-quality transparency from these approaches.

Brands and multi-stakeholder initiatives launched several responses to Rana Plaza. Two we discuss here are the Alliance's Helpline, Amader Kotha, and the ILO's Better Work Bangladesh (BWB) program. These approaches are covered in more detail in Chapters 5 and 6, respectively, so we only discuss them briefly, here.

Amader Kotha was a helpline funded by the Alliance for Bangladesh Worker Safety, and implemented by a consortium of three organizations—hotline consultancy Clear Voice, local NGO Phulki, and then-nonprofit technology program Laborlink[6]—under the project management of supply chain consultancy Elevate. Elevate was also the executive body of the Alliance, itself. According to Amader Kotha publications, the helpline suffered severe misrepresentation among workers, with 71% of callers being men,[7] from an industry where 90% of workers are women.[8] Amader Kotha suffered a large fraction of "test calls", where over 90% of the incoming calls were not germane to the helpline's focus.[9] Finally, both internally and in public reporting, Amader Kotha had no sophisticated reporting. Statistics on individual facilities were nonexistent or severely delayed, either by the design of information management systems, or because of a paucity of reliable data. It was really hard, if not impossible, to compare reports versus the past—creating useful trend lines—or to compare factories among peers—creating useful benchmarks—to understand what changes, if any, had occurred. Reports were uploaded as PDFs and no attempts were made to parse them or otherwise summarize changes.[10]

BWB is a program supported by the ILO, under the broader Better Work program. Over 12 years of operation, the Better Work program globally has reached some 1.9 million workers,[11] a slow growth path encumbered both by fitful adoption of technology and by the ILO's tripartite consensus-based approach. In addition, while Better Work programs in Cambodia and Indonesia have been supported by trade policy mandates, requiring suppliers to participate, BWB was established without such an accelerant. Despite this proliferation of initiatives and approaches, these solutions still don't suffice. Roughly, these initiatives can be divided and analyzed as *corporate initiatives* and *multilateral initiatives*.

Corporate initiatives commonly have five failure modes. First, they are not sector-wide, covering only suppliers connected to funding corporations. This means they miss dangerous situations like unauthorized subcontracting—a phenomenon that is opaque by design. They also fail to keep up with rapidly changing sourcing relationships. Second, data collection is top-down, involving factory management. Management tends to both throttle the volume of data collected and taint data collection mechanisms as "management-controlled". Top-down data collection also precludes modern technology growth methods. Third, data collected are proprietary to the involved corporations. The data cannot be openly shared or cross-checked for consistency with other data sources. These siloed data don't support open competition among suppliers. Fourth, siloed, single-use data collection is expensive, and is very taxing on small, volatile, corporate CSR budgets. This limits data collection to the "latest and loudest" of the most problematic suppliers. Factory management then has an incentive to wait-out brand concerns, certain in the knowledge that budgetary focus, or the sourcing relationship itself, will shift over time. Similarly, CSR executives have limited political capital, can present no "clean" supplier alternatives for sourcing colleagues, and can only rule out suppliers after demonstrating a history of CSR noncompliance. Finally, corporate initiatives, because of the reasons above, cannot design interventions for scale—rather, they perpetuate small, volatile, custom solutions for each corporate customer. These solutions are built on a consulting business model, where consultants have every incentive to over-customize offerings and continually inflate costs.

Similarly, multilateral initiatives have five failure modes of their own. First, they often focus primarily on building government capacity through training programs. This ignores the fact that well-trained government staff have every incentive to leave for the private sector, eliminating the effect of capacity-building efforts. They also attempt to replicate structures from high-governance countries, rather than leapfrogging to more appropriate governance methods. Second, they often have a low capacity to innovate, especially when the latest technology needs to be evaluated and adopted. Staff of these initiatives are often easily distracted by shiny-new technology (augmented reality/virtual reality, artificial intelligence, blockchain). They also get distracted by technology consultants rather than launching fast-cheap experimentation. Third, they have a similar dependency on top-down models for engaging factory management, with similar failures as noted above. Fourth, they operate extremely slowly, usually on the basis of consensus between all parties. This means that they remain vulnerable to political pressure from local government and government-capturing interests. Finally, these weaknesses lead multilateral initiative staff to avoid innovation altogether. Structurally, they have no tolerance for failure, no real reward for success, and only penalties for risk-taking. This leads to little real experimentation, as well as the initiatives losing frustrated expert staff to private companies and foundations.

Presenting a solution that actually works

At the core of our argument is this: for any solution to be adopted and be truly successful, it has to work for all parties involved. If we look outside the specific issues tackled by this book, examples of this abound. Any of the multitude of platform or community-driven businesses that have sprung up over the last few decades—Waze, Yelp, eBay, to just name a few—work because they deliver value to multiple agents. Looking more closely at examples in the supply chain industry, we have Flexport. Arguably the most promising supply chain startup of the last decade, Flexport has successfully employed technology to automate a dated system of freight shipments, which helps both service providers and corporations—service providers can find work more easily and corporations can save money and make faster decisions.

There's no reason the Silicon Valley approach—knowing your "user(s)", identifying their problems, and designing a solution that works for all of them—needs to stay limited to the confines of technology companies. A solution that works for brands, workers, *and* suppliers (and NGOs, governments) is a solution that will actually work. It will move us past the stale debate of whether traditional governance works (spoiler alert: it doesn't). Keeping this view in mind, we will now outline some characteristics of the ideal solution—aligning incentives to drive market pressure to support labor rights, rather than undermine them (Figure 11.1).

Sector-wide and ubiquitous

Existing attempts at responsible sourcing have, sometimes by choice and sometimes by compulsion, restricted themselves to subsectors of industries and/or geographies. The Alliance and Accord in Bangladesh are good examples of this. Several initiatives have chosen to only focus on a small part

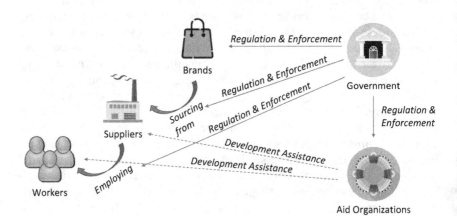

Figure 11.1 Stakeholders in a typical apparel supply chain.

of the industry, for instance tier 1 suppliers.[12] While it can be tempting to look at subsectors since they imply reduced complexity, this strategy hurts long-term sustainability because the full picture is missing.

A single, industry-wide solution ensures that everyone speaks the same language and refers to the same source of truth. Also, by looking at the *entire* sector, instead of just a few regions, or just the first tier suppliers, we ensure full visibility into the supply chain. This is especially important given that often the harshest conditions exist at the periphery of a brand's supply chain, where subcontractors and smaller suppliers reside.

Additionally, the solution needs to be international in scope in order for it to really work for brands. Most of the big name apparel brands produce from dozens of countries. A "Bangladesh only" solution is hence restrictive and simply won't see serious adoption. Brands, as users, need a global engagement strategy, instead of custom, one-off projects for every country.

A bottom-up approach

The most common modus operandi we have seen involves getting suppliers to sign on to a program, usually under some form of pressure from one or more brand customers. This "top-down" process is fraught with delays. Often, there is distrust from suppliers and a feeling of being surveilled. In some cases, suppliers claim they are operating in full compliance, and therefore need no monitoring or capacity-building. What this means, in effect, is that there is a tremendous amount of red tape involved in getting—and keeping—suppliers involved with any initiative.

The other, and perhaps even more serious, implication of reaching workers via suppliers is trust. As noted above, evidence of collusion and corruption abounds. Suppliers get informed about "surprise" visits ahead of time. Workers are coached on how to respond to questions, and in many cases management is in the room as they are interviewed. It is hard to imagine a system designed for less reliability.

There is a very straightforward solution to this problem. Using technology and the workers' existing mobile phones, we can reach them directly. Several apps that workers use today—Facebook, Google, Yelp—have already achieved this. Additionally, there are ways to collect information from them in ways that don't require smartphones. This is key in regions like Bangladesh where smartphone penetration is relatively low, even though mobile penetration is quite high. By establishing a direct communication line with the worker, we can get to reliable data on the situation in the factory, and get it a lot faster—a matter of days versus months.

Independent and open

The audit industry is built on siloed data. Once a year or so, an auditor visits the factory and checks off a list. Reports are delivered to a single brand, and then locked away in their internal data stores. The same process is then repeated for another brand sourcing from the same factory. Each report is already outdated by the time it gets to the brand. There is little to no collaboration or sharing of data,[13] making the reports even more rapidly obsolete.

This can only change if there is an independent platform that is accessible to everyone, a platform that doesn't need to rely on other stakeholders to exist or collect information. Reuse and collaboration is only the beginning of the gains from this approach, however. On an independent platform, factories get benchmarked against each other on a range of social responsibility metrics. This inspires a race to the top among factories, and it gives the good guys—suppliers doing right by their employees—a chance to differentiate themselves from the rest. Brands, by extension, gain by being able to select the lowest risk suppliers industry-wide. Additionally, recommendations and best practices can be shared with a much greater degree of sophistication, e.g.: "based on other factories in the region, we suggest that you train your workers on how overtime is calculated".

Worker-centered design

Audits and other top-down approaches see brands as users of their services. Workers are a means to an end. This approach means that auditors can provide cheap, streamlined, checklists to brands at a large scale. As we've established earlier, however, data collected this way cannot be trusted. Why would workers trust an auditor with confidential information? When a small fraction of the workforce does get a chance to share their insights on working conditions, assuming they don't experience coercion, they don't have any visibility into what this means for them. At the end of the day, what does any of this really do for the worker?

Workers are a key stakeholder in the supply chain, and need to be treated as such to enable a successful outcome. That is not only the primary premise introducing this chapter, it is also the missing piece in existing solutions. When workers feel empowered by the same information that is being shared with brands, they have a compelling reason to share the full, true story. The only way to collect reliable data is to deliver value to the source—workers, themselves.

Long-term thinking is also essential in attracting and retaining workers as a part of the solution. Fleeting attempts to reach workers don't work because workers don't trust that anything will ever be done about their problems, since they don't know what happens next. Making them a part of the process means that they will actually participate and provide reliable data on a continuous basis, which is a lot more valuable than a one-off conversation every other year.

A worker-focused solution gives them a say in their own working conditions. When data collected en masse is fed back to workers, it gives them a chance to vote with their feet and migrate toward the best possible work environments for them. When a solution like this spreads, it works for new workers entering the workforce as well, potentially eliminating bad actors—both suppliers and recruiters—in the system. Workers, armed with market information, can effectively boycott bad actors out of the market.

Long-term sustainability

Audits, despite several defects, operate in a successful billion-dollar ecosystem. Other initiatives, particularly multi-stakeholder approaches, have failed to get things done and, unsurprisingly, are now winding down. Designed in response to the Rana Plaza tragedy, they were reactive in nature, and focused on responding to the bad public relations generated for US and European brands.

A value-driven approach can and will outlast and out-scale other solutions born out of short-term thinking or pure philanthropy. We have seen elsewhere in the supply chain that brands will pay for access to important data, and hence a solution that works for workers can also work for them, instead of needing to be bankrolled by foundations or governments in the long-term. The sustainability problem, then, is limited to generating seed funding, as we describe later in the chapter.

Government as a key stakeholder

Regulators have been traditionally singled out as enemies in the responsibility debate, often seen as turning a blind eye to problems in the supply chain. As per the UN "Protect, Respect and Remedy" Guiding Principles, it is "the state duty to protect against human rights abuses by third parties, including business". Regulators largely face the same challenge as brands, however: they simply don't know where and how violations are occurring.

Providing government organizations with macro- and factory-level data gives them the tools to detect problems and focus their efforts accordingly. The same data can then be used to drive accountability among citizens and civil society at large, by creating awareness and education about labor issues and what can be done to resolve them.

Our theory of change is summarized as follows (Figure 11.2).

Crowdsourced worker voice in action

We have been working to make this solution a reality, and several key components are already in place. In this section, we present a handful of first-hand accounts of the results for workers, brands, and suppliers. In only a few years of work, we have seen some excellent validation for the design principles laid out earlier.

Detecting and defeating forced labor in Turkey

In late 2017, LaborVoices partnered with a large athletic wear brand to monitor working conditions for some of their suppliers amidst an increasingly

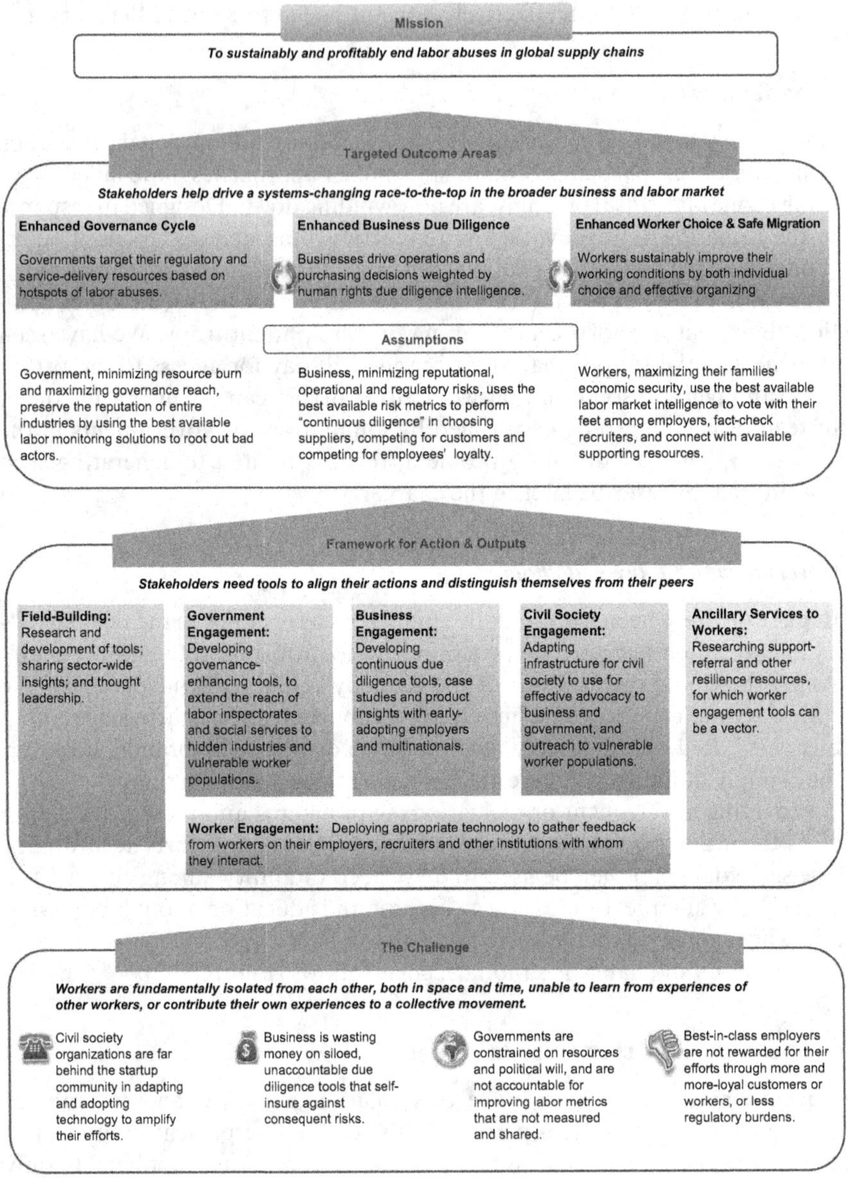

Mission

To sustainably and profitably end labor abuses in global supply chains

Targeted Outcome Areas

Stakeholders help drive a systems-changing race-to-the-top in the broader business and labor market

Enhanced Governance Cycle

Governments target their regulatory and service-delivery resources based on hotspots of labor abuses.

Enhanced Business Due Diligence

Businesses drive operations and purchasing decisions weighted by human rights due diligence intelligence.

Enhanced Worker Choice & Safe Migration

Workers sustainably improve their working conditions by both individual choice and effective organizing

Assumptions

Government, minimizing resource burn and maximizing governance reach, preserve the reputation of entire industries by using the best available labor monitoring solutions to root out bad actors.

Business, minimizing reputational, operational and regulatory risks, uses the best available risk metrics to perform "continuous diligence" in choosing suppliers, competing for customers and competing for employees' loyalty.

Workers, maximizing their families' economic security, use the best available labor market intelligence to vote with their feet among employers, fact-check recruiters, and connect with available supporting resources.

Framework for Action & Outputs

Stakeholders need tools to align their actions and distinguish themselves from their peers

Field-Building: Research and development of tools; sharing sector-wide insights; and thought leadership.

Government Engagement: Developing governance-enhancing tools, to extend the reach of labor inspectorates and social services to hidden industries and vulnerable worker populations.

Business Engagement: Developing continuous due diligence tools, case studies and product insights with early-adopting employers and multinationals.

Civil Society Engagement: Adapting infrastructure for civil society to use for effective advocacy to business and government; and outreach to vulnerable worker populations.

Ancillary Services to Workers: Researching support-referral and other resilience resources, for which worker engagement tools can be a vector.

Worker Engagement: Deploying appropriate technology to gather feedback from workers on their employers, recruiters and other institutions with whom they interact.

The Challenge

Workers are fundamentally isolated from each other, both in space and time, unable to learn from experiences of other workers, or contribute their own experiences to a collective movement.

Civil society organizations are far behind the startup community in adapting and adopting technology to amplify their efforts.

Business is wasting money on siloed, unaccountable due diligence tools that self-insure against consequent risks.

Governments are constrained on resources and political will, and are not accountable for improving labor metrics that are not measured and shared.

Best-in-class employers are not rewarded for their efforts through more and more-loyal customers or workers, or less regulatory burdens.

Figure 11.2 Proposed theory of change.

turbulent political climate in Turkey. Our ground team connected with workers outside the factory and introduced them to our data collection platform. Within a few weeks, dozens of workers had started sending us reports.

Almost immediately, we started receiving complaints from workers about one of the suppliers employing migrant labor. Workers reported that unknown workers would arrive at the factory late at night, after the regular shift was over. These unknown workers were Syrian migrants, and the supplier was paying them exploitative wages and taking advantage of their undocumented status. We alerted the brand right away, who were in turn assured by the factory management that these reports were false. A few weeks passed and the reports kept coming in. At this point the brand organized a surprise late night visit to the factory and confirmed our prior reports. In response, the brand intervened and worked out a transition plan with the supplier. Within a few weeks, the brand prevented significant brand damage via bad public relations by discreetly detecting and responding to an issue that would have simply been missed using other methods. The supplier, responding to pressure from the brand, did away with exploiting undocumented labor.

Reaching workers directly and outside the factory allowed them to share this critical information, without fear of retribution. Not only were we able to uncover a serious issue, we were able to get to it in weeks. At scale, this solution will do more to help these migrant workers as well, by pointing them toward the best available jobs, as rated by their peers.

Predicting large-scale disruption and labor unrest in Bangladesh

In January 2017, widespread riots and labor unrest occurred in Ashulia, near Dhaka. Workers from hundreds of factories were impacted, and over a thousand were sacked from their jobs. Since June 2016, LaborVoices had been reaching hundreds of workers in the region, outside the factories and in the communities where they live. Workers reported information about their working conditions, including wages, working hours, and any abuses experienced.

LaborVoices detected a relationship among the factors that affect the satisfaction of the workers and the events that unfolded in Ashulia. A closer examination of the data we had collected revealed that the wages score dropped significantly in January 2017 compared to the past three months for these factories. Additionally, there was a significant rise in abuse reports and forced labor issues compared to December 2016. These factors may have led to the overall upheaval in January 2017.

These results, applied in the right context, might have prevented a loss of jobs and millions of dollars in supply chain disruption costs. Additionally, they validate several aspects of the solution we have discussed earlier. Worker-generated data can be gathered before the fact and used to prevent issues if the data are collected continuously. By looking closely, indicators for disruption make themselves visible. Additionally, it demonstrates the value of collecting data sector-wide instead of focusing on sections of the worker population.

Understanding human trafficking indicators in Bangladesh

After first introducing the worker outreach model in 2016 and reaching a critical mass of workers and factories in our database, we partnered with a few public and private funders[14] to focus on domestic trafficking in Bangladesh. Starting in late 2016, we reached hundreds of workers via our platform and conducted interviews to understand how they were being recruited and what problems they were facing.

In a matter of weeks, we learned the ins and outs of the recruiting process for the Bangladesh apparel sector. We found that most recruiting was informal, via a friend or someone in the extended family. This meant workers weren't always forthcoming about migration details, as they felt protective of their friends and family. At the same time, several problems surfaced, with training centers being at the center of many of them. Almost two-thirds of the workers reported these centers took possession of their ID cards, and almost a third of workers had to pay the centers to find jobs.

Based on these observations, we reached out directly to training centers, to gather some insights from them. Much to our surprise, many of them were excited about our worker platform, and wanted to use it to reach workers. This gave us the idea to kill two birds with one stone—by featuring the best recruiting centers as rated by workers, we can solve the problem for both sides.

This experiment was another example of how we can extract deeper insights from workers, that go well beyond monitoring day-to-day conditions in factories. At a macro-level, we were able to identify causal factors for the domestic trafficking problem. While tracking the informal sector will continue to be a challenge, we found that applying worker-sourced data can create a solution that entirely sidesteps informal and uninformed recruitment. Lastly and most importantly, we proved that recruiters and training centers can do better, when they are provided the right incentives.

Scaling and sustainability: how do we get there from here?

Potential solutions like the few described above face several hurdles to realizing the above promise, particularly around experimentation and scaling up. Once overcome, several interesting future use cases open up, as well.

Experimentation

Effective tool design requires extensive experimentation and testing. We find the current testing environment constrained by seed funding and scalable approaches to worker outreach. The seed funding available—via public and private donors, corporate sponsorships, and investors—for experimentation and testing is constrained in several ways. First, funders typically lack the technical capacity to distinguish between viable approaches on the one hand, and approaches that perpetuate the above failures on the other. This "signal-to-noise" problem results in, for example, top-down, selective, closed initiatives dominating the landscape.[15] Similarly, funding is often overly constrained, requiring certain types of academic or corporate partners,[16] with only a passing nod to declared theories of change. Finally, funding very rarely supports the establishment of lasting infrastructure for further experimentation, beyond the initial interests of the funder.

Partly because of these funding constraints, pilot experiments are often based on one–off interactions with workers. This means that most initiatives make no effort to present a long-term value proposition to workers—a product that workers actually value. To create an effective, sustainable, and scalable user base of workers, such product focus is critical. Unfortunately, getting to such a product requires rapid experimentation, unsuited to one-off pilots. Faced with these one-off interactions, whether by exhausting workers or funders, "survey fatigue" and "donor fatigue", key stakeholders eventually lose interest.[17]

Scaling up successes

Where initiatives have shown early success, they face three hurdles to scaling up: volatile CSR budgets, poor government integration, and limited international reach.

First, individual company sponsors' CSR budgets are small and volatile. Consortia of corporate sponsors—collaborating in a "precompetitive space"—are typically even more risk-averse in budgeting for innovative experiments. While these CSR sponsors are useful for early stage pilots, they simply aren't suited to build lasting infrastructure and economies of scale.

As per the UN Guiding Principles, integrating with a robust governance system should be a long-term design goal. Government decision-making is slow and often fickle, depending on elections and prevailing economic conditions. Innovators should pursue integration with government carefully, and on multiple fronts, simultaneously.

Ideally, as suppliers compete internationally as well as with domestic competitors, and as multinational corporations dominate the buying landscape for supply chains, innovators should also be building solutions with transnational reach. This yields an enhanced value proposition for government and corporate stakeholders, for making meaningful comparisons and benchmarks at the regional and country level.

New uses for an enhanced toolset

With the above hurdles overcome, new use cases open up for workers, advocates, and governments. For an example worker-facing tool, LaborVoices is described above as one instance that generates value across stakeholders. Ideally, many such tools would exist, and, crucially, all be working toward shared open data ownership models and interoperability. Open data, as described above, are critical to maintaining long-term accuracy and integrity among worker-facing tools. When toolmakers can cross-check results, the result is a race toward accuracy and reliability.[18]

Advocates have an opportunity to use advocate-facing tools to take data seriously. We can now measure on-the-ground social conditions, continuously, allowing advocates to measure real-time impact from advocacy efforts. There is now space for result-oriented advocates to use data to: target their efforts on the worst-in-class offenders, not just the most-prominent multinational brands; measure the results of campaign tactics, for their own operational improvement and for their donors; accelerate a race-to-the-top competition among employers; offer real, practical solutions to workers—such as better jobs and legal aid—based on the best available data. Similarly, results-oriented donors can require advocates to build internal capacity, or create long-term partnerships with tool builders.

Government can now use tools to facilitate the rule of law, as mentioned above. As well, public- and government-facing tools can help in holding government actors accountable for failing to enforce the law. On the international stage, these tools can enhance both formal mechanisms like the ILO complaints process, and less-formal mechanisms like the human rights reporting process.[19] Locally, citizens can use these tools to highlight which districts and agencies are most effective, and which not, following up on politicians' claims of increased enforcement resources, and measuring the resolution of worker-reported issues. The business community can also help, by demonstrating to government stakeholders via these tools that low-governance areas generate real social risks for business. Conversely, these tools can help highlight previously unknown best-in-class suppliers, diamonds in the rough, and distinguish them from low-road competitors.

Conclusion

There is plenty of space for multiple tools to handle each of the above needs, and exploit these new capabilities. As long as each of them is built with interoperability in mind, innovators have a chance to cost-effectively share common infrastructure. By embracing reality and sharing infrastructure, we can eliminate surprises like Rana Plaza, save lives, and improve the entire market of employment opportunities for workers, sustainably and scalably.

It is worth noting that the full-fledged solution discussed here today is not academic in nature. Several key pieces exist already. The "why" and "how" are clear, as we lay in wait for the right parties to recognize the pattern and change the way we look at sourcing.

Bibliography

Alliance for Bangladesh Worker Safety, 2018, *Helpline Call Statistics*, www.bangladeshworkersafety.org/progress-impact/helpline-statistics.

Amader Kotha Worker Helpline, 2018, *Our Voice Special Edition Amader Kotha Newsletter Volume 5, Number 2*, www.bangladeshworkersafety.org/files/newsletters/AmaderKotha_Q22018.pdf.

bdnews24.com, 2018, *Alliance for garment workers' safety leaving Bangladesh by December*,https://bdnews24.com/business/2018/07/22/alliance-for-garment-workers-safety-leaving-bangladesh-by-december.

Better Work, 2018, *About Us*, https://betterwork.org/about-us/the-programme/.

BSCI, 2013, *BSCI saddened by the collapse of Rana Plaza in Savar, Bangladesh*, www.amfori.org/news/bsci-saddened-collapse-rana-plaza-savar-bangladesh.

Clean Clothes Campaign, 2005, *Looking for a quick fix*, https://cleanclothes.org/resources/publications/05-quick-fix.pdf/view.

CSRWire, 2017, *ELEVATE Acquires Laborlink*, www.csrwire.com/press_releases/40236-ELEVATE-Acquires-Laborlink.

Rashed Al Mahmud Titumir, 2003, *Spinning the Chain; Lost in the Queue*, P. 6, www.unnayan.org/documents/RightsParticipation/Spinning_the_Chain_Lost_in_the_Queue.pdf.

Vikas Bajaj (The New York Times), 2012, *Fatal Fire in Bangladesh Highlights the Dangers Facing Garment Workers*, www.nytimes.com/2012/11/26/world/asia/bangladesh-fire-kills-more-than-100-and-injures-many.html.

Notes

1 Clean Clothes Campaign, 2005, *Looking for a quick fix*, P. 12, https://cleanclothes.org/resources/publications/05-quick-fix.pdf/view.

2 SGS, Bureau Veritas, and Intertek, from Clean Clothes Campaign, 2005, *Looking for a quick fix*, P. 56, https://cleanclothes.org/resources/publications/05-quick-fix.pdf/view.

3 Clean Clothes Campaign, 2005, *Looking for a quick fix*, P. 25, https://cleanclothes.org/resources/publications/05-quick-fix.pdf/view.

4 BSCI, 2013, *BSCI saddened by the collapse of Rana Plaza in Savar, Bangladesh*, www.amfori.org/news/bsci-saddened-collapse-rana-plaza-savar-bangladesh.

5 Vikas Bajaj (The New York Times), 2012, *Fatal Fire in Bangladesh Highlights the Dangers Facing Garment Workers*, www.nytimes.com/2012/11/26/world/asia/bangladesh-fire-kills-more-than-100-and-injures-many.html.

6 Laborlink was itself a program run by nonprofit Good World Solutions (GWS), a subsidiary of Fair Trade USA. GWS was acquired in 2017 by for-profit consultancy Elevate, a subsidiary of private equity firm EQT. Source: CSRWire, 2017, *ELEVATE Acquires Laborlink*, www.csrwire.com/press_releases/40236-ELEVATE-Acquires-Laborlink.

7 Alliance for Bangladesh Worker Safety, 2018, *Helpline Call Statistics*, www.bangladeshworkersafety.org/progress-impact/helpline-statistics.

8 Rashed Al Mahmud Titumir, 2003, *Spinning the Chain; Lost in the Queue*, P. 6, www.unnayan.org/documents/RightsParticipation/Spinning_the_Chain_Lost_in_the_Queue.pdf.

9 Note that "Substantive" calls number less than 10% of total calls. Amader Kotha Worker Helpline, 2018, *Our Voice Special Edition Amader Kotha Newsletter Volume 5, Number 2*, P. 3, www.bangladeshworkersafety.org/files/newsletters/AmaderKotha_Q22018.pdf.

10 Communications with Amader Kotha staff who chose to remain anonymous, 2016.

11 Better Work, 2018, *About* Us, https://betterwork.org/about-us/the-programme/.

12 Typically, "tier 1 supplier" refers to the last entity performing manufacturing or assembly on a product, before it is shipped further in a multinational corporation's supply chain for sale to customers. Tier 1 suppliers buy their inputs from tier 2 suppliers, and so on.

13 Shared data systems, such as SEDEX, the Fair Factories Clearinghouse, and the Sustainable Apparel Coalition, rely largely on either self-reported data and outdated audit reports. None has any significant worker-reported data component.

14 This work was supported in part by the United States Agency for International Development, Humanity United, C&A Foundation.

15 See, for example, Geopoll www.geopoll.com, Laborlink https://portal. elevatelimited.com, MicroBenefits www.microbenefits.com, Ulula http://ulula. com, and Workplace Options www.workplaceoptions.com.

16 See, for example, The Global Fund to End Modern Slavery www.gfems.org/ portfolio/#prevalence.

17 bdnews24.com, 2018, *Alliance for garment workers' safety leaving Bangladesh by December,* https://bdnews24.com/business/2018/07/22/alliance-for-garment-workers-safety-leaving-bangladesh-by-december.

18 Here again, this stands in stark contrast to principle- and standard-setting initiatives such as WEST https://westprinciples.org, lacking any accountability mechanism.

19 See, for example, *Human Rights Watch World Report 2018* www.hrw.org/ world-report/2018 and *U.S. Department of State Country Reports on Human Rights Practices 2017* www.state.gov/j/drl/rls/hrrpt/humanrightsreport/index. htm#wrapper.

12 Fast fashion, production targets, and gender-based violence in Asian garment supply chains

Shikha Silliman Bhattacharjee

Introduction

Radhika, a line tailor, stitches garments for the export market on a production line in Bangalore, Karnataka, India. In order for brands to offer new styles in their stores year-round, orders to suppliers have to be completed fast. Supplier factories are required to meet accelerated production time lines, sometimes without much advance notice. Production starts with a sample made by a highly skilled sample tailor. The time taken for the sample tailor to make one piece is used to calculate hourly production targets. Radhika, like the majority of workers from across Asian garment production networks, is under sustained pressure to meet targets at the expense of taking breaks to rest, using the restroom, and even drinking water.

For Radhika and other women on her production line, pressure to meet production targets drives workplace violence. Radhika described being thrown to the floor and beaten by her batch supervisor:

> At 12:30 pm, my batch supervisor came up behind me as I was working on the sewing machine, yelling "you are not meeting your target production." He pulled me out of the chair and I fell on the floor. He hit me, including on my breasts. He pulled me up and then pushed me to the floor again. He kicked me.

Singled out from a line of around 38 tailors, this public corporal discipline terrorized not only Radhika, but the women around her. Violence on the production line is so normalized that no supervisor or coworker intervened on her behalf.

Radhika filed a written complaint with the human resources department at the factory. She described the meeting between herself, the supervisor, and human resources personnel:

> They called the supervisor to the office and said, "last month you did the same thing to another lady—haven't you learned?" Then they told him to apologize to me. After that, they warned me not to mention this further. The supervisor and I left the meeting. I went back to work.

In Radhika's meeting with human resources, it became clear that her supervisor was a repeat offender: this was at least the second time he assaulted a woman worker on the factory floor, but this did not lead to his termination. Radhika reported that though the abuse from her manager did not stop, she continued to work at the factory because she needs the job.

Radhika's experience of violence is not an isolated incident. During January–May 2018, Asia Floor Wage Alliance (AFWA) and Global Labor Justice (GLJ) researchers documented gender-based violence reported by 150 women garment workers in Bangladesh, Cambodia, India, Indonesia, and Sri Lanka—including workers from 37 different supplier factories within the Gap, H&M, and Walmart supply chains.[1] Women garment workers reported facing sexual harm and suffering; gendered industrial discipline practices—including physical violence, verbal abuse, coercion, and threats; physically extractive labor practices with severe health consequences—a practice termed *mining of the body* (Nathan et al. 2018); unsafe workplaces; and the production of insecurity through reliance on contract workers, threats of termination, barriers to freedom of association and collective bargaining, and retaliation for reporting violence. Gendered cultures of impunity among perpetrators further undermine accountability for violence.

Gender-based violence in the garment industry is not simply a factory-level problem, but is instead rooted in gendered segmentation of the garment workforce. In-depth factory profiles of 13 garment supplier factories from Bangladesh, Cambodia, and India revealed consistent distribution of workers by gender across departments and roles.[2] Women workers are concentrated in low-wage production jobs where they are hired on short-term contracts. Within these roles, they are driven to reach unrealistic production targets through excessive hours of work in unsafe workplaces. These risk factors for violence[3] stem from the structure of garment supply chains, including asymmetrical relationships of power between brands and suppliers, brand purchasing practices driven by fast fashion trends and pressure to reduce costs, and proliferation of contract labor and subcontracting practices among supplier firms. In short, gender-based violence in the garment industry is a by-product of how multinational brands do business. The structure of production in global production networks (GPNs), involving several companies across multiple countries, allows brands and retailers to dictate sourcing and production patterns while deflecting accountability for how purchasing practices drive severe violations of rights at work.

What approaches might prove effective in eliminating gender-based violence in garment supply chains? This chapter makes a case for substantive obligations on lead firms through binding, contractually enforceable agreements. In order to address gender-based violence at the intersection of patriarchal social norms and supply chain employment practices, such an approach should be led by women workers and require brands to meaningfully invest in addressing risk factors for violence in their supply chains.

Women workers in Asian garment supply chains

Globally, Asian garment suppliers top apparel exports worldwide. In 2016, more than 55.4% of $443 billion in global apparel exports originated from seven Asian countries—in order of market share: China, Bangladesh, Vietnam, India, Hong Kong, Indonesia, and Cambodia (WTO 2017). Across Asia, women make up the vast majority of garment workers. Women between the ages of 18 and 35 dominate the Cambodian garment production sector, comprising an estimated 90%–95% of the industry's estimated 700,000 workers (Barria 2014; Kashyap 2015). In Bangladesh and Sri Lanka, 85% of garment workers are women (Madurawala 2017; Moyeen 2018). In Indonesia, women comprise 80% of the garment workforce (Oktaviania 2017). In India, women account for between 60% and 75% of the garment workforce (Kane 2015; Mohan 2017). These numbers do not include women engaged in seasonal, home-based garment work (Kashyap 2015).

Working conditions for women producing garments at the base of Asian garment supply chains are informed by the structure of the Textile, Clothing, Leather and Footwear (TCLF) GPN.[4] The evolution of production processes to include several companies across multiple countries has precipitated shifts in employment relationships and control over production processes. Brand purchasing practices, driven by fast fashion trends and pressure to reduce costs, structure employment relationships for women workers. These features of work in the garment supply chain have significant consequences for a gendered global labor force.

Buyer-driven value chains

The TCLF GPN is characterized by geographically dispersed production and rapid, market-driven changes. Brands engage in high-value market research, design, sales, marketing, and financial services. They typically outsource garment production to geographically disbursed Tier 1 companies that may, in turn, subcontract some or all of the garment production process to manufacturing companies known as suppliers. This structure allows brands and retailers to drive coordinated production of goods by capitalizing upon new technology, relaxed regulatory frameworks, and a supply of low-wage labor in developing countries (Ghosh 2015). While brands and retailers do not produce garments, they drive sourcing and production patterns overseas. This production model has been characterized as a buyer-driven value chain (Gereffi 1994).

Due to diminished government and brand accountability—especially among unregistered suppliers—working conditions in garment factories lack oversight and consistently fall below decent work standards (Kashyap 2015). Poor government capacity, limited resources, infrastructural needs, and, in some cases, adverse disposition toward protective labor standards have weakened national labor standards in producing countries. This decline in labor standards is linked to dominant global policy frameworks that prescribe labor deregulation as a prerequisite to attracting investment capital (Ghosh 2015). Further eroding accountability for working conditions, brands typically make distinctions between their liability for authorized and unauthorized subcontracts. Unauthorized subcontractors may be unregistered and therefore outside the purview of any remaining government labor regulations.

Fast fashion, production targets, and accelerated work

Business relationships between brands and suppliers are governed by purchasing practices that impact the functioning of supplier firms and, in turn, working conditions. Current purchasing practices reflect the rise of fast fashion. Where the norm was four style seasons each year, the Zara brand pioneered monthly styles and even two-week cycles. Today, brands commonly release between eight and ten style seasons each year (Nathan and Kumar 2017), accelerating production cycles and shortening lead time. Short lead times, high quotas, and irregular, repeat orders for high-demand items require supervisors and line managers to demand high-speed turnover, drive worker productivity, and hold workers' overtime (Vaughan-Whitehead and Caro 2017).

Reliance on contract labor

Since 2010, garment brand and retail members of the UK Ethical Trading Initiative (ETI) have reported increasing reliance on contract labor within garment value chains. Contract workers cost less to employ per unit, often receive lower wages, rarely receive nonwage benefits, including paid leave and social security, and can be fired according to shifting employer needs. These terms of employment leave contract workers particularly vulnerable to exploitation when compared to directly employed workers (Chan 2013).

Rise in employment of contract workers has been attributed to buyer purchasing practices. Downward pressure on prices, combined with increasingly unpredictable seasonal variation in production, requires garment suppliers to employ a flexible, low-wage work force. The result: a workforce of predominantly women workers with unstable employment, making garments for low wages to meet fast fashion demands.

Gendered segmentation of the garment workforce

Scholarship on gender in the global economy has documented how in varied, locally specific ways, international capital relies upon gendered ideologies and social relations to recruit and discipline workers, producing segmented labor forces within and between countries (Mills 2003). Women in the Asian garment workforce migrate for employment to garment production hubs due

Table 12.1 Gendered production roles in garment supply chains in Bangladesh, Cambodia, and India

Gendered hiring by department, range across factories					
Department	Fabric Store	Cutting	Fusing/ pasting	Production	Finishing/packing
Management	Manager male	Supervisor male - female	Supervisor male	Supervisor 80-100% male 0-20% female	Supervisor 90-100% male 0-10% female
	In-charge male	Quality Control 60-100% male 0-40% female		Quality Control 20-100% male 0-80% female	Quality Control Male - Female
	Supervisor male			Line In-Charge 70-100% male 0-30% female	
				Group leaders (lower level managers in Cambodia) 0-30% male 70-100% female	
Specialized roles	Store Keeper male	Sticker Master 0%-100% male 0-100% female	Fusing machine Operator 20-100% male 0-80% female	Record Keeper 20-100% male 0-80% female	
		Cutting Machine male			
		Layer Man male - female			
Checkers		Checker 0%-100% male 0-100% female		Checker 0%-100% male 0-100% female	
Machine operators		Button Machine 0%-100% male 0-100% female		Line Tailor 0%-40% male 0-100% female	
Helpers		Male and female workers in varied proportions, including all male and all female departments	Helper 20-70% male 30%-80% female	Helper 0-30% male 70-100% female	Male and female workers in varied proportions, including all male and all female departments

to lack of opportunity in their home provinces, family debt, and inability to sustain themselves and their families. Within garment factories, the vast majority of women workers are employed in the production department in subordinate machine operator, checker, and helper roles (Table 12.1).

Departments segregated by gender may also be spatially separate, creating multiple working environments within a factory. For instance, within one Indonesian supplier factory, the first floor includes the production department and accessory warehouse, comprised of women workers supervised by both male and female supervisors. While some men work on the first floor,

212 Shikha Silliman Bhattacharjee

they work in a physically separate warehouse for final products. The second floor houses the cutting unit, staffed by a mix of male and female workers and supervisors. In this arrangement, women production-line workers are concentrated not only in subordinate roles, but also in segregated spaces.

Women garment workers may be further segregated by demographic categories. For instance, in a garment supplier factory in Gurugram (Gurgaon), Haryana, India, women workers described being separated by age during a routine morning practice of labor segmentation:

> As we enter the factory, we are asked to form two separate lines: one of young girls and another of elder women. They keep us segregated. Young girls work on a different floor than the older ladies. So, in the end, we have no idea how they behave with young girls.

This compounded spatial, role, and age segregation prevents elder women intervening on behalf of younger women who may face violence and harassment. Sri Lankan women workers also identified young, unmarried girls as particularly vulnerable to sexual harassment from both male managers and coworkers.

While younger women are targeted for sexual advances, pregnant women and senior women employees may face alternate forms of life-stage-related discrimination. Women are routinely fired from their jobs during pregnancy. Even permanent workers report being forced to take pregnancy leave without pay. Contract, piece rate, and casual workers reported that although most of the time they are reinstated in their jobs after pregnancy, they receive new contracts and forfeit seniority, reinforcing concentration of women in subordinate low-wage roles.

Further reinforcing concentration of women in subordinate low-wage roles, in Bangladesh, India, and Indonesia, women reported that senior women employees face heightened levels of abuse after they become eligible for seniority benefits. A woman worker in Bangladesh explained:

> Four the first four years that I worked as a sewing machine operator, I had a reputation for skill and dedication. After my fourth year, when I was eligible for gratuity, the line chief and supervisor increased my production targets, shouted at me, and referred to me in derogatory terms. I reported to human resources, but they did not intervene. Work became so unbearable that I left the factory.

Women workers in Bangladesh reported that targeting women workers who are eligible for seniority benefits is common. Women who resign due to harassment are considered to have resigned voluntarily, relieving the employer from paying legally mandated benefits.

Gender-based violence may be further intensified for women from socially marginalized communities. In India, women garment workers include migrant scheduled caste, scheduled tribe, and Muslim women. Their intersecting status as migrants, women, and members of marginalized communities increases risk of exploitation and exclusion from decent work, and undermines accountability through formal legal channels (Shah 2009).

Gender-based violence in Asian garment value chains

Violence in Asian garment value chains is gendered not only because women workers may be singled out for violence and harassment, but because violence and harassment disproportionately impact women workers.[5] This chapter presents five analytic categories to understand gender-based violence: sexual harm and stigma; gendered industrial discipline practices; mining women's productive capacity—or *body mining* (Nathan et al. 2018); unsafe workplaces; and the production of vulnerability through job insecurity, barriers to freedom of association and collective bargaining, and retaliation for reporting violence. These categories of violence are not discrete but layered and intersecting—a palimpsest of violence at the intersection of supply chain employment practices and patriarchal norms.

Sexual harm and stigma

Patterns of sexual violence and harassment reported by women garment workers reflect power asymmetries between men and women (Lin et al. 2014). Women garment workers reported sexual harm from men in positions of authority within the factory as well as coworkers. While perpetrators traverse hierarchical and nonhierarchical employment relationships with women workers, reports of sexual harm most commonly featured employment relationships where women held subordinate roles in relationship to male supervisors, line managers, and mechanics tasked with fixing their machines.

In factories where majority male supervisors and line managers oversee an overwhelmingly female workforce, male monopoly over authority can contribute to a culture of impunity around sexual violence and harassment. Women workers employed in a supplier factory in Gurugram described being moved from line-to-line depending upon the desires of male supervisors. One woman explained:

> If the supervisor likes a girl and has some influence over the floor incharge, then he will arrange to shift that girl under his supervision. If she refuses she will be fired—they will blame *her* for being unable to achieve targets.

In Gurugram, supervisors, floor incharge, and line managers within a factory are often relatives. This interconnected web of male supervision further undermines avenues for relief for women who are targets of sexual advances. Reports of sexual advances by men in positions of authority are not limited to India. Bangladeshi women reported that it is common for supervisors and managers to pursue sexual relationships with women workers by offering benefits including salary increases, promotions, and better positions. Women rejecting these offers face retaliation, including being fired. Sri Lankan trade union leaders reported that women employed through "manpower"—or temporary work agencies—face routine sexual advances from supervisors who make hiring within the factory contingent upon receiving their overtures. Women reported retaliation from supervisors if they resist advances: a woman who does not meet the sexual desires of the supervisor may get more overtime hours, denied legally mandated breaks or leaves, or even fired.

Control over working hours by male supervisors provides opportunities for sexual violence and harassment to extend beyond legal working hours and the factory floor. In Tirupur, Tamil Nadu, India, women workers reported supervisors abusing control over working hours to make sexual advances after long night shifts. One woman explained:

> It is a trap. If a supervisor is interested in a woman, he can make her work the half-night shift which gets over at midnight. Then, he may offer to drop her home on his bike. She may not have another option to reach home at night. In this situation, it is easy for the supervisor to exploit the woman targeted.

Women workers in this position face a double bind: either submit to sexual advances from supervisors; or risk harassment, robbery, or worse during a solo late-night commute.

In Sri Lanka, women working in supplier factories reported being at risk of sexual harassment from male mechanics tasked with fixing their machines. One woman recounted:

> A machine mechanic asked me to spend the night with him. I refused. When my machine stopped working, I asked him to repair it. He refused. Then he asked me to spend the night with him. He said if I agreed, he would fix my machine.

While women workers are not directly subordinate to machine mechanics, they are functionally subordinate to these male workers because their ability to meet production targets depends upon machine maintenance.

Further undermining accountability, women reported reluctance to report sexual harassment, advances, and violence due to social stigma that may manifests as either restriction on their mobility or victim blaming. One woman worker described the social consequences that prevented her from reporting sexual advances at work and at home:

> I did not report at work because it is the woman who is blamed. No one sees the man as at fault. I thought, if my husband comes to know about this he will not let me work anymore. So, I decided to resign quietly without telling anyone anything.

In this instance, social stigma, rooted in family and community patriarchal norms, threatened yet another level of consequences for unwanted sexual advances faced at work: barriers to future employment outside the household. Fear or reporting due to stigma and victim blaming further constrains access justice in cases of sexual harm.

For those who decide to seek relief through legal channels, social authority wielded by male supervisors and coworkers may be reinforced through gaps in legal protections and gendered policing practices. Notably, women employed in the garment production hub of Phnom Penh, Cambodia, have no avenue for redress under Cambodian Labor Law for sexual harassment from male colleagues.[6] Even where sexual harassment is an actionable offense, women report barriers to accountability, beginning at the police station. When a woman sewing machine operator in Bangladesh reported repeated sexual overtures from her manager to the police, the police refused to file her case. When she returned to work the next day, she was fired from her job. She learned that the police informed the accused manager that she had visited the police station to report sexual harassment.

Gendered industrial discipline practices

Women workers in divisions ranging from sewing, trimming excess thread, quality checking, and packaging are assigned production targets. Production targets vary by garment type, but typically require workers to be accountable for every minute they are at work. Women in Phnom Penh described group production targets of 380 pieces per hour per line— with 38 workers per line.[7] In India, Indonesia, and Sri Lanka, women more commonly reported individual production targets. Indian women in Gurugram described typical targets as 30–40 pieces per hour. However, during heavy production periods, they may be driven to meet inflated and unreachable[8] targets of up to 100 pieces an hour. In Indonesia, women reported being required to produce 90–120 pieces every 25 minutes, with timed intervals to determine if targets were met. In Sri Lanka, production targets can escalate to 200–250 pieces every 30 minutes. Across Asian garment production networks, women reported that workers who fell short of their targets may be prevented from taking lunch breaks or forced to stay overtime.

The daily race to meet production targets is sustained through gendered industrial discipline associated with *operatory labor practices*: referring to the role of workers as basic sewing machine operators, operatory labor practices correspond with hierarchical work relationships, sweatshop discipline, and anti-union management practices (Nathan, Saripalle and Gurunathan 2016). Tied to their ability to reach production targets, women workers reported physical and verbal abuse, coercion, threats, and deprivations of liberty. While both women and men reported these forms of workplace violence, discipline is disproportionately directed at women workers due to their concentration in machine operator, checker, and helper roles within production departments.

Physical violence reported by women workers included slapping, push-ing, kicking, and throwing heavy bundles of papers and clothes, especially during high-stress production times. Bundles may weigh between two and four kilograms—a projectile that is approximately the weight of a brick, but unlikely to leave visible marks that would allow the victim to seek redress. Workers reported that physical discipline practices spiked after second tier management came out of meetings with senior management driving produc-tion targets.

In Cambodia, where local workers are managed by Chinese managers, women reported that physical and verbal abuse escalated due to frustra-tion with communicating across language barriers. One woman worker recounted:

> Chinese managers pressure the Cambodian team leaders to shout at the workers to make them work faster. We are called stupid and lazy. Sometimes they beat workers.

A Cambodian woman described an incident where a translator slapped a female worker and later claimed he was joking. No action was taken against the perpetrator. As with Radhika, whose experience of violence opened this chapter, public corporal discipline terrorizes not only the direct victim, but also women around her. Consequently, violence on the production line is both looming and normalized—a constant threat that drives production with fear.

In addition to targeted physical aggression, women reported rough treat-ment from male supervisors and relentless verbal abuse. One woman from a supplier factory in Gurugram, Haryana, India, described being physically pushed to work: "The supervisor and master push us by our shoulder or shake it abruptly and roughly with their hand ordering us to work."

Women garment workers in Bangladesh, Cambodia, and Indonesia described constant and relentless verbal abuse that continues from the be-ginning to the end of their shifts. An Indonesian woman described the stress and humiliation associated with yelling and mocking from her supervisor:

> If you miss the target, all the workers in the production room can hear the yelling:
> "You stupid! Cannot work?"
> "Watch out, you! I will not extend your contract."
> "You don't have to come to work tomorrow if you can't do your job!"
> They also throw materials. They kick our chairs. They don't touch us so they don't leave a mark that could be used as evidence with the police, but it is very stressful.

Industrial discipline practices may intersect with sexual harassment and threats of violence on the factory floor. A woman worker, employed in a supplier factory in Gurugram, explained: "It's very common for the in-charge manager to say, 'finish the target or I will …' —using any number of sexual connotations. They do not say this to men." The categories of gender-based violence described in this chapter are not discrete. Rather, these types of violence are intersecting, overlapping, and mutually reinforcing.

Body mining

The combination of low wages and relentless working hours in the garment industry violently extract labor from women's bodies. Introduced by Nathan et al. (2018), the term *body mining* refers to the physical toll on women that results from poor nutritional intake, no weekly rest day, and the physical demands of work. Their study found that among 38 garment workers (21 women and 17 men) in two garment factories in India, 33.3% of women fainted at work and 28.6% received a glucose drip within the last year. All of the women reporting fainting had worked overtime. No man reported fainting—a finding contextualized by the authors in relationship to anemia among Indian women, a common condition due to discrimination in access to food; and women's heavy burden of unpaid work at home. According to a randomized survey conducted by India's Employees State Insurance Corporation in 2014, 60.6% of garment workers surveyed were anemic (Ceresna-Chaturvedi 2015).

The concept of body mining has expansive application in understanding the impact of excessive working hours across garment supply chains. Women from Bangladesh, Cambodia, India, Indonesia, and Sri Lanka all reported being forced to work overtime to meet short production time lines. Women workers in Manesar, Haryana, India reported that overtime hours for most workers amount to a minimum of three hours per day and routinely stretched till late at night. To take Sunday off, workers report being made to work as late as 4 am on Sunday to complete their Saturday shift. While Indian legal standards require suppliers to compensate workers for food expenditures during overtime work hours, this supplier factory provides a mere Rs. 79 [USD 1.22] to workers engaged in overtime late into the night. During high-intensity production cycles, women may work days on end without a break. A woman tailor from a supplier factory in Gurugram described having to work 21 days continuously without a break.

Women garment workers labor under caloric and nutritional deficits because the food they can afford does not sustain the length and rigor of their work day. Data gathered by tracking monthly food purchases by 95 workers employed in a range of garment factories in Cambodia, compared with recommended amounts and workers' Body Mass Index, revealed that workers were found to intake an average of 1,598 calories per day, around half the recommended among for a woman working in an industrial context (McMullen and Majumder 2016).

Body mining is intimately tied to wages and working conditions in supplier factories, competing to win production bids from brands and retailers. Suppliers project labor costs based upon minimum wages, rather than living wages;[9] and ten-hour days, including two hours of overtime, rather than eight-hour working days. Due to this practice, suppliers routinely pay only normal wages for overtime rather than the double-wage rate required under many labor law regimes (Nathan and Kumar 2016). The costs of inadequate wages and excessive hours of work are born by women workers, subjected to dangerous and deadly tolls upon their bodies.

Unsafe workplaces

Body mining is compounded by unsafe working conditions, including long hours performing repetitive manual tasks under exposure to heat, noise, dust, and chemicals. Long hours sitting hunched over machines leads to back pain, ulcers, piles, and reproductive health issues (irregular period and excessive bleeding). Women working as checkers report varicose veins as a result of long hours standing and checking garments. Other routine health consequences for women garment workers include respiratory illnesses like tuberculosis, irritation of the upper respiratory tract and bronchi, and silicosis from sand blasting. Prolonged exposure can progress to chronic, obstructive pulmonary disease. According to a randomized survey conducted by India's Employees State Insurance Corporation in 2014, 80% of all tuberculosis cases registered in 2009 were from Indian garment workers; largely internal migrants between the ages of 18 and 45 years with lower socioeconomic status faced difficulties accessing medical attention (Ceresna-Chaturvedi 2015).

In Cambodia, mandatory overtime during the production high season overlaps with Cambodia's hottest season. From April to August, workers report being forced to work up to 14 hours a day—as well as on Sundays and national holidays—in sweltering heat, without adequate supply of clean drinking water or any breaks. Exposure to high temperatures and high levels of chemical substances, exacerbated by poor ventilation systems and inadequate nutrition among workers, make episodes of mass fainting a regular occurrence. In 2017, the Cambodian National Social Security Fund identified 1,603 cases of fainting across 22 factories. One thousand five hundred ninety-nine—or 98%—of these cases were women.

Cases of fainting include individual workers, and multiple workers within a factory fainting at once. On August 4, 2017, Meas Sreyleak, a 25-year-old Cambodian woman, died on her way from the factory to the hospital after she fainted at work and hit her head on the sewing table. Women who worked with Sreyleak reported she had been feeling unwell on the day she died. She had a sore throat, but was made to work two hours overtime. Her family received $1,000 from the factory to help defray funeral expenses. On July 6, 2017, Neom Somol saw a colleague faint in the factory and attempted to help her get to a medical clinic. In the process of doing so she fainted herself, her head hit a wall, and she died at the factory. At another factory in Phnom Penh, 150 workers fainted over two days (30th and 31st of August 2017) due to the combination of high heat and exhaustion.

The extreme health consequences associated with extractive labor practices in garment supplier factories are well known to major garment brands. As early as 2011, Swedish fashion brand, H&M, responded to 284 Cambodian workers fainting at M&V International Manufacturing in Kompong Chhnang Province—an H&M supplier. More than 100 workers were hospitalized. H&M reported launching an investigation (McPherson 2011). The investigative report commission by H&M blamed the fainting on "mass hysteria" caused by work-related and personal stress (Butler 2012). This explanation capitalizes on gendered tropes that blame women workers for the consequences of extractive labor. Investigation by labor researchers revealed a more robust explanation at the intersection of body mining and unsafe workplaces: malnutrition, prevalent among Cambodian garment workers, makes them more susceptible to exposure to harmful environments (McMullen and Majumder 2016).

Mass cases of fainting among garment workers in Cambodia are the most widely reported to date, but are not isolated to Cambodia. On March 19, 2018, 52 workers collapsed from breathing toxic fumes in a garment supplier factory in Ekala, Sri Lanka. That day, the Branch Union Secretary for the factory encouraged workers to leave the workplace due to widespread difficulty breathing, nausea, stinging eyes, and vomiting. Instead, workers continued to work to meet their production targets. The Assistant Factory Manager attributed the smell to machine maintenance and took no action to address worker complaints. By 10:40 am that day, workers began collapsing and 52 workers were rushed to the hospital.

Unsafe workplace practices extend beyond the factory gates. Workers in Cambodia stand crowded together in the back of open-air trucks to reach their factory shifts. On November 10, 2017, Campost, a Khmer language newspaper, reported an accident involving a truck carrying 68 garment workers on their way to garment supplier factory Juhi Footwear Co. Five workers were seriously injured. The paper attributed the accident to negligence by the driver, leading the truck to flip over.

Producing vulnerability

Violence in the garment industry occurs amidst cultures of fear and isolation for women perpetually at risk of termination.[10] Ongoing employment insecurity undermines accountability for workplace violence and other rights violations. Women workers reported choosing not to report violence due to the high consequences—job loss and social stigma—and few viable avenues for redress. The potential for collective action to address working conditions is undermined by retaliation against workers seeking to build unions, strict control over workplace solidarity, and high turnover among workers. Without avenues for redress that disrupt workplace violence, women garment workers remain vulnerable to the spectrum of violence presented in this chapter.

Retaliation for reporting workplace rights violations

Women workers from Bangladesh, Cambodia, India, Indonesia, and Sri Lanka all described fearing retaliation if they complained about any violations of rights at work, including but not limited to gender-based violence. One woman worker in Gurugram, Haryana, India, explained:

> Whoever speaks against any injustice is fired. Once I, along with others, went to the manager because our wage was not being paid properly. They did not remove us all together, but within ten days, they used some reason or another to remove each and every one of us.

Routine and ongoing threats of employment termination discourage women workers from seeking relief. For instance, a woman in Phnom Penh explained not reporting the Chinese team leader who threw heavy bundles of clothes at her. Fearing retaliation for reporting the violence, she kept quiet.

Barriers to freedom of association

Constant threats of termination create a significant barrier to organizing a union. Workers and union organizers in Indonesia explained that high turnover undermines unionization, worker solidarity, and collective action. Within garment production units, very few workers hold continuous employment for more than a year. By hiring workers on short-term contracts, the contractor and the factory can fire workers in retaliation for engaging in union activities.

The structure of work in garment supplier factories further undermines freedom of association. Long working hours deny workers opportunity to engage with one another. In Manesar, Gurgaon, India, workers are prevented from speaking with one another during breaks in the workday. Workers are forbidden to leave factory premises—during their tea and lunch break they are required to eat at the canteen inside the unit. Prohibitions on leaving the factory for breaks during working hours, combined with extended working hours—at times up to 17 hours a day—functionally eclipse the potential for workers to exercise their fundamental rights to freedom of association and collective bargaining.

Denying freedom of association and collective bargaining forecloses important pathways for redress by women workers. Barriers to freedom of association and collective bargaining prevent workers from responding collectively to violence, furthering cultures of impunity around gender-based violence.

Conclusion: interventions to eliminate gender-based violence

Ending gender-based violence in garment supplier factories that manifests at the intersection of patriarchal norms and supply chain employment practices calls for three types of interventions: to hold apparel brands and retailers at the top of the supply chain jointly responsible for risk factors for violence; to challenge the concentration of women workers in subordinate roles; and to address gendered cultures of impunity for workplace violence. This approach reflects core strategies from tri-partite "jobber" agreements negotiated in the United States in the middle part of the twentieth century by the International Ladies Garment Workers Union (ILGWU) and companies called jobbers—individuals and firms that designed or sold, but did not manufacture apparel. Precipitated in part by a fire at the Triangle Shirtwaist Company in 1911 that killed 146 workers, by 1935, agreements negotiated between ILGWU, contractors, and jobbers led to a widespread decline in sweatshop working conditions for women garment workers, a largely female and immigrant workforce (Anner, Bair, and Blasi 2013).[11]

On April 4, 2013, the Rana Plaza building, housing five garment factories in Dhaka Bangladesh, collapsed, killing 1,129 workers (Manik and Yardley 2013). Widespread media coverage and campaigning by a coalition of unions and NGOs resulted in more than thirty-five large apparel brands and retailers signing the Accord on Building and Fire Safety in Bangladesh ("Accord")(Greenhouse 2013). The Accord builds upon the success of historical trade union initiatives in securing supply chain accountability and also represents new innovations to secure transnational accountability in context of global garment production networks—by collectivizing global brands and requiring their dedicated investment in factory infrastructure. The Accord has been acclaimed as a "new model of corporate accountability" in contrast to corporate social responsibility reliance on voluntary standards for brands and retailers (Anner, Bair, and Blasi 2013). Although the Accord is a step forward in providing a contemporary model of corporate accountability, as documented in this volume, the enforceability of this agreement has been limited, due in part to reliance on third-parties for enforcement. The combined strength of enforceable brand agreements, and accountability located in the leadership of women garment workers and their trade unions, however, provides a promising avenue for ending gender-based violence in garment factories.

Risk factors for gender-based violence must also be addressed through targeted commitment by brands and retailers. Gendered industrial discipline practices can be alleviated through enforceable prohibitions against unrealistic production targets that accelerate production speed, extend working hours, and create high-stress work environments. Enforceable commitments to supplying only from factories that pay living wages and respect working hours can address body mining and other physically extractive labor practices. Brand and buyer commitments to sourcing from suppliers that provide employment security; prohibit workplace retaliation; protect workers from environmental and occupational health hazards; and uphold fundamental rights to freedom of association and collective bargaining have the potential to make strong inroads into addressing cultures of impunity for workplace violence. Research provides preliminary evidence that initiatives to address workplace violence stand to benefit brands and suppliers by increasing individual efficiency, production quantity, and ultimately revenue (Rourke 2014).[12]

For enforceable brand agreements to intervene in patriarchal subordination and stigma that fuel gender-based violence in supplier factories, they must take conscious measures to disrupt gendered power relationships in the workplace and beyond. Recent initiatives for racial justice that align worker interests within the workplace and community offer an instructive model for addressing gendered relationships of power. For instance, AFSCME 3299, representing 24,000 patient care and service worker on University of California campuses—half of whom are Latinos, with a supermajority being people of color—took measures to address attacks against members based on race and nationality. AFSCME 3299 formed a racial justice working group where workers shared personal stories about racism and police violence, and demanded an end to outsourcing, improved job security, benefits, increased wages, and training programs to improve working conditions for people of color (JWJ 2018; Howard, Manzanarez, and Patel 2017). This approach raised the visibility of racial injustice among union members and provided a foundation for collective action to address racial injustice in the workplace and beyond. This model of worker leadership in addressing racial injustice aligns with calls by trade unions and labor organizations to position workers at the front and center of negotiating enforceable contractual obligations on garment brands and retailers (e.g., AFWA 2017).

On May 28, 2018, the International Labour Organization (ILO) convened a Standard Setting Committee to begin the historic work of creating a global standard protecting workers from violence and harassment in the work of work, with a specific mandate to address gender-based violence. As the Committee entered deliberations on the definition of the term "gender-based violence," a delegation including trade union leadership from AFWA and the GLJ research and legal team released factory level research reports documenting gender-based violence in H&M, Gap, and Walmart Asian garment supply chains (AFWA/GLJ 2018a-c)—these findings form the research core of this chapter.[13] The reports were covered by more than 50 news outlets across 17 countries and described by The Nation as a "#MeToo Movement for the Global Fashion Industry."[14] This campaign built upon the successes of ten years of organizing by AFWA, including establishment of the only Asian-led alliance of workers and allies, widespread legitimacy around a regional living wage for Asian garment workers, and the role of trade unions in bargaining for brand accountability. On June 5, 2018, H&M and Gap publicly declared support for a binding ILO Convention on workplace violence, including gender-based violence in garment supply chains. In the public realm, AFWA and GLJ established widespread recognition of the spectrum of gender-based violence and associated risk factors in the garment industry, and the need for solutions which include collective worker voices.

In order for enforceable bargaining agreements to address unequal power relationships that subordinate women garment workers, bargaining must include an important role for *women* leaders at supply factories—supported by enforceable brand agreements. To that end, in June 2018, AFWA and GLJ called upon Gap, H&M, and Walmart to address gender-based violence documented in their supply chains by proactively working with the AFWA Women's Leadership Committee (WLC) to pilot enforceable brand agreements in supplier factories with trade unions aimed at eliminating gender-based violence and discrimination, and expanding broader indicia of women's collective empowerment. Such initiatives, led by women garment workers' collectives, have the potential not only to identify context-specific risk factors for violence, but also to address gendered imbalances of power within supplier factories.

Notes

1 In advance of the 107th Session of the International Labour Conference, a global coalition of trade unions, worker rights and human rights organizations, which includes AFWA, CENTRAL Cambodia, GLJ, Sedane Labour Resource Centre (LIPS) Indonesia, and Society for Labour and Development India released factory-level research detailing gender-based violence in Walmart, Gap, and H&M Asian garment supply chains. This study was designed and coordinated by Shikha Silliman Bhattacharjee; J. D. Field research conducted during January–May 2018 was completed by Faisal Bin Majid, Immanuel Dahaghani, Jenny Holligan, Patrick Lee, Monower Mostafa, Thy Phalla, Sar Mora, Linda Nop, Aparna Roy, Anjum Shaheen, Abiramy Sivalogananthan, Yang Sophorn, and Wiranta Yudha.
2 Researchers developed profiles for five factories from Bangladesh, five factories from Cambodia, and three factories from India.
3 The October 2016 report on the outcomes of the ILO Meeting of Experts on "Violence against Women and Men in the World of Work" presents a detailed set of risk factors for violence in the world of work that lends insight into the conditions under which violence is more likely to occur. These include risk factors associated with the nature and setting of work as well as the structure of the labor market. The report calls for an international labor law instrument that can respond to the new challenges and risks which might lead to violence and harassment in the world of work, such as those arising from changing forms of work and technology (GB.328/INS/17/5, Appendix I, para. 18).

4 GPN is a term that describes contemporary production systems that involve several companies across multiple countries. Companies linked through GPNs are related through various legal forms, with exchanges between firms structured so that multinational or transnational corporations (TNCs) do not legally own overseas subsidiaries or franchisees but only outsource production to them. GPNs shift market relationships between firms from trade relationships to quasi-production relationships without the risks of ownership. Within this model, TNCs drive coordinated production of goods while disbursing risk associated with market fluctuations across global value chains. By 2013, GPNs accounted for some 80% of global trade (UNCTAD 2013).

5 This framework for understanding gender-based violence aligns with the definition of gender-based violence by the CEDAW Committee, in General recommendation 19, that identifies gender-based violence as not only instances when women are targets of violence on the basis of their gender, but also disproportionate impact of particular forms of violence upon women, rooted in structural inequalities. Under this standard, gender-based violence includes (1) violence which is directed against a woman because she is a woman; and (2) violence that affects women disproportionately. Forms of gender-based violence include acts that inflict physical harm, mental harm, sexual harm or suffering, threats of the any of these acts, coercion, and deprivations of liberty (CEDAW, General recommendation 19, Article 1). Over the last 25 years, this interpretation of gender-based violence has been endorsed by judicial opinions and state practices, and has evolved into a principle of customary international law (CEDAW, General recommendation No. 35, para. 2).

CEDAW General recommendation No. 35 emphasizes that gender-based violence is a social rather than an individual problem, requiring comprehensive responses that extend beyond specific events, individual perpetrators, and victims/survivors (para. 9). The CEDAW Committee further underscores that gender-based violence against women is one of the fundamental social, political, and economic means by which the subordination of women with respect to men is perpetuated (para. 10). General recommendations No. 28 and No. 33—on the core obligation of States parties under Article 2 of CEDAW and women's access to justice, respectively—confirm that discrimination against women is inextricably linked to other axes of discrimination.

6 Sexual harassment from male colleagues is not included under Article 172 of the Cambodian Labor Law which governs sexual harassment in the workplace perpetrated by supervisors. Exclusion of sexual harassment from male colleagues under Labor Law, combined with a restrictive definition of sexual harassment in the Cambodian Criminal Code, strips female workers from protection against sexual harassment perpetrated by male colleagues.

7 While prior to increases in the Cambodian minimum wage there had been up to 50 workers per line, at the time of writing this number decreased to around 38.

8 At a maximum, women workers in Gurugram reported being able to produce 90–95 pieces per hour, 5%–10% short of the required targets.

9 AFWA, a global coalition of trade unions, workers' rights and human rights organizations, provides a detailed formula for calculating living wages across national contexts. The AFWA definition of a living wage specifies that living wage calculations must include support for all family members, basic nutritional needs of a worker and other basic needs, including housing, healthcare, education, and some basic savings. AFWA's living wage calculation is based on the following considerations: a worker needs to support themselves and two other consumption units (one consumption unit supports either one adult or two children); an adult requires 3,000 calories a day in order to carry out physically demanding work in good health; within Asia, food costs amount for half of a

worker's monthly expenditure. Based upon these assumptions, the Asia Floor Wage is calculated in Purchasing Power Parity $ (PPP$). This fictitious World Bank currency is built upon consumption of goods and services, allowing standard of living between countries to be compared regardless of the national currency. Accounting for high inflation, Asia Floor Wage figures are calculated annually based upon regular and ongoing food basket research. For instance, the 2017 Asia Floor Wage figure is PPP$ 1181. These wage figures are then converted into local currency: Bangladesh, 37,661 Takas; Cambodia, 1,939,606 Riel; India, 23,588 Rupees; and Indonesia, 5,886,112 Rupiah.

10 The proposition that gender-based violence has social roots that belie specific events, individual perpetrators, and victims/survivors has been sufficiently well established that it has been recognized by the United Nations Committee on the Elimination of Discrimination against Women. CEDAW General recommendation No. 35 emphasizes that gender-based violence is a social rather than an individual problem, requiring comprehensive responses that extend beyond specific events, individual perpetrators, and victims/survivors (para. 9). The CEDAW Committee further underscores that gender-based violence against women is one of the fundamental social, political, and economic means by which the subordination of women with respect to men is perpetuated (para. 10). General recommendations No. 28 and No. 33—on the core obligation of States parties under article 2 of CEDAW and women's access to justice, respectively—confirm that discrimination against women is inextricably linked to other axes of discrimination.

11 Anner et. al. both provide a historical account of the negotiation of jobber agreements and their role in the decline of sweatshop conditions in the U.S. apparel industry by the middle part of the twentieth century, and distinguish both parallels and distinctions between U.S. domestic subcontracting networks and contemporary global supply chains. Key distinctions between the historical context of jobber agreements and contemporary supply chains include relatively high union density in the Northeast of the U.S. by the mid-twentieth century, and willingness by the U.S. government to enforce labor laws. Both union density and government enforcement of strong labor laws are currently lacking in major garment export countries, including in Asia.

12 Rourke's analyzes worker productivity as it relates to verbal abuse in garment factories in Indonesia, Jordan, and Vietnam, providing preliminary evidence that verbal exhortation actually diminishes individual efficiency, productivity, and revenue. She finds that verbal abuse in firm incentive structures has the opposite of its intended motivational effect

13 These reports followed the May 24 release of factory level research documenting gender based violence in Walmart Asian garment supply chains. These reports are available at https://www.globallaborjustice.org and https://asia.floorwage.org/workersvoices.

14 Access to this global coverage is available at Global Labor Justice, "In the News", available at https://www.globallaborjustice.org/press/.

Bibliography

Anner, M., Jennifer Bair, and Jeremy Blasi (2013). Toward Joint Liability in Global Supply Chains: Addressing the Root Causes of Labor Violations in International Subcontracting Networks. *Comparative Labor Law and Policy Journal*, 35:1, p. 1–44.

Barria, S. (2014). National People's Tribunal on Living Wage for Garment Workers in Asia, Asia Floor Wage Campaign: Delhi.

Butler, S. (2012). "Cambodian workers hold 'people's tribunal' to look at factory conditions: H&M and GAP criticised for not agreeing to attend hearings next week investigating pay, working hours and 'mass faintings.'" The Guardian, February 2, 2012, accessed August 31, 2018: www.theguardian.com/world/2012/feb/02/cambodian-workers-peoples-tribunal-factory.

Ceresna-Chaturvedi, L. (2015). A Study of Occupational Health and Safety in the Garment Industry in Bangalore. Cividep, accessed August 31, 2018: http://cividep.org/wp-content/uploads/2017/04/25-2-Occupational-health-safety-13.pdf.

Chan, M. (2013). Contract Labour in Global Garment Supply Chains: Key Characteristics and Recent Trends, Wiego 2013, accessed August 31, 2018: http://wiego.org/sites/wiego.org/files/publications/files/Chan_Contract_Labour_Report_final_2013.pdf.

Gereffi, G. (1994). "The Organization of Buyer-Driven Global Commodity Chains: How U.S. Retailers Shape Overseas Production Networks," in ed. Gary Gereffi and Miguel Korzeniewicz, *Commodity Chains and Global Capitalism* (Praeger: Westport Connecticut and London).

Ghosh, S. (2015). "Global Value Chains and the Garment Sector in India," *Towards an Asia Floor Wage: A Global South Labour Initiative for Garment Workers* (Bangalore: Books for Change).

Greenhouse, S. (2013). Major Retailers Join Bangladesh Safety Plan, N.Y. TIMES, May 13, 2013. A full list of signatories is available at INDUSTRIALL, Bangladesh, www.industriall-union.org/tags/bangladesh (last visited Sept. 10, 2013).

Howard, L., Maricruz Manzanarez, and Seth Newton Patel (2017). "How we're setting our contract bargaining tables to advance racial justice." Labor Notes, March 15, 2017, accessed August 31, 2018: http://labornotes.org/2017/03/setting-our-bargaining-tables-advance-racial-justice.

Jobs with Justice (2018). Expanding the Frontiers of Bargaining: Building Power in the 21st Century (forthcoming).

Kane, G. (2015). "Facts on India's garment industry." Clean clothes campaign, accessed May 6, 2019: https://cleanclothes.org/resources/publications/factsheets/india-factsheet-february-2015.pdf/view.

Kashyap, A. (2015). "Work faster or get out: labour rights abuses in Cambodia's garment industry," Human Rights Watch.

Lin, X, Laura Babbitt, and Drusilla Brown. (2014). *Sexual Harassment in the Workplace: How Does It Affect Firm Performance and Profits*. Better Work Discussion Paper Series No. 16. Stable URL: betterwork.org/global/wp-content/uploads/2014/11/DP16.pdf. Accessed on October 1, 2018.

Madurawala, S (2017). "The dwindling stitching hands: labour shortages in the apparel industry in Sri Lanka," accessed May 20, 2018: www.ips.lk/talkingeconomics/2017/04/03/the-dwindling-stitching-hands-labour-shortages-in-the-apparel-industry-in-sri-lanka/.

Manik, J. & Jim Yardley, "Building collapse in Bangladesh leaves scores dead," N.Y. TIMES, Apr. 25, 2013, at A1.

Mills, Mary Beth. (2003). Gender and Inequality in the Global Labor Force. *Annual Review of Anthropology*, 32, pp. 41–62.

McMullen, A. and Sanjita Majumder. (2016). Do We Buy It?: A supply chain investigation into living wage commitments from M&S and H&M. Labour Behind the Label, Cividep, Stand up Movement, Center for Alliance of Labour and Human Rights (CENTRAL), accessed August 31, 2018: http://labourbehindthelabel.net/wp-content/uploads/2016/02/DoWeBuyIt-spreadssml-1.pdf.

McPherson, P. (2011). Hundreds of workers collapse at Cambodian H&M clothing factory. Independent. August, 29, 2011, accessed May 9, 2016: www. independent.co.uk/news/world/asia/hundreds-of-workers-collapse-at-cambodian-hampm-clothing-factory-2345537.html/

Mohan, R. (2017). "Bengaluru garment hub's dirty secret: Sexual harassment in the workplace," Scroll.in, September 19, 2018, accessed August 31, 2018: https://scroll. in/article/840363/bengaluru-garment-hubs-dirty-secret-sexual-harassment-at-the-workplace.

Moyeen, S. (2018). "Redefining women's empowerment in Bangladesh," World Bank, accessed August 31, 2018: http://blogs.worldbank.org/endpovertyinsouthasia/ redefining-womens-empowerment-bangladesh.

Nathan, Dev et al. (2018). Defining and Achieving a Living Wage: Garment Workers (forthcoming).

Nathan, Dev and Purushottam Kumar. (2017). Purchasing Practices of Global Brands: Their Impact on Supplier Firms and Employment Conditions of Workers. Global Production Network Studies Working Paper (on file with author).

Nathan, D., Madhuri Saripalle and L. Gurunathan. (2016). "ILO Asia Pacific Working Paper Series: Labour Practices in India."

NDTV (2016). "Truth v. hype: brands of shame," July 9, 2016, accessed August 31, 2018: www.ndtv.com/video/news/truth-vs-hype/truth-vs-hype-brands-of-shame-423115.

Oktaviania, Z. (2017). Pekerja Pabrik Garmen Ketakutan Saat Hamil, Ini Alasannya. *Republika*, December 19, 2017, accessed February 24, 2018: http:// nasional.republika.co.id/berita/nasional/hukum/17/12/19/p174ky382-pekerja-pabrik-garmen-ketakutan-saat-hamil-ini-alasannya.

Rourke, Emily L. 2014. *Is There a Business Case Against Verbal Abuse? Incentive Structure, Verbal Abuse, Productivity and Profits in Garment Factories*. Better Work Discussion Paper Series No. 15. ILO: Better Work, February.

Shah, Naureen. (2009). Broken System: Dysfunction, Abuse, and Impunity in the Indian Police. Human Rights Watch, accessed 14 October 2018: www.hrw.org/ sites/default/files/reports/india0809web.pdf.

United Nations Conference on Trade and Development (UNCTAD) (2013). World Investment Report, 2013-Global Value Chains: Investment and Trade for Development, accessed August 31, 2018, http://unctad.org/en/PublicationsLibrary/ wir2013_en.pdf.

Vaughan-Whitehead, Daniel and Luis Pinerdo Caro. 2017. Purchasing practices and working conditions in global supply chains. INWORK Issue Brief No. 10, Geneva: IL). www.ilo.org/wcmsp5/groups/public/---ed_protect/---protrav/---travail/ documents/publication/wcms_556336.pdf. Last accessed September 9, 2017.

World Trade Organization (2017), "World Trade Statistical Review 2017: Statistical tables," accessed May 13, 2018: www.wto.org/english/res_e/statis_e/wts2017_e/ WTO_Chapter_09_tables_e.pdf.

Part V
A way forward

13 The evolving politics of labor standards in Bangladesh

Taking stock and looking forward

Naila Kabeer

Introduction

In this chapter, I provide a brief history of more than three decades of national and international efforts to improve labor standards for workers in the Bangladesh export garment industry. I will examine the different forms it took in different phases of this history and will conclude with some comments on the future of the industry. As someone who has been carrying out research on the industry on and off almost since its inception, I will be drawing on my own findings as well as the wider literature to narrate this history.

Any account of achievements and failures in the efforts to improve labor standards in the Bangladesh industry has to be embedded in the wider context in which it is located because it helps us to understand why working conditions continue to fall short of international conventions and national regulations. While the country faces the typical difficulties of any under-developed country with a very limited history of industrialization, it has been given unusual prominence in international efforts to promote labor standards in global value chains. For this reason, it provides an important case study of the challenges encountered by these efforts when the apparent protectionism of powerful global actors encounters the apparent intransigence of those with relative power at the local level.

The emergence of the export garment industry in Bangladesh

The fact that protectionism is a major theme in this chapter is to be expected. It is dealing with a sector of manufacturing that has long been granted protected status in international trade by advanced industrialized countries, despite their stated commitment to trade liberalization. The General Agreement on Tariffs and Trade (GATT) was set up in 1948 precisely to promote this objective through the gradual reduction of barriers to trade. By 1974, tariffs on trade had been reduced from an average of 40% in the immediate post-war period to 6% in 1974 (World Bank, 1987). However, that same year, trade in garments and textiles was removed from the trade liberalization framework of GATT and placed under the framework of the Multi-Fibre Arrangement (MFA) signed by the USA, Canada and a number of European countries.

The MFA was originally represented as a short-term measure to 'facilitate' the process of trade liberalization by allowing signatory countries time to make an orderly adjustment to rising imports from the fast-growing East Asian economies. In fact, it turned into a longer-term measure, which was renewed every four years on increasingly restrictive terms until it was finally phased out in 2005. Under the MFA's 'anti-surge' clause, signatory countries were allowed to impose quotas on items imported from another country if the annual rate of growth in imports in these items exceeded 6% a year. However, in recognition of their particular development needs, the MFA allowed exemption from these quotas for imports from poorer developing countries.

The recession that followed the oil price hikes in the early 1970s led several countries to invoke MFA quotas, primarily to curb imports from East Asian countries. At the same time, a number of their trade unions began to lobby for the insertion of a social clause into the rules of the MFA. This would allow sanctions against countries whose exports were made in conditions that violated internationally agreed labor standards. Although efforts to link trade sanctions to labor standards were over a century old, the renewed interest in the social clause was a response to re-emergence of structural unemployment in advanced industrial countries (Bairoch, 1999).

The imposition of quotas gave rise to the practice of 'quota hopping' as East Asian capital went in search of new low-wage sites which were still 'quota-free'. The export garment manufacturing industry in Bangladesh emerged as a result of this practice. A small number of subcontracting factories were set up in the country by the late 1970s with the assistance of South Korean capital and know-how. Expansion in the early years was slow so that even in 1983, there were only 47 such units in the country.

This changed with the adoption of the 1982 New Industrial Policy by the Bangladesh government, which, in conformity with IMF conditionalities, adopted a strategy of export-oriented growth. The nascent garment industry was seen as a viable alternative source of foreign exchange to the country's declining jute industry. Various incentives were offered by the government to encourage local entrepreneurs to invest in the industry. Combined with low capital requirements and an apparently unlimited supply of poor female labor unable to find work in the countryside, the industry offered the prospect of easy profits. In the absence of purpose-built industrial centres, factories were opened wherever space could be rented, very often in residential buildings. The industry had expanded to 700 factories by 1985 and grew rapidly thereafter. Estimates of the number of jobs created varied between 80,000 and 250,000 in 1985, but it was generally agreed that 85% of them were held by women (World Bank, 1990).

Despite the ad hoc beginnings of the industry, garment employers were able to organize themselves very early on to deal with the challenges of operating in the global economy, setting up the Bangladesh Garment Manufacturing Exporters Association (BGMEA) in 1987. The close relationship between the BGMEA and successive governments has allowed it to extract various concessions from successive governments as well to exercise a certain degree of autonomy in the governance of the industry (Khan, 2013).

By contrast, there was very little effort by the state to support labor in the industry. Existing labor legislation, which included around 51 labor laws, had been inherited largely intact from the days of British rule, applied only to 3% of the workforce that were in the formal sector (Mondol, 2002, p. 121). Provisions for labor inspections to ensure compliance with national regulations were minimal as were efforts to enforce the international conventions on labor that the government signed up to.

While the right to form unions was recognized by law, it was subject to various bureaucratic obstacles, including a 30% membership threshold requirement to register a new union. As a result, trade unions were virtually absent, not only from the garment industry but from the economy at large. Trade union membership accounted for less than 5% of the total workforce and only one-third of the formal workforce (Mondol, 2002, p. 121).

Other factors contributed to the low levels of unionism in the garment sector. One was the hostility of employers who regarded them as a disruptive force and sought either to co-opt them through paternalistic relationships or to repress them through a range of coercive tactics. The other was the fact that the unions did indeed have a history of disruptive politics. The major unions in the country were affiliated to its main political parties and partisan interests generally dominated over those of their membership (Rahman and Langford, 2012).

Given the absence of a history of industrial development, an industrial work force and an independent trade union movement, both employers and workers constructed their relationships in the emerging export garment industry along the informal lines which prevailed in the rest of the economy. As a result, great deal of the industry was characterized by the absence of written contracts and by the routine violations of health and safety regulations, long hours of overtime often without pay, low levels of unionization and high rates of turnover in the work force. Not surprisingly Bangladesh began to feature prominently in the concerns expressed at international level about working conditions in the export garment sector.

The MFA and the call for quotas

The Bangladesh industry had its first encounter with these concerns almost as soon as it took off. In 1985, Britain, France and the USA all invoked the 'anti-surge' clause of the MFA to impose quotas on clothing imports from Bangladesh. They argued that the rapidity with which these imports had grown was threatening to disrupt the domestic markets of these countries. The imposition of quotas was extremely punishing for an industry that was still in its infancy: 'Shipments of garments were stopped on their way to the docks, investors panicked and the bottom fell out of the booming market. With no experience of quotas and no system in place to manage them, there was chaos' (Jackson, 1992, p. 29). As quota-induced uncertainty spread, around two-thirds of the factories closed down within three months and over 100,000 women workers had been thrown out of work (Ahmed and Rahman, 1991, cited in Jackson, 1992).

Within the UK, views supporting and opposing quotas divided along predictable lines. Associations of UK garment employers, trade unions and the Labour Party, which was then in opposition, argued in favour of renewing the MFA on more restrictive terms to insulate the domestic industry while it underwent a process of planned restructuring. They also favoured the introduction of a social clause in trade agreements to penalize countries which violated labor standards, arguing that the extremely exploitative conditions which prevailed in Third World factories gave their employers an unfair advantage in the international market.

The opposition to a restrictive MFA came from the Thatcher government, then in power in the UK, who strongly espoused a free market philosophy. It pointed out that the restrictive practices permitted by the MFA militated against the efficient allocation of resources along lines of comparative advantage and represented a net cost to British consumer, who had to pay for more expensive locally produced goods.

Opposition also came from sections of civil society but on somewhat different grounds. The World Development Movement (WDM) in Britain launched an influential campaign against the imposition of any quotas on imports from the 50 poorest countries of the world (Jackson, 1992). It argued that the production of clothing and textiles for a wider export market offered a promising and indeed, at that time, the only route, out of the 'trade trap' which bound so many poor countries into dependence on a limited range of primary commodities whose prices on world market had been in steady decline. It also pointed out that although 'cheap imports from the Third World' were frequently cited as the major cause of job losses in Britain, fuelling public and political support for an ever-more restrictive MFA stance towards the Third World, the major factor in job losses was the prevailing economic climate in which crippling interest rates, a soaring exchange rate and slump in domestic demand had all adversely affected domestic production, employment and capacity.

Around this time, and broadly in support of the WDM position, a number of us became involved in a campaign organized by Tower Hamlets International Solidarity, a group based in the East End of London, the heart of the British clothing industry. In a report by the group, which was co-authored by Nick Chisolm, Swasti Mitter, Stuart Howard and myself (1986), we argued that that the quota system symbolized the way in which powerful countries not only wrote 'the rules of the game' in international trade, but interpreted them in their own interests. Bangladesh, for instance, was an obvious candidate for exemption from anti-surge quotas under the special provision of the MFA which required participating countries to be conscious of the problems posed by quota restrictions on exports from poorer countries. It was at the time one of the world's poorest countries, second only to Ethiopia, with an annual per capita income of $150, less than one-hundredth of that of the USA.[1] Moreover, the 'surges' in question started from a very low base. In the UK, for instance, the rate of growth in imports from Bangladesh had indeed exceeded 6% permitted under the MFA, but in actual terms, it took Bangladesh's share of total clothing imports into Britain from a mere 0.01 of total imports in 1980 to 0.11 in 1985, a share that was totally dwarfed at all times by the more established suppliers (Jackson, 1992).

We called for a renewal of the MFA on terms which would facilitate a planned restructuring of the UK clothing industry to improve its own working conditions and adjust to growing competition from cheaper import. We also supported the continuation of special provisions to encourage industry in the poorest countries. In addition, we supported the call by the Trade Union Congress for a social clause in international trade agreements in order to strengthen the ability of workers' organizations in lower wage economies to resist exploitation – but we added that the role of the international labor movement should be one of solidarity rather than covert support for protectionism.

The outcry against quotas on clothing imports from Bangladesh led to them being lifted by Britain and France in 1986. By contrast, almost all items of ready-made garments exported to the USA, and many into Canada, continued to be governed by quotas.

The campaign against the quotas gave me my first encounter with the power of symbolic politics, the use of words, metaphors and images to frame particular arguments in ways that increased their persuasive power, regardless of what bearing they had on the realities they claimed to depict. For instance, the support of the UK trade unions for quotas on imports from developing countries was justified at the time in terms of their opposition to the exploitation of 'cheap' Third World women workers. Elson (1983) provided a perceptive deconstruction of the meanings embedded in this persistent, and stigmatizing, equation of 'Third World women' with 'cheap labour'. She noted how the equation served to legitimize demands by workers in the First World for greater protection from 'unfair competition':

Women workers in the Third World are often stigmatised as 'cheap labour', willing to work in appalling conditions which undermines the position of women workers in the First World countries of North America, Western Europe and Australasia. There is often a feeling that Third World women are at fault; that they won't stand up for their rights, and thus jeopardise any attempt by women in the First World to stand up for theirs. Tighter restrictions on imports of garments and textiles are often seen as the only strategy for women in the First World to protect themselves against the supposed menace of 'cheap labour' founded on 'oriental submissiveness'.

(p. 6)

She went on to point to the pejorative subtext of the discourse of 'cheap labour':

The term 'cheap labour' carries with it condemnation of the workers themselves. There is something of an implication that workers who are cheap labour must be lacking in self-respect. ... Frequently, it also has racist implications when applied to non-white people – the implication that people of colour are 'cheap labour' because they are culturally backward. When used to describe women in the Third World (or of Third World origin) sexism and racism are often combined – as in the myth of the submissive Oriental girl.

(p. 10)

This form of symbolic politics, with its persistent tendency to conflate the characteristics of work at the lower end of the global value chain with the characteristics of workers who did it, has, as this chapter argues, remained the hallmark of Northern-led campaigns to promote labor standards in developing countries.

My own position on the social clause shifted after I carried out detailed qualitative research in 1988 with some of the women who were working in the export garment industry (Kabeer, 2000). It was not simply that their accounts of their lives and struggles bore no relationship to the stereotypes of docile victims that would be regularly invoked in the international politics of representation. Certainly, these women had been drawn into the industry because it promised a better option to working for a casual daily wage in the fields or other people's home, the only other options available to women with little or no education. Certainly, they had defied patriarchal traditions that required them to remain secluded within the shelter of the home and dependent on a male breadwinner for their entire life course. And certainly they were able to carve out some degree of agency and a better life for themselves and their families, despite the exploitative conditions under which they had to work. But much more importantly, it had become clear to many of us that that the growing support for the social clause among influential sections of the international labor movement was, for all its rhetoric of compassion and solidarity, motivated by protectionism.

The Harkin Bill: protecting children or protecting jobs?

The next major controversy to hit the Bangladesh industry came hard on the heels of the quota campaign. The neo-liberal policies promoted by the Thatcher government in the UK were mirrored in the policies of the Reagan administration. They led to a decline in manufacturing jobs in the USA, as these jobs were moved to low-wage, non-unionized offshore locations, and to a decline in union membership. The AFL-CIO (American Federation of Labour-Congress of Industrial Organizations), the leading federation of US unions, had begun to lobby sympathetic politicians for protectionist trade measures to halt this movement of jobs. In August 1992, in response to these efforts, Senator Harkin of Iowa introduced the Child Labour Deterrence Bill into the US Senate to ban imports into the USA of any products made partly or wholly with child labor. The bill combined a concern with the rights of the child with the assertion that 'adult workers in the USA and other developed countries should not have their jobs imperilled by imports produced by child labor in developing countries' (cited in Brooks, 2007, p. 6).

American unions had already been drawing attention to the issue of child labor in the Bangladesh industry and in December 2002, National Broadcasting Company (NBC) aired a programme on the use of child labor in Bangladeshi factories that supplied Walmart (Nielsen, 2005). Along with its concern for these children, the programme also promoted another message. This was communicated by a prominent American trade unionist who appeared on the programme to declare: 'for every child working in a Bangladesh garment factory, there is an adult American out of a job'.

The programme was described by observers on the ground as a 'highly unbalanced and sensationalised account' of the situation of children in the garment industry (Bissell and Sobhan, 1996) but it had the desired effect. Various supporters of the Harkin Bill, which included AAFLI (Asian-American Free Labour Institute), the international division of AFL-CIO as well as the US Child Labour Coalition were able to mobilize public opinion behind the call for a boycott of Bangladeshi clothing imports.

Employers reacted immediately to this unwelcome publicity, laying off child workers *en masse*. It quickly became clear to development organizations within Bangladesh that this would not end child labor, but merely push it into far more hazardous and exploitative forms of work (Boyden, 2003; Bissell and Sobhan, 1996). Concern with the fate of retrenched children led United Nations International Children's Emergency Fund and a number of local non-governmental agencies to call for some kind of 'holding' operation until a more satisfactory alternative to immediate dismissal could be worked out.

After prolonged negotiations, in which the BGMEA participated on condition that AAFLI was excluded, an agreement was arrived at (Nielson, 2005). However, the final memorandum that was signed by the BGMEA, the

ILO and UNICEF was not the one that met with the unanimous approval of all three signatories. Their preferred version would have permitted some light, part-time regulated factory work for children in the 12–14 age group along with school attendance. However, this was rejected by US buyers because of 'the perceptions of the Western consuming public' who, it was claimed, would be satisfied only with the complete elimination of all child labor from the factories (Bissell and Sobhan, 1996).

'Unfair' trade: debating the social clause

Nielson has pointed out, the themes that played out during this episode in the history of Bangladesh's export garment industry were reproduced in broader debates about the social clause that were being played out in international forums. Arguments made by US unions in favour of the social clause routinely drew on working conditions and workers in the Bangladesh industry to bolster their case. Thus US trade union leaders seeking to make their case for the social clause referred contemptuously to the 'culturally passive Islamic women toiling 60 hours a week and making less than $30 a month' to swell the profits of US corporations (Collingsworth et al., 1994, p. 8).

At the same time, the issues raised by the case of child labor in the Bangladesh industry were cited by Rao (1999), an advocate of the social clause, as an example of its counterproductive potential when their consequences for workers had not been thought through:

> A social clause that forces employers to improve labour standards would necessitate greater investment in human resources. If employers are not willing to do this or if wages rise, they may resort to greater mechanisation in order to cut down on labour costs. Labour will then be displaced. In other words, there may be a trade-off between the right to better labour standards and the right to work.

In 1995 the newly established World Trade Organization took over from GATT in setting the rules for international trade. The decision had already been taken that the MFA would be phased out by 2005 and the WTO would become responsible for regulating the trade in garment and textiles. The US government led demands at the very first WTO ministerial meeting in 1996 for the insertion of a social clause into WTO rules so that it could exercise oversight of labor standards in exporting countries.

In a review of the debates about the social clause, Pahle (2010) uses as his point of departure the attempt by Van Roozendaal (2002) to pose the divisions between supporters and opponents in terms of a clear-cut ideological dichotomy between interventionist and neo-liberal politics. The reality, as he notes, is far more complex.

There is no doubt that advocates of neo-liberal policies were adamantly opposed to the social clause on the grounds that linking labor standards to trade agreements would distort market forces and erode the comparative advantage of labor-abundant, low-wage economies in the Global South (Bhagwati, 1996). This position was also supported by many governments in the Global South on grounds which echoed the arguments of neoclassical economists but also added concerns about national sovereignty into the mix.

Those in favour of the social clause included a larger number of Northern governments and trade unions, the latter led by the International Confederation of Free Trade Unions (ICFTU), the global voice of organized labor in these debates. The ICFTU had sought to frame the social clause as a measure to uphold basic labor rights of workers within international trade in order to prevent a 'race to the welfare bottom'. The question that Pahle set out to investigate was why, in spite of the ICFTU having conducted 'the most wide-ranging [campaign] in the history of the union movement' (ICFTU, 1999 cited in Pahle, 2010) in support of this position, it 'failed to secure sufficient support for the proposal from its own southern constituents, and from civil society more broadly' (Pahle, p. 390). Why was a proposal that it saw as a kind of 'freedom fighter' on behalf of workers in the Global South regarded by the representatives of these workers as more akin to a 'terrorist'.

He suggests that a major factor behind this outcome was that the most powerful Northern trade unions and the AFL-CIO, in particular, were not at all wedded to the ICFTU position. Their support for the social clause was as a protectionist trade measure that would help to lessen the effects of 'unfair' trade on workers in the north. As Pahle notes, the concept of 'unfair' trade within US trade policy referred unequivocally to what foreign competitors' practices did to US firms and their workers, not to the effects of these practices on firms and workers within the competitors' own national contexts. Consequently, the support of US unions for upholding labor standards in the low-wage economies of the Global South were consistently couched in terms of the interests of American workers – the argument that had featured in the case of the Harkin Bill – making it difficult for the alternative framing of fair trade to defend workers' rights to gain much purchase in the international debates.

It was the dominance of this protectionist framing of social clause arguments over the solidaristic one that explains why resistance to the social clause went beyond governments of developing countries to many trade unions, non-governmental organizations as well as progressive academics. For instance, Bhattacharya (1996), a Bangladeshi economist not known for his neoclassical/neo-liberal sentiments, criticized the steady rise of 'neo-protectionism' by advanced industrialized countries in the shape of 'non-tariff' barriers which explicitly targeted those labor-intensive products in which developing countries had a competitive advantage. He pointed to the MFA as one example of such barriers, the proposed social clause as another.

The intensity of the opposition to the social clause in the run-up to the WTO Ministerial Conference in Seattle, 1999 brought together an unexpected coalition of southern trade unions, civil society organizations, think tanks as well as a number of neoclassical, institutionalist as well as feminist scholars who signed the 'Third World Intellectuals and NGOs Statement against Linkage' (TWIN-SAL) (1999).[2] They declared their unambiguous opposition to the linkage of labor and environmental standards to WTO and trade treaties and took issue with attempts to represent their position in terms of corporate interests and malign governments. They acknowledged that many who supported the social clause may have been sincere and well-intentioned in their concerns about workers' rights but charged that their legitimate concerns were being 'contaminated' by powerful protectionist lobbies who sought to blunt international competition from developing countries by raising their costs of production.

They suggested that failure to reach agreement on the social clause reflected the fact that it was an attempt to use the WTO to achieve two very different objectives: the liberalization of trade and the advancement of social agendas. They supported the idea that the WTO be tasked with the liberalization agenda while recommending that appropriate international organizations, such as the ILO and UNICEF, be made responsible for the social agenda along with civil society organizations in developing countries.

The TWIN-SAL statement also touched on other concerns which had been expressed by those who opposed the social clause. One was the hypocrisy of countries that were calling for the social clause despite evidence that their own track record on labor rights was extremely flawed. For instance only 12% of US labor force was in trade unions at the time, due in no small part to restrictive legislation dismantling workers' rights in that country. Moreover, the USA had systematically failed to sign key ILO conventions on labor rights, including the clause on forced labor, continuing to use prison labor in the manufacture of goods in a violation of ILO conventions. There was also a concern about how asymmetries of power in the international trading system would play out within the WTO. Could smaller, less powerful countries like Bangladesh use the WTO's dispute settlement procedures to demand trade sanctions against the USA for its violation of ILO conventions? What would be the political fallout from doing so (Raghavan, 1996; Thoene, 2014)?

Efforts to incorporate a workers' rights clause into the WTO were defeated at the Ministerial Conference at Doha in 2001 and debates about the issue died down, at least within multilateral trade forums. But the USA increasingly incorporated provisions about labor standards into its bilateral agreements with its trading partners.

Campaigning for corporate social responsibility

While Northern trade unions led advocacy in favour of linking trade and labor standards in international forums, they were also active in the street-level politics of the anti-sweatshop movement which took off in the 1990s. Mainly based in the USA, the movement brought together trade unions, consumer groups, church groups, human rights activists, students and others with the aim of mobilizing consumer outrage about the conditions in which their garments were made in order to put pressure on global brands and buyers to take greater responsibility for working conditions in the factories from which they sourced their garments.

Their strategy to achieve this relied heavily on the politics of representation in a particularly negative form: 'a language of horror, of sensationalized narratives generalized from individual stories that may or may not be representative' (Siddiqi, 2009) but which was crafted to 'inflame' (Ross, 1997, p. 10) the conscience of consumers in the north. Their relentless focus on the victimhood of women and children working in global value chains was not accidental. Research into consumer behaviour had suggested that it was far easier to persuade consumers to avoid commodities that had been produced under negative conditions than to seek out those that had been produced in conditions that respect workers' rights (Elliot and Freeman, 2003). This meant that anti-sweatshop discourses were most likely to be effective in their pressure to get corporations to act when they framed women workers in the Global South as victims of ruthless global capitalism than as agents capable of protesting their conditions of work in solidarity with others.

In a collection of articles brought together to mark the 'Year of the Sweatshop', Bangladeshi workers made an appearance in a particularly sensationalized form. Elinor Spielberg (1997), who was associated with UNITE, the garment workers union within AFL-CIO, offered a contribution based on what appeared to have been a brief and cursory visit to the country in 1994. She began her account with the extraordinary claim that 'there's a saying among the girls in the slums of Bangladesh: if you are lucky, you'll be a prostitute – if you're unlucky, you'll be a garment worker' (p. 113). Despite having done extensive research with garment workers by then, I had found no evidence for this saying either in my own research (Kabeer, 2000) or among other researchers and activists who had been working in the urban slums of Bangladesh for many years (a point also made by Siddiqi, 2009). As in many other countries in the world, particularly in sexually conservative societies like Bangladesh, prostitution remains possibly the most socially stigmatized of occupations.

Spielberg goes onto make a number of other extraordinary statements about the garment workers she met but what stands out among these is her detailed description of the condition of the *feet* of a young garment she encountered, a description she links, improbably, to working conditions in the girl's garment factory:

> Whatever early malnutrition had started doing to her chances of marriage, the garment trade had finished off. The mind cannot register, in the first few seconds, that these appendages are attached to a creature that walks upright on the ground. They have flattened and spread out to such a degree they seem more suited to one that propels itself in

the water. Like fins. Like flounders, but curved in toward each other: bottom fish that got trapped, and grew, inside a kidney-shaped pan. The mind tries to grasp hold of something more noble, something scientific perhaps, to explain why a child, a child who is now admiring her new plastic bangles and smoothing the hem of her best dress, has been cursed with feet like that on which to toil. Compensation: now that's a scientific word. The bones of her feet were too weak to support the weight of the body, so they accommodated the floor.

(p. 114)

While the kind of malnutrition she describes is widespread among poorer children, particularly girls, in Bangladesh, it reflects economic deprivation and gender discrimination since birth in an underdeveloped and patriarchal society rather than the effects of a few years' work in the garment industry. Its inclusion in her account helps to establish her credentials as a caring moral being but it reduces the young girl to the status of 'a creature', almost a different species, while testifying to the dehumanizing conditions that her union claimed to be campaigning against.

The anti-sweatshop movement has, without doubt, been extremely effective in raising awareness among Northern consumers about the conditions in which their clothes were made and helping to invest private acts of consumption with political meaning (Balsiger, 2010). Moreover, it has had an impact beyond the transnational corporations (TNCs) that were the direct targets of their campaigns. Today most corporations with a brand image to protect seek to pre-empt such campaigns by building their own reputation for corporate social responsibility. This has generally entailed developing their own codes of conduct, based on some or all of the ILO's 'core labour standards', and incorporating them into contracts with their suppliers in low-wage economies.

National regulation and corporate codes of conduct

By the late 1990s, Bangladesh industry had experienced the same proliferation of corporate codes of conduct that was occurring in supplier factories across global value chains. Bangladeshi employers were also beginning to realize that compliance with these codes was becoming as important for their ability to compete in global markets as low labor costs and capacity to deliver on time. There was also evidence that the government was making efforts to improve the national regulatory framework, albeit very slowly. A commission had been set up in 1992 with a view to developing a unified labor legislation that would cover workers in both formal and informal sectors. The draft code was drawn up in 1994, but it is indicative of the obstacles it encountered that it was not till 2006 that the law was finalized.

The new legislation included a number of important measures relating to wages and working condition of workers in Bangladesh but it had many shortcomings, including continued restrictions relating to the formation of trade unions. To compensate for the absence of unions, it required employers of establishments with more than 50 workers to set up participation committees, made up of representatives of management and of workers, the latter either nominated by management or elected by workers. This was intended as a platform for social dialogue between management and workers as well as to encourage various forms of training, monitor application of labor laws and ensure production targets were met.

In order to find out whether these various efforts had resulted in progress on workers' rights and working conditions, Simeen Mahmud and I undertook a number of studies between 2000 and 2006. We carried out a survey in 2001 to compare how workers fared in export garment factories and in informal wage labor in urban areas, their most likely alternative. We found evidence of improvement in working conditions in the garment sector, more markedly in the EPZs, where factories were more likely to be joint ventures but also in locally owned factories. These relate mainly to paid leave, maternity leave, overtime pay and medical care. In comparison to informal wage workers, they were more likely to report paid leave, maternity leave, overtime pay and medical care. They also earned more, and while they worked longer hours, they were much less likely to have been without work in the past year and more likely to report an increase in their income. However, there were two telling indicators of the limits to what had been achieved: less than 5% of the garment workers reported a presence of a trade union in their workplace and only around 20% had heard of the country's labor laws (Kabeer and Mahmud, 2004a).

We also carried out qualitative research with various stakeholders in the garment industry in 2004 (Mahmud and Kabeer, 2006). Our interviews with employers suggested that while membership of the BGMEA had helped to formalize their relationships with each other and with the state, their relationships with their workers remained rooted in the culture of the informal economy. Some had been shamed into improving working conditions by the negative image that the industry had acquired in the international arena but they were a minority.

Many of the employers we interviewed expressed the belief that their workers had no discipline and did not expect or deserve to be treated like a formal work force: '...they don't like to work under any rules. They work for some days, if they need to go home they leave without any notice and come back to join another factory' (p. 232). Yet these employers had benefited as a group from considerable state support, more than any other group of employers and, according to the laws of the country, they owed a great deal more to their workers than the simple generation of jobs. Seen in this light, corporate codes of conduct could be interpreted as attempts on the part of international buyers to enforce the social responsibility obligations of their suppliers, given their failure to do so voluntarily and the failure of the state to compel them.

From the employers' perspective, on the other hand, corporate codes of conduct were simply another set of conditions imposed by global brands and buyers, along with production deadlines and quality control, the costs of which they were forced to bear in order to stay in business. They saw the codes as a public relations exercise on the part of global brands that were concerned about their public image so as to maintain a facade of social responsibility for their consumers while covertly passing the cost of compliance onto their suppliers. They complained with bitterness about the double standards of companies who combined their demands for increasingly onerous and expensive quality and labor standards with a steady reduction in the prices they offered to their producers. As one employer who has been in the industry for many years commented:

> There is no such thing as a permanent contract in this business. None of the buyers will give you a permanent contract and say okay, we have booked orders with your factory for at least the next two years.... They will work from contract to contract and demand shorter and shorter delivery times.
>
> (p. 233)

Thus, if local suppliers profited from keeping their relationships with their workers as informal as possible, using the threat of dismissal to discipline their workers, international buyers in turn exercised their monopsony-like power in the global market for clothing to keep their relationship with their producers as informal as possible, using the constant threat of relocation to create a permanent condition of insecurity among suppliers across the world.

Nor did we find much grounds for hope that the main trade unions in the country would step in on behalf of workers. As Dannecker had noted in her research, many of their leaders viewed female garment workers as passive products of rural backgrounds, illiteracy and general lack of awareness:

> Since the women are illiterate they do not understand what a labour union is and that we are trying to improve their working conditions. We visit them but they hardly listen to us because they cannot grasp the idea of solidarity and unity.
>
> (Dannecker, 2002, p. 222)

But our conversations with workers suggested that they had not remained untouched by the forces of change in the larger society. Intense media coverage of their working conditions and increased attempts to mobilize them by a wide range of actors, including local and international trade unions, labor rights organizations and women's organizations, had all served to raise their knowledge and awareness of their rights. The workers we interviewed reported various cases when they had come together, sometimes spontaneously, sometimes in a planned and coordinated way, to undertake factory-wide protests which often spilled out onto the streets.

We concluded on the basis of their accounts:

> There is …no linear story of progress that emerges out of these accounts, of victories gained leading on to further victories. Some workers felt that conditions had improved after a protest, some felt they had worsened. Employers made promises in order to quell a disturbance, but used every pretext subsequently to victimise or get rid of the leaders. However, changes in consciousness were often permanent and the leadership that developed did not simply fade away when a struggle was lost but went on to other factories to start the job of organisation once again
>
> (p. 240)

In fact, very soon after we had completed out research, these piecemeal and isolated protests escalated in 2006 into the largest mobilization of garment workers in the history of the RMG sector in Bangladesh. It was led by two independent leftist unions – neither part of the mainstream movement nor of the organizations being promoted by international trade unions (Rahman and Langford, 2012). The government responded to these protests by raising the minimum wage which had been frozen since 1994. They raised them again in 2010, in 2014 and then again in 2018. Each such raise was preceded by a period of agitation by workers.

From compliance to cooperation: multi-stakeholder initiatives after Rana Plaza

Codes of conduct have become an accepted part of doing business in global value chains but their effects in Bangladesh – as elsewhere – have been mixed. The improvements we noted in our study, and those that have taken place subsequently, have taken place in an ad hoc and uncoordinated way, manifestations of what we called a 'culture of compliance' with corporate codes of conduct rather a 'culture of accountability' to national legislation (Mahmud and Kabeer, p. 240). Furthermore, these improvements were largely focused on various aspects of working conditions within the factories, rather than on infrastructural conditions, despite the series of fires and industrial disasters that occurred periodically over the industry's history.

The scale of the tragedy at Rana Plaza in April 2013 provided a much needed wake-up call. The death of over a thousand garment workers and the injury of many more galvanized a range of institutional actors at global and local levels into action. Pressure from Western governments, especially the suspension of the Generalized System of Preferences facility by the USA and threats to do so by the EU, prompted the Bangladesh government to act. In July 2013, it signed a Sustainability Compact with the EU, the USA,

Canada and the ILO whereby it agreed to take immediate and longer term measures to address health and safety in the RMG sector.

The Bangladesh Labour Act 2006 was amended to promote work place safety and to bring into line with international conventions. Among various changes, it made it obligatory that workers' representatives on the WPCs were elected rather than nominated by management. Health and safety committees had to be set up in factories with more than 50 workers, with worker representatives drawn from trade unions or the WPCs. However, it left the 30% threshold requirement to form unions intact. There was a rise in the number of new unions that were registered in the aftermath of these changes (Anner, 2018), but the momentum could not be maintained in the face of resistance from government and employers.

The other major response to Rana Plaza was the adoption of the two major multi-stakeholder agreements.[3] These were seen as exemplifying a new cooperation-based, multi-stakeholder approach to CSR in place of the buyer-driven, compliance-based approach of the codes of conduct. The Accord was signed by more than 200 international brands from 20 mainly European countries, two European-based international unions (UNI Global Union and IndustriAll Global Union) and eight of their associated labor federations in Bangladesh. It represented a departure from past agreements of this kind in its legally binding nature: all signatories agreed that arbitration awards or the enforcement of fees could be pursued in the relevant national legal systems. A counterpart agreement, the Alliance, was signed by 28 mainly US-based firms: it had limited union participation and, due to the reluctance of US firms, was not legally binding.

The initiatives were envisioned to last till 2018.[4] Funding was provided through annual contributions by buyers. The objective was to list all firms supplying the signatory companies, to send inspection teams to ensure that their structural and safety conditions complied with national building regulations and to draw up corrective recommendations where necessary to be implemented by managers within a prescribed time frame. Factories that did not comply were disqualified from further business with the signatory firms. As of April 2018, Accord had inspected 2,022 factories while Alliance had inspected 836 factories, around 50% of which were shared with Accord (Barrett et al., 2018).

In 2017, Simeen Mahmud and I joined a larger team of researchers to assess the impact of these initiatives from the perspective of workers, while others on the team explored the managers' perspectives.[5] We found that many of the health and safety requirements associated with the Accord and Alliance had been carried out, not only but most significantly in factories affiliated with these initiatives. We also found significant evidence of 'spill over' effects on outcomes which were not covered by the agreements, including higher wages, more permanent contracts, greater likelihood of elected participation committees and greater knowledge of both labor laws and codes of conduct (Kabeer et al., 2019).

Based on the workers' survey alone, our conclusion would have been that the new multi-stakeholder approach to corporate responsibility had achieved some important outcomes – or at least made them more likely. But this account of change was made more complex by the findings reported by the study of managers of AA-affiliated factories carried out as part of the same project (Rahman and Rahman, 2018). Their initial response to the AA agreements had been favourable: they welcomed what promised to be a coordinated framework for improving health and safety conditions in their factories and the opportunity to improve the country's international reputation.

But this gave way to considerable dissatisfaction. While they complained about various technical problems that had proved costly for them, their greatest bitterness was reserved for the fact that while buyers paid for the costs of inspections, the costs of expensive remediation or relocation measures had to be borne by the employers (Barret et al., 2018).

The expectation on the part of suppliers that these costs would be shared was based on the terms of the Accord agreement which had spelt out the responsibilities of the signatory companies towards their suppliers. According to Article 28 of Accord: 'participating brands and retailers will negotiate commercial terms with their suppliers which ensure that it is financially feasible for the factories to maintain safe workplaces and comply with upgrade and remediation requirements instituted by the Safety Inspector'. Yet none of 109 managers interviewed by Rahman and Rahman had received any assistance in implementing the recommendations advised by inspectors. While larger factories were generally able to finance these measures through profits or loans, small and medium firms found it a major struggle, many going out of business.[6]

Furthermore, lead firms had continued to pursue 'business as usual' purchasing practices that went directly against the financial feasibility of local suppliers. Not only did they fail to increase the procurement prices paid to local suppliers, one way to have offset some of the remediation costs incurred by the latter, but the prices they paid to their suppliers in Bangladesh continued their long-term decline. According to the results of a survey of factory managers by Anner (2018):

> the average FOB price was USD 4.64 in 2016, which is a 7.79% decline from a FOB price point of USD 5.03 in 2011. If we look at exports to the United States, the price point declined by 10.67%. For European buyers, the price point came down by 9.04%. Indeed, in all major product categories we find a decline in nominal prices paid per unit.

Evidence from other sources supports this trend of declining prices which continued after Rana Plaza, a decline that could not be explained by the rising price of raw materials or fluctuations in exchange rates (Anner, 2018). Also part of the 'business as usual' approach was the continued reduction of delivery times. In 2011, the major global brands had given Bangladesh fac-tories an average of 94 days to complete an order. By 2016, it had declined to 86 days. With production costs, including wages, going up and purchasing prices declining, the only way that supplier factories could remain in business was by reducing their profit margins. This was indeed the case. Anner's sur-vey (2018) of 223 managers found that profit margins had decreased by 13.3% between 2011 and 2016 leaving managers with a mean profit margin of 7.69%.

It would appear therefore that while the shift from a compliance to cooperation-based model of CSR had improved structural safety in the garment industry, it had left intact certain fundamental asymmetries in rela-tionships within global value chains. The externalization of corporate social responsibility by the buyers associated with the new agreements and the com-plaints they gave rise to on the part of managers were uncannily similar to our findings in relation to the codes of conduct that we had reported earlier.

The persistence of these asymmetries of power within the garment sup-ply chain helps to explain what emerged as certain key sticking points in the processes of change that were recorded by our workers' survey. These related to the level of wages, with the majority of workers reporting them to be inadequate; long working hours and the use of compulsory overtime; the mistreatment of workers, generally associated with the failure to meet production targets; and the continued hostility towards trade unions that might seek to challenge these practices. Some of this resistance to change can clearly be attributed to the continued intransigence of a group of em-ployers who refused to accord dignity and respect to those who worked for them. But it also reflected the continuing insecurities associated with com-peting in the global market for clothing with no assurance that compliance with CSR requirements would improve the terms on which they do business with global buyers.[7]

'Looking in the wrong place?' from spotlight to flood light perspectives

The key 'sticking points' in processes of change that we recorded through our workers' survey related to conditions at work that might well be worse in Bangladesh than other garment exporting countries, but they are by no means unique to it. Rather they are endemic to the organization of global supply chains. As Locke (2013) pointed out on the basis of his study of these supply chains, despite initiatives of various kinds, include private compli-ance programmes as well as efforts at capacity building, 'poor working con-ditions, excessive working hours, precarious employment practices and low wages persist in factories producing for global supply chains' (p. 126).

He suggested that if we wanted to understand why problems of work-ing conditions are so pervasive and persistent in garment value chains, we would be looking in the wrong place if we focus only on the factories where these problems are manifested. We need to move from a narrow 'spotlight' perspective on working conditions in global value chains, a perspective that draws our gaze to the locus of production alone, to a 'flood light' approach which illuminates the broader political economy of supply chain capitalism within which these production processes are located.

Bangladesh entered the global garment industry at a time when the retail sector became increasingly concentrated, particularly in the USA and Europe, investing a small number of global brands and retailers with disproportionate bargaining power vis-à-vis the large, and growing, number of suppliers dispersed in low-wage economies across the developing world. Competition in the global apparel industry further intensified when the quotas permitted under the MFA were phased out, effectively marking the end of the MFA by 2005. The increased liberalization of trade expanded the number of countries from which buyers could source, allowing them to play suppliers in increasing numbers of countries against each other (Anner et al., 2012).

This was also a period that saw the rise of a new 'fast fashion' business model based on a greater variety of cheap clothing delivered faster and more frequently to retail outlets. Studies have shown that the fast fashion retailing has been particularly inimical to the observance of decent wages and working conditions across the global industry (Anner et al., 2012). Global brands and buyers have been able to use the increasingly unequal distribution of bargaining power within these chains to pressure their suppliers to meet the competitive pressures within the industry by producing smaller batches of increasing varieties of products more rapidly and at decreasing prices.

Even if some global buyers did make efforts to improve labor standards among their suppliers, and even if some suppliers were responsive to these efforts, the 'upstream' business practices associated with fast fashion retailing inevitably undermined its 'downstream' CSR efforts. Faced with CSR practices which increased the production costs of suppliers, and purchasing practices which reduced the prices they received, suppliers had a limited range of options: to reduce their profit margins, pay their workers lower wages, demand longer hours of work, subcontract out their work to lower cost units and take short cuts in safety standards.

The implications of these sourcing practices for labor standards within value chains have been by Anner et al. (2012) using US data. They found that the nominal price per square metre of imported clothing into the USA increased from $3.48 in 1989 to $3.77 in 1997 but had declined to $2.89 in 2010. This represented a drop of 23% in nominal dollar prices but 48% in real dollar price over this period. In addition, they found that while respect for the rights to freedom of association and collective bargaining was relatively steady in the 1990s among the top 20 garment exporters to the USA, it began to decline significantly after 2001. In fact, prices, and presumably respect for workers' rights, were highest in 2010 among those countries who had faced greatest decline in their share of US markets.

Consumers have been mobilized to put pressure on global brands to improve conditions in their supplier factories but the strength of their stake in this outcome is not clear. Some authors believe that consumers have demonstrated their willingness to pay higher prices for clothes made in decent working conditions (Ross, 1997; Prasad et al., 2004). It is certainly the case that consumer outrage, or the fear of it, was a driving force behind the various CSR efforts that have come into existence since the 1990s. Yet consumer outrage has not been sustained enough or powerful enough to force a change in business practices.

Other authors have been less sanguine about the power or motivation of consumers. An early OXFAM report (2004) appears to suggest that they may have been co-opted into the fast fashion model: '...consumers have come to expect high quality and year-round availability at "value" prices. Many retailers and brands compete to capture their loyalty through new products, short fashion cycles, and price wars, and so increase their own market share' (p. 36). And more recently, Taplin (2014) observes, 'Western consumers have become accustomed to cheap fashion and for the most part appear unwilling to pay more for items that are untainted by exploitative practices' (p. 73).[8]

Reviewing the confluence of forces that led to Rana Plaza, Taplin concludes that the fast fashion business model that dominates global value chains has created a situation 'where the "villains" are many and the innocent caught up in the manifold uncertainties that such a model produces' (p. 73). In such a situation, industrial disasters like Rana Plaza are not only highly likely, but almost inevitable.

Assessing recommendations for the way forward

The question that this raises is what can be done to protect 'the innocent'? One of the striking features of successive efforts to enforce labor standards in developing countries is the extent to which the main burden of proposed change generally devolves almost entirely on stakeholders in the Global South. The campaign around the 'social clause' in the 1990s, for instance, placed the responsibility for upholding labor standards on the governments of developing countries. While anti-sweatshop campaigns put pressure on global buyers and brands to adopting corporate codes of conduct, the actual responsibility and costs of implementing these codes fell squarely on supplying factories. And as we noted, the Accord and Alliance agreements have also externalized the costs of making the factories safer to local suppliers.

Locke suggests the need for new institutional arrangements and political coalitions which would reallocate costs and rewards among *all* stakeholders engaged in these value chains, thus transcending traditional boundaries between producers and consumers, buyers and suppliers, NGOs and corporations, advanced and developing countries. Given the power dynamics that characterize supply chain capitalism, it is difficult to envisage what these arrangements might be and how they might emerge but the proposal does at least represent a shift from a 'spotlight' perspective on the problem to a 'floodlit' one. By way of conclusion, we discuss some recent recommendations for advancing the transition to a fairer set of institutional arrangements. We will draw in particular on Sobhan (2014) to discuss the specific challenges of the Bangladesh context.

We begin with the proposal put forward by the Stern Centre for Business and Human Rights for what they call a 'shared responsibility model'. It is intended to respond to the immediate challenge of addressing remaining health and safety conditions in the RMG industry in Bangladesh after Accord and Alliance agreements come to an end (Barrett et al., 2018). It calls for an international task force, led by Bangladeshi stakeholders, to coordinate efforts to raise the funds necessary to complete this task and to oversee the implementation process. Along with the Bangladeshi government and RMG employers, the proposal envisages financial contributions from international actors, including Western buyers and the countries that import garments from Bangladesh – mainly EU and the USA who account for 64% and 18% of Bangladesh's garment exports respectively.

While there are self-evident reasons why the Bangladesh government and employers should take lead responsibility for improving conditions in the RMG sector, the case made by the Stern proposal for involving Western buyers and governments is based on appeals to their sense of fairness and their 'special obligations'. Yet the commitment expressed by these actors to economic justice for workers in global value chains calls for a stronger and more institutionalized model of shared responsibility, one based on a fairer distribution of rights and responsibilities across the value chain, rather than on special pleading.

Estimates of the distribution of gains across the value chain have shown that local suppliers retain a very small share of the final retail price of their products. An attempt by Asia Foundation (cited in Kabeer and Mahmud, 2004b) to break down the cost components of a shirt made in Bangladesh and retailing in the USA for $13 found that just 38% of the value of the final retail price was retained by Bangladeshi suppliers. This had to cover all their costs, including fabric (23%), labor (1.2%), trim (0.24%), and all other operating costs, including their profits (2.01%).

Norfield (2011) carried out a similar exercise for a T-shirt retailing in H&M stores in Germany for 4.95 euros. He estimated that H&M paid the Bangladeshi supplier 1.35 euros for a T-shirt (around 27%). This had to cover 0.40 euro for raw cotton material purchased from the USA, leaving 95 cents to cover labor costs, power costs, the cost of materials other than cotton, depreciation of machinery and other items as well as the suppliers' own profit. The rest of the final price of the shirt was made up of 0.06 euro for shipping costs to Germany, 2.00 euros for transport, shop rents, sales force, marketing and administration in Germany, 0.60 euro net profit per shirt and then an additional 0.70 euro, representing the 19% VAT levied by member states in EU countries on all goods and services bought and sold within the EU.

Similar estimates are provided by Sobhan with regard to shirts made in Bangladesh and retailed in Walmart stores in the USA. He estimates that 29% of the final retail price was retained by the Bangladeshi supplier to cover the cost of fabric; rental, local transport, administrative overheads; and the suppliers' profit. But he makes the additional point that there is generally very little information on how much of the final retail price that goes to Walmart was used to cover its costs and how much represented the political rents it was able to enjoy by virtue of its monopsony power within the global value chain.

Western buyers have not shown much inclination to redistribute some of their profits as their contribution to sharing the costs of corporate responsibility but their governments are in a position to make a difference. As Norfield's estimate shows, a sizeable portion of the revenue generated by garment value chain production is claimed by EU governments in the form of VAT. In the case of the USA, government revenue is collected in the form of tariffs on imports, with higher tariffs (15%) being imposed on textile and garments than any other imports. As Bain (2018) points out:

> The reason for the high tariffs is classic—and many might say outdated—protectionism....[E]ven though the US textile industry has dwindled to a tiny share of what it once was, the small manufacturers that remain exert a strong hold on their political representatives, who fight for them in trade deals.

One consequence of this, as Bain (2018) notes, is that Bangladesh has been paying higher tariffs than any of the other 232 countries that export to the USA because it is primarily an exporter of garments. As Sobhan points out, the tariff revenue of around $720 million raised annually from Bangladesh by the US government is considerably greater than $200 million a year that the USA provided in overseas aid to Bangladesh[9]: 'the paradox of a net transfer of resources from Bangladesh, a least developed country, to the budget of the world's wealthiest country' (Sobhan, p. 6).

The concern that governments in the USA and the EU have expressed about the rights of workers in the countries from which they import their clothing surely implies commensurate obligations on their part. These could be met by routinely redistributing some of the revenue they collect from imports from Bangladesh and other lower-income exporting countries back to the countries in question both to ensure that their exporting industries have the resources to provide decent working conditions and to promote mechanisms, including those exercised by civil society, to hold the industry accountable.

Aside from the recommendations contained in the Stern Centre, the literature on labor standards contains a variety of studies and recommendations relating to various local-level efforts to improve working conditions and build skills and organizational capacity in garment factories by national and international trade unions, labor rights NGOs as well as by multi-stakeholder initiatives such as the ILO's Better Works Programme. Others have stressed the importance of strengthening and enforcing national regulations. As Locke suggests, each of these has limited impact on its own but can mutually reinforce each other to amplify impact.

However, the question of the national regulation is clearly problematic in Bangladesh. The failures of government oversight that have contributed to the conditions prevailing in the garment sector are part of a broader crisis of governance failure within the country. While there is no doubt that the government needs to take much greater responsibility for the rights of its workers, as it must for the rights of all its citizens, the present state of governance in the country means that this is unlikely to happen in the foreseeable future.

On the other hand, if the objective of these efforts is to build the export garment sector in Bangladesh as 'an island of good governance ...in an ocean of mal-governance' (Sobhan, p. 5), this may well be within the realms of possibility. Whether the BGMEA can provide the horizontal form of governance that has helped it to pursue its membership's interests in the past (Khan, 2013) to compensate for state regulatory failure in relation to workers' rights is not clear since it is largely led by those most resistant to regulation. But employers would need to take coordinated action, with or without the BGMEA, to work towards achievable labor standards within the industry as their contribution to a shared responsibility model.

These efforts, if successful, will have repercussions for the structure of industry. It is likely that only the elite segment of the RMG sector can meet the necessary standards of 'good governance'. The suggestion by Barret et al. that buyers reform their purchasing practices and reward high-performance suppliers with longer-term contracts, larger-order volumes and more favourable pricing is likely to hasten the bifurcation of the industry. Smaller factories that are unable to meet the necessary standards will either close down or disappear into the ocean of unregistered informal activities that make up the bulk of the country's economy. It is not clear how many factories have closed down because of inability or delay in addressing current remediation requirements under AA but media estimates suggest around 400 factories had closed by 2014 with repercussions for about 150,000 workers (Hossain, 2014).

Civil society has also featured in various recommendations about the improvement of labor standards in Bangladesh. Labor activists tend to focus primarily on trade unions as best placed to fight for workers' rights. Here again, given the history of trade unionism in Bangladesh, progress has been slow. However, a 'floodlight' perspective on the problem would take account not only of the vertical dimension of value chains but also of their horizontal dimensions, namely the broader socio-economic context in which production takes place. From this perspective, efforts to build politically independent unions, however discouraging, would not be regarded as futile but part of the painful process of building a strong and active civil society.

Zajak (2017), for instance, points out the presence of Accord provided a 'shadow of protection' to efforts by some of the newer unions in the garment sector to stand up for workers' grievances. She also notes that interaction with international organizations and alliances also increased the strategizing skills of union leaders. These skills and experiences are unlikely to disappear when Accord and Alliance come to an end just as the struggle for workers' right did not come into existence with their inception. As we noted, our earlier study had found sporadic examples of workers engaging in factory-wide collective actions, sometimes planned, sometimes spontaneously, which frequently spilled over into the streets. Such actions testified to the growth of 'practical' as opposed to a 'discursive' class consciousness among these workers (Rahman and Langford, 2012), one that was not in evidence in the 1980s and 1990s but had clearly evolved over time. It is this practical consciousness that was at play in the massive strike that took place in 2006 and has continued to be at play in subsequent agitations.

Nevertheless, as FNV Mondial (2016) concluded, Bangladesh trade unions do not currently represent a strong countervailing power when it comes to promoting and enforcing labor legislation despite several years of efforts by international labor organizations. Efforts to build trade unions are likely to continue, but for local activists, it is important to broaden efforts to build voice and organization beyond trade unions and beyond the garment sector because what happens to workers' rights in the garment sector is closely bound up with what happens to the rights of citizens in the wider society. Other sectors of civil society engaged with the promotion of democratic processes and legal justice in Bangladesh have frequently engaged with the garment sector as part of their activities. They can be instrumental in helping to strengthen and expand the potential held out, for instance, by the setting up of elected WPCs within garment factories. In short, the process of building state accountability for the rights of workers in Bangladesh needs to be carried out as part and parcel of efforts to build a broader culture of rights within the country.

Conclusion: diversify and conquer?

Bangladesh moved into the export garment sector when the opportunity arose not simply because of its *comparative* advantage in garment manufacturing but because of its *absolute* advantage, given that it was, and remains, a low-wage, labor-abundant economy. The rapid development of the sector, and its contribution to the country's growth rates and foreign exchange earnings, appeared to hold out the promise of helping the country to transition from aid dependency to greater self-reliance through trade. But while it has gone from the handful of factories that existed in its early years to becoming the second largest exporter of garments after China, it is evident that the market conditions under which it has to compete have steadily worsened as the fast fashion business model has come to dominate global value chains. It is by no means clear that employers in the industry would have voluntarily improved labor standards in their factories if the terms on which they supply their garments had improved over time but what is clear is that their ability to do so has been severely constrained by the increasingly exploitative business practices of global buyers.

Moreover, access to the markets of the richer countries of the world remains governed by such instruments as the Generalized System of Preferences and the EU's Everything But Arms which allow the richer countries to determine how they will interpret the rules of trade that they have helped to put in place. Smaller countries like Bangladesh, especially those with little geo-political significance, are compelled to maintain 'politically serviceable relationships' (Sobhan, p. 6) with these countries in order to receive trade privileges, but are always aware that these can be withdrawn at the political discretion of their governments. Consequently Bangladesh has moved from a position of aid dependence to one of trade dependence as it seeks to lobby countries like the USA to remove tariff barriers to its exports (Sobhan, 2003).

The future of the Bangladesh export garment sector as a source of jobs does not look bright. We have noted that many factories have closed down as a result of recent efforts to improve health, safety and working conditions in the industry. Many workers have lost their jobs and more are likely to do so as efforts to build the industry as an island of good governance continue: without a fairer distribution of profits, improvements in the quality of jobs in the garment sector inevitably imply fewer jobs.

Not surprisingly, there have been efforts by the Bangladesh government itself and by others to explore the options for diversification into other higher value-added manufacturing industries that can help to reduce its dependence on garments. It is beyond the scope of this chapter to discuss what these might be but diversification is unlikely to be easy. I will conclude by quoting from an Action Aid report (2015) as to the challenges that Bangladesh faces in any effort to 'diversify and conquer', given its position as a rule-taker rather than a rule-maker in the global economic order:

Today, the provisions of World Trade Organisation (WTO) law and trade and investment agreements prevent developing countries from using many of the policy tools that today's rich economies relied on to industrialise, such as import quotas, subsidies and tariffs. LDC leaders' hands are tied and cannot easily target economic activities to transform the economy. For example, Bangladesh is highly constrained by having to reduce tariffs and custom duties, remove quantitative restrictions and relax local content requirements of products. Other WTO rules are medium constraining, and include government procurement, intellectual property and export subsidies in agriculture. A third set of rules, regulating devaluations, investment incentives, trade finance and export taxes are the least constraining of them all but are nonetheless there. An economy that is increasingly open to free trade and regulated by the rules listed above makes it difficult for domestic businesses to enter the market: they are put out of business before they have any chance to become competitive.

(p. 11)

Notes

1 www.nationmaster.com/country-info/stats/Economy/GDP-per-capita-in-1973.
2 www2.bc.edu/james-anderson/twin-sal12.pdf.
3 The government took responsibility for oversight over factories that did not have business with the members of Accord and Alliance under the National Tripartite Plan of Action for Fire and Structural Integrity, now known as the National Initiative. There is less information on the number of factories that come under government overview, much of it is contradictory but it seems clear that the initiative has not made much headway (Barret et al. 2018).
4 The Alliance has now come to an end. The extension of Accord is under negotiation.
5 The Garment Supply Chain Governance project was funded by Volkswagen Foundation in co-operation with the Riksbankens Jubileumsfond and the Wellcome Trust. (http://www.wiwiss.fu-berlin.de/forschung/Garments/index.html)
6 www.reuters.com/article/us-bangladesh-garments-insight/safety-overhaul-puts-strain-on-bangladesh-garment-industry-idUSKBN0KD0N820150104.
7 A 2018 survey of 156 suppliers across 24 countries which asked about their experiences with 65 buyers found that over 60% of suppliers were not incentivized for being compliant to buyer codes of conduct, despite many observers believing incentives are essential to improving purchasing practices. Purchasing practices by apparel brands were unaffected by the length of relationship with supplier. https://apparelinsider.com/survey-raises-questions-purchasing-practices/.
8 A survey of 2,025 respondents carried out a month after Rana Plaza, by *Retail Week*, an industry publication, found that only 13% said they were a lot more likely to ask retailers where their clothes were produced than before the collapse of the building while 44% of consumers were no more likely to ask retailers and 22% said that they were 'little more likely'. As Quelch and Rodriguez (2013) note concern among some observers that consumer preference for low prices might outweigh their preference for workplace safety.
9 The US withdrawal of Bangladesh's GSP status after Rana Plaza was a purely symbolic gesture since it had not enjoyed duty-free access on any of its exports prior to Rana Plaza.

References

Action Aid (2015) *Diversify and Conquer: Transforming Bangladesh into an Industrial Country.* London: Action Aid.
Anner, M. (2018) *Binding Power: The Sourcing Squeeze, Workers' Rights, and Building Safety in Bangladesh Since Rana Plaza* Research Report, Centre for Global Workers' Rights Pennsylvania.

Anner, N., J. Bair and J. Blasi (2012) *Buyer Power, Pricing Practices, and Labor Outcomes in Global Supply Chains* Institute of Behaviour Science Working Paper Series, August. University of Colorado.

Bain, M. (2018) *The US imposes its highest tariffs on Bangladesh and other poor countries* Quartz April 6th. https://qz.com/1246556/the-highest-us-tariffs-arent-on-china-theyre-on-its-poor-neighbors/.

Bairoch, P. (1999) "A Brief History of the Social Clause in Trade Policy." In N. Dewatripont, A. Sapir and K. Sekkat (eds.) *Trade and Jobs in Europe: Much ado About Nothing?* Oxford: Oxford University Press.

Balsiger, P. (2010) "Making Political Consumers: The Tactical Action Repertoire of a Campaign for Clean Clothes." *Social Movement Studies: Journal of Social, Cultural and Political Protest*, 9(3): 311–329.

Barrett, P. M., D. Baumann-Pauly and A. Gu (2018) *Five Years after Rana Plaza: The Way Forward*. New York: NYU Stern Center for Business and Human Rights.

Bhagwati, J. (1996) "Trade Liberalisation and Fair Trade demands: Addressing the Environmental and Labour Standards Issue." *The World Economy*, 18: 745–759.

Bhattacharya, D. (1996) "International Trade, Social Labelling and Developing Countries: The Case of Bangladesh's Garment Export and Use of Child Labour." *Annuaire Suisse de politique de development*, 15: 215–238.

Bissell, S. and B. Sobhan (1996) Child labour and education programming in the garment industry of Bangladesh: experience and issues, Report from UNICEF, September.

Boyden, J. (2003) "Postscript: Implementing the Convention on the Rights of the Child – Who Decides About Children's Welfare?" In A. James and A. Prout (eds.) *Constructing and Reconstructing Childhood. Contemporary Issues in the Sociological Study of Childhood*. London: Falmer Press.

Brooks, E. C. 2007. *Unravelling the Garment Industry. Transnational Organizing and Women's Work*. Minneapolis: University of Minnesota Press.

Chisolm, N., N. Kabeer, S. Mitter and S. Howard (1986) *Linked by the Same Thread: The Multi-Fibre Arrangement and the Labour Movement*. London: Tower Hamlets International Solidarity and Tower Hamlets Trade Union Council.

Collingsworth, T., J. W. Gould and P. J. Harvey (1994) "Time for a Global New Deal." *Foreign Affairs*, 73(1): 8–13.

Dannecker, P. (2002) *Between Conformity and Resistance: Women Garment workers in Bangladesh*. Dhaka: University Press Ltd.

Elliot, Kimberly A. and Richard B. Freeman. (2003). *Can Labour Standards Improve under Globalization?* Washington, DC: Institute for International Economics.

Elson, D. (1983) "Nimble Fingers and Other Fables." In W. Enloe and C. Chapkis (eds.) *Of Common Cloth: Women in the Global Textile Industry* (pp. 5–14). Amsterdam: Transnational Institute.

FNV Mondial (2016) *Country Report Bangladesh Endline 2016*, Ede, The Netherlands.

Hossain, A. (2014) "About 400 RMG Factories Shut from Loss of Orders, Compliance Issues." *The Daily Independent*, 10 September.

ICFTU (1999). *Building Workers' Rights into the Global Trading System*. Brussels: ICFTU.

Jackson, B. (1992) *Threadbare: How the Rich Stitch Up the World's Rag Trade*. London: World Development Movement.

Kabeer, N. (2000) *The Power to Choose: Bangladeshi Women and Labour Market Decisions in London and Dhaka.* London: Verso Press.

Kabeer, N. and S. Mahmud (2004a) "Globalization, Gender and Poverty: Bangladeshi Women Workers in Export and Local Markets." *Journal of International Development,* 16(1): 93–109.

Kabeer, N. and S. Mahmud (2004b) "Rags, Riches and Women Workers: Export-oriented Garment Manufacturing in Bangladesh." In M. Carr (ed.) *Chains of Fortune: Linking Women Producers and Workers with Global Markets.* London: Commonwealth Secretariat.

Kabeer, N., L. Huq and M. Sulaiman (2019) *Multistakeholder Initiatives in Bangladesh after Rana Plaza: Global Norms and Workers' Perspectives,* International Development Working Paper Series No. 19-193, London School of Economics, London (www.lse.ac.uk/international-development/Assets/Documents/PDFs/Working-Papers/WP193.pdf).

Khan, M. H. (2013) "Bangladesh. Economic Growth in a Vulnerable Limited Access Order." In D. North, J. Wallis, S. Webb and B. Weingast (eds.) *Violence: Politics, Economics and the Problems of Development* (pp. 24–69). Cambridge: Cambridge University Press.

Locke, R. (2013) *The Promise and Limits of Private Power: Promoting Labor Standards in a Global Economy.* Cambridge: Cambridge University Press.

Mahmud, S. and N. Kabeer (2006) "Compliance versus Accountability: Struggles for Dignity and Daily Bread in the Bangladesh Garment Industry." Chapter 11 in P. Newell and J. Wheeler (eds.) *Rights, Resources and the Politics of Accountability* (pp. 223–244). London: Zed Press.

Mondol, A. H. (2002) "Globalization, Industrial Relations and Labour Policies: The Need for a Renewed Agenda." In M. Muqtada (ed.) *Bangladesh: Economic and Social Challenges of Globalization.* Dhaka: University Press Ltd.

Nielsen, M. E. (2005) "The Politics of Corporate Responsibility and Child Labour in the Bangladesh Garment Industry." *International Affairs,* 81(3): 559–580.

Norfield, T. (2011) *Economics of Imperialism. What the 'China Price' Really Means.* https://economicsofimperialism.blogspot.com/2011/06/what-china-price-really-means.html.

Oxfam (2004) *Trading Away Our Rights. Women Working in Global Supply Chains.* Oxford: Oxfam International.

Pahle, S. (2010) "The Rise and Demise of the "Social Clause" Proposal in the 1990s: Implications of a Discourse Theoretical Reading." *Labor History,* 51(3): 389–410.

Prasad, M., H. Kimeldorf and R. Meyer (2004) "Consumers of the World Unite: A Market-Based Response to Sweatshops." *Labour Studies Journal,* 29(3): 57–80.

Rahman, S. and K. M. Rahman (2018) *Multi-actor co-responsibility initiatives after Rana Plaza: perspectives from the Bangladesh garment factory management,* Draft report, Global Governance Report.

Rahman, Z. and T. Langford (2012) "Why Labour Unions Have Failed Bangladesh's Garment Workers." In S. Mosoetsa and M. Williams (eds.) *Labour in the Global South* (pp. 87–106). Geneva: International Labour organization.

Raghavan, C. (1996). *Barking Up the Wrong Tree: Trade and Social Clause Links.* www.twnside.org.sg/south/twn/title/tree-ch.htm.

Rao, R. (1999) 'Social clauses: here to stay': Part 2' Global Policy Forum. www.globalpolicy.org/component/content/article/219/46739.html.

Ross, A. (1997). 'Introduction.' In Ross Andrew (ed.) *No Sweat: Fashion, Free Trade and the Rights of Garment Workers*. London: Verso.

Siddiqi, D. (2009) "Do Bangladeshi Factory Workers Need Saving? Sisterhood in the Post-Sweatshop Era." *Feminist Review*, 91: 154–174.

Sobhan, R. (2003) "The Shift from Aid Dependence to Trade Dependence." *Weekly Holiday*, 39th Anniversary Edition, October 31, 2003.

Sobhan, R. (2014) *Bangladesh's Disaster: Perspectives on the Political Economy*, Indian Review of Global Affairs March 20, 2014. https://cpd.org.bd/bangladeshs-disaster-perspectives-on-the-political-economy-rehman-sobhan/.

Spielberg, E. (1997) "The Myth of Nimble Fingers." In A. Ross (ed.) *No Sweat: Fashion, Free Trade and the Rights of Garment Workers* (pp. 113–122). London and New York: Verso.

Taplin, I. M. (2014) "Who is to Blame? A Re-examination of Fast Fashion after the 2013 Factory Disaster in Bangladesh." *Critical Perspectives on International Business*, 10(1/2): 72–83.

Thoene, U. (2014) "The Strategic Use of the Labour Rights Discourse – Revisting the "Social Clause" Debate in Trade Agreements." *Justicia Juris*, 10(2): 59–70.

Van Roozendaal, G. (2002) *Trade Unions and Global Governance: The Debate on a Social Clause*. London: Continuum.

World Bank (1987) World Development Report. Washington: World Bank.

World Bank (1990) Bangladesh Strategies for Enhancing the Role of Women in Economic Development. World Bank: Washington DC.

Zajak, S. (2017) "International Allies, Institutional Layering and Power in the Making of Labour in Bangladesh," *Development and Change*.

Index

Note: **Bold** page numbers refer to tables; *italic* page numbers refer to figures and page numbers followed by "n" denote endnotes.